Layman's
BIBLE
Commentary

Matthew &

Volume
8

Contributing Editors:

DR. IAN FAIR
DR. STEPHEN LESTON

Consulting Editor:

DR. MARK STRAUSS

BARBOUR
PUBLISHING

© 2008 by Barbour Publishing, Inc.

ISBN 978-1-62029-781-0

All rights reserved. No part of this publication may be reproduced or transmitted for commercial purposes, except for brief quotations in printed reviews, without written permission of the publisher.

Churches and other noncommercial interests may reproduce portions of this book without the express written permission of Barbour Publishing, provided that the text does not exceed 500 words and that the text is not material quoted from another publisher. When reproducing text from this book, include the following credit line: "From *Layman's Bible Commentary, Vol. 8: Matthew and Mark,* published by Barbour Publishing, Inc. Used by permission."

Scripture quotations marked NIV are taken from the HOLY BIBLE, NEW INTERNATIONAL VERSION ®. NIV ®. Copyright © 1973, 1978, 1984 by International Bible Society. Used by permission of Zondervan. All rights reserved.

Scripture quotations marked NLT are taken from the *Holy Bible*, New Living Translation copyright © 1996. Used by permission of Tyndale House Publishers, Inc., Wheaton, Illinois 60189. All rights reserved.

Scripture quotations marked NLV are taken from the Holy Bible, New Life Version, Copyright 1969, 1976, 1978, 1983, 1986, Christian Literature International, P.O. Box 777, Canby, OR 97013. Used by permission.

Scripture quotations marked CEV are taken from the Holy Bible, Contemporary English Version Copyright © 1995, 1997 by the American Bible Society. Used by permission. All rights reserved.

Scripture quotations marked NKJV are taken from the New King James Version ®. Copyright © 1982. Used by permission of Thomas Nelson Publishers, Nashville, TN. All rights reserved.

Scripture quotations marked MSG are taken from *THE MESSAGE.* Copyright © 1993, 1994, 1995, 1996, 2000, 2001, 2002. Used by permission of NavPress Publishing Group.

Scripture quotations marked GWT are taken from *GOD'S WORD*, which is a copyrighted work of God's Word to the Nations. Quotations are used by permission. Copyright 1995 by God's Word to the Nations. All rights reserved.

Scripture quotations marked TLB are taken from The Living Bible by Kenneth Taylor, © 1971 by Tyndale House Publishers, Inc. Used by permission. All rights reserved.

Scripture quotations marked NRSV are taken from the New Revised Standard Version Bible, copyright 1989, Division of Christian Education of the National Council of the Churches of Christ in the United States of America. Used by permission. All rights reserved.

Scripture quotations marked ESV are taken from The Holy Bible, English Standard Version, copyright © 2001, Wheaton: Good News Publishers. Used by permission. All rights reserved.

Scripture quotations that do not reference a specific translation use the same wording that is common to multiple translations.

Produced with the assistance of Christopher. D. Hudson & Associates. Contributing writers include Carol Smith and Stan Campbell.

Published by Barbour Publishing, Inc., P.O. Box 719, Uhrichsville, Ohio 44683, www.barbourbooks.com

Our mission is to publish and distribute inspirational products offering exceptional value and biblical encouragement to the masses.

Member of the
Evangelical Christian
Publishers Association

Printed in the United States of America.

TABLE OF CONTENTS

INTRODUCTION TO THE GOSPELS

THE GOSPEL OF MATTHEW

THE GOSPEL OF MARK

INTRODUCTION TO THE
GOSPELS

THE GOSPELS

The first three Gospels in our New Testament—Matthew, Mark, Luke—are considered the synoptic Gospels. The word *synoptic* denotes that the separate Gospels were written "from a common view." These three narratives follow a similar chronological or structural outline, whereas the Gospel of John follows a different chronological or structural outline.

Although all four Gospels tell the story of Jesus carefully and accurately, they differ somewhat in content and considerably in what they want to say about Jesus. Each of the gospel writers adopted a different form or literary style, and even vocabulary. They each had a different theological purpose or intention. Furthermore, they each had a different audience in mind. Still, each individual writer was empowered by the Holy Spirit to use his specific giftedness to record faithfully the purpose of God.

The Gospels of Mark and Matthew are very similar in their narrative accounts. Luke is only slightly different, but still has much in common with Matthew and Mark. (It has been estimated that over 90 percent of the verses of Mark are found in Matthew.)

Both Matthew and Luke follow Mark's basic narrative form. Mark was probably the first of the Gospels written, then Matthew, followed by Luke. Matthew and Luke supplemented Mark's narrative with additional material to meet the unique theological purpose and audience each had in mind.

THE GOSPELS IN THE LIFE OF THE CHURCH

The most likely dates for writing the synoptic Gospels range from the early 60s AD to the mid-70s AD. Even if Matthew was written earlier, as some believe to be true, several of Paul's epistles (Galatians, 1 and 2 Thessalonians, Romans, 1 and 2 Corinthians) were likely written before the Gospels. In the early days of the mission and expansion of the church, the need for the Gospels was not as great since the apostles and other apostolic men were still alive and active. Then, as the church spread and as the apostles were dying, the gospel message needed to be formalized.

Furthermore, as the gospel spread to distant lands and among different Gentile cultures it became necessary to explain the story of Jesus in terms the new communities of believers or would-be believers could understand. It became necessary to interpret the significance of Jesus for a second generation of believers, namely, Gentile Roman and Greek seekers. Hence there arose a need for Gospels that would explain Jesus to a Roman audience (Mark), a Jewish audience (Matthew), and a Greek audience (Luke). Some years later, in the region of Asia (Turkey), it became necessary for John to retell the story of Jesus to a church that was being challenged by new false doctrines about Jesus' divinity and human form (John).

The Gospels are often described as accounts of Jesus' death, burial, and resurrection with extended introductions to provide backstory. They explain why the death of this seemingly marginal Jew, Jesus, was so significant. The Gospels give reasons why people should respond to a radical call to discipleship, surrender their lives to this Jesus, and follow Him wherever that might lead, possibly even to a martyr's death. (Remember that martyrdom for Jesus was a real threat to Christians during the first three centuries.)

Although we cannot date the four Gospels precisely, all four were certainly written before the end of the first century AD. They are the only early and reliable historical accounts of the life and ministry of Jesus. The later so-called "apocryphal Gospels"—such as the Gospel of Thomas, the Gospel of the Truth, and the Gospel of Phillip—either borrowed from the four canonical Gospels or were created from legendary stories.

THE NATURE OF THE GOSPELS

It is important to understanding that we ask this question: "What kind of literature do we have in these Gospels?"

The four New Testament Gospels are fundamentally a different kind of literature from the New Testament Epistles. The Gospels incorporate a number of literary styles (parables, teaching materials, narrative materials) as they tell their stories. Keeping these literary styles in mind gives us a framework to interpret the Gospels accurately.

BIOGRAPHIES?

The Gospels don't fit the category of modern biographies in that they describe only a short period of Jesus' life. They do fit in the category of ancient biographies in that ancient hero biographies did not attempt to tell everything about a hero, but only those matters that were important to the story. Nevertheless, to simply define the Gospels as biographies comes up short.

HISTORY

Some have attempted to define the Gospels as historical narratives. Although there was an interest in setting the story of Jesus into a historical context, there is obviously more than mere historical facts in the Gospels. Jesus was a historical person who actually lived, died, and rose again, although outside of scripture it would be difficult to prove the historical nature of His resurrection. However, there is enough other material in the Gospels that touch history to affirm that the Gospels are accurate. The Gospel writers were concerned with reliable testimony as they told the significant facts of Jesus' life and ministry. So, do the Gospels relate the story of Jesus in historical terms, constructs, or contexts? The answer is yes, but this is not their primary concern.

THEOLOGY

The Gospels are in fact theological writings, telling the story of Jesus (biographical facts significant to their purpose) and placing Him into a historical context (historical testimony significant to their story), but more importantly, explaining why He had the right to be considered the Son of God, the Messiah, and the Christ ("the anointed").

Some have suggested that the Gospels are really the story of Jesus' suffering, death, burial, and resurrection—with extended introductions. These lengthy introductions explained who this Jesus was, why His life was significant, and what discipleship of Jesus entails.

THE THEOLOGICAL FOCUS OF THE INDIVIDUAL GOSPELS

Each of the synoptic Gospels was written for a particular audience or community, with the purpose of explaining how the message of Jesus related to that group's needs and interests.

Mark wrote to a group of persecuted believers to demonstrate that Jesus was the mighty Messiah and Son of God, but that He suffered and died to pay for sins. His is a call for believers to take up their own crosses and follow Jesus through suffering to victory.

For the Jewish mind-set, and especially those Jewish Christians that were displaced after the destruction of Jerusalem, Matthew wrote to establish Jesus' rightful claim to be the Messiah, the King of God's kingdom.

For a mainly Gentile audience, Luke wrote demonstrating that Jesus was the Son of God who was truly interested in people and who had died to save people from sin. Jesus, in Luke, is the Savior of the world—He is the healer of mankind.

THE NEED AND PURPOSE OF THE GOSPELS

Several factors lay behind the need for the gospel story to be written down in reliable form. We can group them under the following categories:

- **Apostolic Preaching**. The need to preserve the preaching message of the apostles was becoming urgent as the apostles were being persecuted and dying as martyrs for the cause and message of Christ. In time, our four Gospels became a form of apostolic presence.
- **Gentile Missions and Expansion of the Church.** The dramatic expansion of the New Testament church created a situation that demanded a firm and reliable record of the apostolic preaching in the form of the written message. It was simply impossible for the apostles and apostolic evangelists to cover all of the new bases and churches in the Gentile world.
- **False Teaching.** There was a need to correct false ideas about Jesus and His mission that began to arise in the church.

We continue to need the perspective of all four Gospels to this day. They teach us that Jesus was a real person of history and that God, from even before His birth, was involved in the events that took life in the person of Jesus. They teach us that Jesus performed miracles to prove His divinity and mission, that He died according to the plan and will of God, that He was resurrected in history on the third day, that He now reigns in God's kingdom, and that He will return as predicted in scripture to judge the world in righteousness.

THE GOSPEL OF
MATTHEW

INTRODUCTION TO
MATTHEW

Although this is a commentary on the Gospel of Matthew, and this Gospel can stand alone as an independent witness to Jesus, it is helpful to our understanding of it to see it in relation to the other Gospels, especially Mark and Luke. As noted in the introduction to this volume, Matthew, Mark, and Luke are referred to as the synoptic Gospels because they are similar accounts and see the story of Jesus "through the same eyes." The Gospel of John had a unique view or approach to the gospel story.

Although Mark's Gospel appeared first and was early accepted by the church, Matthew soon became the church's favored Gospel. For a number of reasons, throughout the centuries Matthew has continued to be the most prominent of the three synoptic Gospels (Matthew, Mark, and Luke). Here are some possible reasons:

- It is commonly believed to have been written by one of the original apostles.
- It is more comprehensive than Mark, containing messianic genealogy, birth narratives, and a considerable amount of Jesus' teaching material.
- It contains more than 90 percent of Mark's Gospel since Matthew used Mark as a basis for his Gospel.
- Its incorporation of large blocks of Jesus' teaching material, especially the Sermon on the Mount, has met the educational and liturgical needs of the church through the centuries.

AUTHOR

Our earliest records claim that the apostle Matthew wrote this Gospel. Early church tradition was almost unanimous in this regard. While there remains some continuing discussion about Matthew's authorship, the Gospel itself was accepted without question by the early church and incorporated into the New Testament canon.

PURPOSE

It is obvious that Matthew's Gospel was addressed to a Jewish-Christian audience or community. Matthew presented Jesus to this audience as God's messianic King.

HISTORICAL CONTEXT

Some scholars date Matthew after AD 70, sometime after the destruction of Jerusalem, while others date it earlier, in the 60s.

In this commentary we will follow the view that Matthew's community was a group of Jewish Christians or Jewish church communities who had escaped Jerusalem between AD 66 and the destruction of Jerusalem in AD 70. Needing to know that their faith should not be focused on Jerusalem and the temple, which was now destroyed, but on Jesus the Messiah, Matthew wrote for these dislodged Jewish Christian communities who needed to refocus their faith and discipleship.

THEMES

Several characteristics of Matthew's Gospel are immediately apparent:

A strong Jewish interest. Matthew used a number of literary devices that indicate a Jewish audience.

A strong sense of messianic expectation and fulfillment in Matthew. Matthew made much of fulfilled prophecy in his narrative. Quoting heavily from the Old Testament, Matthew claimed that fifteen Old Testament prophecies were fulfilled in Jesus' ministry. He showed great interest in Jesus' teaching on the Law of Moses. Jesus' statement that He came to fulfill the law rather than abolish it is found exclusively in Matthew (5:17-20).

Universalism and Missions. Although Matthew wrote for a Jewish community, he was not a Jewish zealot. He saw Christianity reaching beyond the Jewish nation to the Gentiles. (Note his condemnation of the Jewish leadership in Matthew 23 and the Great Commission in 28:18-20.)

Pastoral and Ecclesiastical Interest. Matthew is in every sense of the word a church Gospel:

- It is the only Gospel to include the term *ekklesia*, meaning "church" (16:18; 18:17).
- Matthew was interested in the church's corporate life and the issues of living in a close-knit body (18:15-20).
- Matthew emphasized Jesus' role as an authoritative teacher (7:29).
- Matthew emphasized Jesus' instruction regarding the kingdom (Chapter 13).

Messianic Kingdom Interests. From the first paragraph of the Gospel, Matthew was concerned with Jesus as the Messiah, the King of God's kingdom. His purpose was to show that Jesus was the long-expected Messiah.

Eschatological Interests. Matthew manifested significant interest in the final age of history, the end times. He included several parables that had themes relating to the final judgment, including:

- The parable of the tares (13:24-30)
- The parable of the ten virgins (25:1-13)
- The parable of the talents (25:14-30)

Matthew described the destruction of Jerusalem in much greater detail than Mark and Luke. In Matthew, three chapters are devoted to the destruction of Jerusalem and the confusion of the disciples over the final end of the age (23-25). Mark and Luke used only one chapter for this discussion (Mark 13; Luke 21).

Careful examination of the Gospel of Matthew reveals a deliberate and careful literary structure with a specific theological purpose. The literary structure of Matthew alternates between six blocks of narrative material, five of which are each followed by a block of sayings or discourse material. Many draw a parallel between the five books of Moses (the Law) and the five discourses of Jesus. In Matthew's case, these discourses were not discussions of Christian law, as the books of Moses are, but teachings discussing the meaning of discipleship in the kingdom.

NARRATIVE 1	Matthew 1:1–4:25	Preparation for Ministry
Discourse 1	Matthew 5:1–7:29	The Sermon on the Mount
NARRATIVE 2	Matthew 8:1–9:38	The Authority of the Messiah
Discourse 2	Matthew 10:1–42	The Limited Commission
NARRATIVE 3	Matthew 11:1–12:50	Opposition and Rejection
Discourse 3	Matthew 13:1–58	The True Nature of the Kingdom
NARRATIVE 4	Matthew 14:1–17:27	Final Days of Preparation
Discourse 4	Matthew 18:1–35	Community—Humility and Forgiveness
NARRATIVE 5	Matthew 19:1–22:46	Toward Jerusalem—The Final Week
Discourse 5	Matthew 23:1–25:46	The Apocalyptic Discourse
NARRATIVE 6	Matthew 26:1–28:20	The Messiah's Final Week

OUTLINE

MATTHEW 1:1–4:25
NARRATIVE 1: PREPARATION FOR MINISTRY

Setting Up the Section

This first block of narrative in Matthew is sometimes overlooked in the misconception that it's not quite as important to the Gospel as, say, the Sermon on the Mount of Matthew 5–7 or the great Kingdom Parables of Matthew 13. It may be seen as simply the backdrop or story setup. However, it actually presents one of the most striking and significant theological emphases of the Gospel. This narrative lays the foundation for Matthew's arguments regarding the messiahship of Jesus.

📖 1:1–17

THE GENEALOGY OF JESUS

Matthew begins his theological argument for the messiahship of Jesus in proper Jewish style, with an appropriate genealogy—although it is a theologically shaped one. It is obvious from a comparison of other Old Testament genealogies (1 Chronicles 1–9) that Matthew leaves out some levels of Jesus' family tree and repeats some names.

Because Matthew's genealogy underlines matters of fundamental theological importance, he grounds his narrative upon several Old Testament quotations and intends to provide a strong sense of fulfillment. To further emphasize the theological impact of this genealogy, he begins with its most significant elements—"Jesus Christ the son of David, the son of Abraham."

Matthew numbers the generations from Abraham to Jesus as three groups of fourteen. This has generated much speculation. Though we cannot be certain of Matthew's meaning, he seems to take it for granted that his first century Jewish readers will understand.

Most importantly, in Matthew's carefully constructed genealogy, it is obvious that Jesus is the descendant of Abraham and David, two significant persons in the genealogy of Israel. By the time Matthew wrote his Gospel, *Son of David* had become a messianic title. Matthew is clearly demonstrating through this historical/theological genealogy that Jesus is the rightful

Son of Abraham and Son of David, namely, the Messiah.

Furthermore, it is Mathew's purpose to demonstrate that the promises to Abraham were fulfilled through Jesus. This would be important for a Jewish believer to know. (In his letter to the Galatians, Paul makes a similar argument—that Jesus is the seed of Abraham, thus fulfilling the promise of God to Abraham.) For Matthew's Jewish audience, Jesus' being the seed of Abraham has both messianic and promise implications. You can read God's promises to Abraham in Genesis 17:5-7.

The genealogy of Matthew differs from that of Luke. Matthew traces a heritage from Abraham through David to Jesus through the royal or legal lineage. His goal is to show that Jesus is the legitimate king of Israel. Luke also follows the line of David and Abraham, but traces his genealogy from Jesus through Mary all the way back to Adam. Luke's genealogy, like Matthew's, is meant to fulfill a theological purpose, demonstrating that Jesus is the Savior for all people everywhere.

📖 1:18–25

THE VIRGIN BIRTH

Joseph is pledged (NIV) to Mary. This indicates something similar to modern engagement, only with a stronger legal implication. It was, in fact, the beginning of the marriage "ceremony." The pledge was as legally binding as the marriage contract. It could only be broken according to the Jewish laws of marriage and divorce. In this case, since it appears that Mary is no longer considered clean since she is pregnant with Jesus, it is within the law for Joseph to divorce her. Imagine the sensitivity of Joseph in this matter. When it is revealed by an angel that Mary's pregnancy is the work of the Holy Spirit and part of God's purpose, Joseph takes her as his wife.

The virgin birth of Jesus is fundamental to the Christian faith and to Matthew's theology. Throughout this section, Matthew emphasizes the role of the Holy Spirit. He wants his readers to know that this conception is unusual, that it transcends the purely historical or earthly, that Jesus' conception and birth involve the direct involvement and action of the divine. The central point in this birth narrative is not simply that Jesus is born of a virgin, true as that may be, but that His conception and birth is the result of direct divine intervention (the Holy Spirit), and that it forms an integral part in God's saving activity in history.

To reinforce this point, Matthew argues that Jesus' birth is a fulfillment of prophecy, namely, Isaiah 7:14. For Jewish ears, this is a powerful argument demonstrating that Jesus is a fulfillment of God's prophetic activity, that He has a legitimate place in God's promises to Abraham, and that He, in fact, stands in the direct line of God's redemption.

Critical Observation

As early as Matthew 1:22, we are introduced to a fascinating aspect of Matthew's theological style. We encounter the first of ten significant fulfillment passages in Matthew. Although Matthew quotes from or cites many Old Testament and prophetic texts, these ten are unique because they are introduced as fulfillments. Singling them out in this manner, Matthew draws out their theological

CONTINUED

implications for Jesus' ministry as Messiah. The other nine similarly unique citations are: 2:15, 17, 23; 4:14; 8:17; 13:35; 21:4; 26:56; and 27:9. Matthew's use of these quotes fits with his determination to demonstrate that Jesus legitimately fulfills the role of Messiah.

In his opening chapter Matthew makes two significant theological claims regarding Jesus.

1) He is the son of Abraham and David, thus supporting Matthew's claims that Jesus is legitimately the Messiah.

2) His birth is not ordinary; it is the result of the direct intervention of God.

2:1-12

THE WISE MEN

With this narrative, Matthew sets the scene for a major theme he will develop throughout the Gospel. It concerns those who acknowledge Jesus and worship Him. The ones you would anticipate as welcoming and worshiping Jesus as the Messiah, do not. It is those from whom one would least expect worship that Jesus receives homage.

Matthew sets this account of the Wise Men in a historical context—during the reign of Herod the king (Herod the Great, AD 47–4 BC). Because we know the date of Herod's death, a key event in this story, we have a firm time marker—one that is somewhat surprising. If Jesus was born while Herod was still ruling, then Jesus was born before 4 BC.

Herod the Great was not popular with the Jews for several reasons.

1) He was not a pure Jew, but an Idumean. (Idumea lay to the south and southeast of Judea and the Dead Sea. Some associate Idumea with Edom and the Edomites, but this is only part of the Idumean heritage).

2) He had been appointed by the Roman government to rule over Israel.

3) He was a harsh ruler. Even the Roman Emperor, Augustus, acknowledged the ruthlessness of Herod.

It is difficult to identify the Wise Men with any degree of certainty. The word used to describe them here is *magoi* (*Magoi* could refer to magicians or a priestly caste from Persia). In all probability, they are a group of Persian priests familiar with reading the formations of the stars. When the Wise Men (not necessarily three wise men, since Matthew does not actually number them) see the star in the East and follow it, they come to Jerusalem and Bethlehem, anticipating something important. They recognize that a new king has been born.

Did they really understand the significance of this baby to Israel? We do not know all that this realization involved—only that it was significant enough to bring them to Jerusalem to inquire about the new king. Word of this disturbs Herod so much that he assembles the chief priests and asks where the Christ was to be born. Fascinating. Herod immediately identifies this new king with the messianic expectation of Israel. So do the chief priests, since they immediately cite the prophecy in Micah 5:2. Matthew's use of this text is in keeping with the Jewish rabbinic practice of making an indirect theological emphasis by the giving of a narrative account. The fact that Herod and the chief priests immediately consider a messianic text in this situation is an indirect support for Matthew's argument that Jesus is indeed the same

Messiah that had been prophesied to be born in Bethlehem, a small town about five miles south of Jerusalem.

The Wise Men (Persian Gentiles) acknowledge Jesus as the king and worship Him and give Him gifts of costly aromatic herbs or ointment. Many have seen a symbolic significance in these three gifts: gold for royalty, incense for deity, myrrh for burial. It is unlikely that the Magi saw this significance, but Matthew's readers may have seen it.

Being warned in a dream not to return to Herod, the Wise Men leave for their own home country. Herod and the chief priests do not receive Jesus and pay Him homage, but Gentiles from afar worship Him. Matthew continues to work this theme into his Gospel.

2:13–23

THE FLIGHT TO EGYPT

Again we have divine intervention—an angel of the Lord warns Joseph to flee into Egypt.

Matthew cites Hosea 11:1 as his second fulfillment prophecy. While this Hosea text pertains to the nation of Israel, Matthew uses it in regard to the Messiah. In doing this, he emphasizes that what is happening to Joseph, Mary, and Jesus is not an accident; it is part of God's ongoing work of salvation throughout history.

Herod's response to the possible presence of the Messiah is to have all male children in Bethlehem who are two years old and under killed. Matthew cites Jeremiah 31:15 as a prophetic reference for this. Again, Matthew takes an Old Testament text and paraphrases it. This text is the third of the fulfillment texts in Matthew. Jeremiah 31:15 is in the specific historical context of the deportation of the Hebrews to Babylon. Matthew applies the prophecy regarding that historical situation to the grief and the weeping over the cruel work of Herod. He again uses this parallel to connect the events surrounding Jesus' birth with an Old Testament fulfillment and God's divine plan.

After Herod's death, God intervenes once again. An angel of the Lord tells Joseph to return to Israel. After Herod's death no one is appointed king, but Herod's son, Archelaus, becomes governor over Judea. Archelaus, like Herod, is not a pure Jew; he is half Idumean and half Samaritan. Because of Archelaus's reputation, Joseph is warned not to return to Judea (which included Bethlehem and Jerusalem), but instead to go to Galilee, the district in the north over which Archelaus is *not* governor. Joseph and his family settle in Nazareth.

Matthew resorts to his fourth fulfillment text to support this (v. 23). The problem is that it is almost impossible to find this prophecy's precise source. This would not be a problem for Jews familiar with first-century application of Old Testament passages. Matthew's purpose is, again, to connect Jesus with, or place Him firmly within, God's saving activity in history. Some say the background behind this text is the Nazarite vows of Judges 13:5, 7 and 16:17, but we can't be sure that the Judges verses are the source.

3:1–12

THE MINISTRY OF JOHN THE BAPTIST

The expression "In those days. . ." (NIV) is a Hebrew statement that draws attention to a period of time that should hold significant interest.

Matthew spends no time explaining who John the Baptist is. He feels no need; every Jew at this time would have known something about John the Baptist, and Matthew is writing for a Jewish-Christian audience. On the other hand, Luke, writing for a Gentile Greek audience, spends considerable time on John's birth (Luke 1:5–25, 39–80). While for Matthew no introduction of John is necessary, John's ministry and his introduction of Jesus are important to Matthew's message.

John the Baptist begins preaching in the wilderness. His message—"Repent, for the kingdom of heaven is near" (NIV)—is a short statement with significant theological content. It is exactly this message that Jesus came preaching (4:17). Each word is loaded with meaning:

- *Repent* (turn to God). Recognizing the time is fulfilled and that Jesus is about to usher in the last days, there is a sense of urgency in the air. God is about to restore His kingdom through His Messiah, Jesus. When the Pharisees and Sadducees come out for baptism not manifesting repentance, John calls them a brood or generation of vipers—in other words, poisonous snakes (3:7).

- *Kingdom of heaven.* It was normal for the Jews to substitute something similar in the place of the word *God*, hence Matthew uses the expression *kingdom of heaven* rather than *kingdom of God*. When the Bible speaks of the "kingdom of God," it is referencing the reign of God. The reign of God from heaven through His messianic king is about to break into human experience in a unique and powerful manner.

- *At hand* (near). This term can mean close or near, but in certain contexts a term can take on heightened importance. In this case, it takes on the sense of something that is already here or something that is so certain that it can be spoken of as if it already exists. In the context of John's preaching, this means that the kingdom of heaven/God is so certain (and in the person of Jesus is already among them) that the Jews need to repent immediately. Later, in Matthew 12:28, Jesus will say, "but if I drive out demons by the Spirit of God, then the kingdom of God has come upon you" (NIV), indicating that the kingdom in His person was already there.

In keeping with his already established policy, Matthew introduces John with a fulfillment passage, but this is not one of the ten specifically formulaic passages. In this case, Matthew (as did Mark and Luke when they cited the Old Testament) quotes from the Septuagint, a Greek version of the Old Testament scriptures.

Matthew's quote stresses that John's ministry takes place in the wilderness, away from the religious establishment. It is in the wilderness that John is preparing for the ministry of the Messiah, whose ministry also begins outside of Jerusalem's influence. Notice that when the Pharisees and Sadducees come out for baptism, John severely warns them to repent because judgment (an axe) is ready to take place over them. They will be judged by God for their rejection of the Messiah.

Even John's clothes set him apart from the religious leaders of the day. His dress is that of a desert monk (and his diet that of a desert survivalist), reminiscent of the great prophet Elijah (2 Kings 1:8). The religious leaders would have worn fine garments reflecting their high position.

John likewise distances himself and his ministry from that of the Messiah. He baptizes in (or with) water based on repentance, but Jesus' ministry and baptism come in the fullness and power of the Holy Spirit. In Matthew 3:6 John preaches a baptism related to the forgiveness of sins. Mark described it simply: "John the Baptist preached in the desert. He preached that people should be baptized because they were sorry for their sins and had turned from them. And they would be forgiven" (Mark 1:4 NLV). What is the difference between this baptism of John and the Christian baptism shortly to be proclaimed by Jesus? Both are based on repentance and are for the forgiveness of sins, yet some of those that are baptized according to John's baptism need to be rebaptized later as Christians (Acts 19:1–5).

Although John's baptism is for the forgiveness of sins, it is a transitory baptism, shortly to be replaced by a baptism that Jesus commands (Matthew 28:19–20; Mark 16:15–16). The difference is the sacrificial system upon which they were built. John's baptism existed under the yearly sacrificial system of animal sacrifices; Christian baptism was, and remains, under the permanent, once-for-all-time, sacrifice of Jesus. John's baptism was under a temporary sacrificial system to last only until the permanent sacrifice of Jesus. Also, Jesus commanded His disciples (apostles) to go and make disciples of all nations (Matthew 28:19–20; Mark 16:15–16). John's baptism was only for the Jews.

John's description of Jesus in verse 12 relates to judgment. A reference to the harvesting and processing of wheat, it describes a procedure in which harvested wheat is gathered onto a threshing floor. The rough wheat is then thrown into the air so that the breeze can catch the lighter chaff and blow it away. In this way, the good, nutritious wheat is separated from the useless chaff.

3:13–17

THE BAPTISM OF JESUS

The baptism of Jesus was so important to His ministry that all three of the synoptic Gospels (Matthew, Mark, Luke) record the event. In convincing John to go through with the baptism, Jesus claims His baptism will fulfill all righteousness, or do everything that God requires of them. Jesus' baptism represents both divine empowerment and divine affirmation for His ministry. It is the inaugural event of His public ministry.

The Gospel of Luke adds an interesting undertone to the significance of the baptism, exemplifying the Pharisees' perspective: "But the proud religious law-keepers and the men who knew the Law would not listen. They would not be baptized by John and they did not receive what God had for them" (Luke 7:30 NLV). In this light, their refusal to be baptized is not simply the rejection of a custom; it is tantamount to rejecting the purpose of God.

God had evidently instructed John to baptize for repentance and forgiveness of sins (Matthew 3:6; Mark 1:4). Baptism as a cleansing rite, based on faith and repentance and for the forgiveness of sins, was important to the ministry of both John the Baptist and Jesus. Christians in the early centuries continued to practice baptism based on faith, accompanied by repentance, for the forgiveness of sins. (See Acts 2:38; 8:34–39; 16:33; 22:16.) From Romans 6:4 and Colossians 2:12 we learn that baptism is a symbolic burial with Jesus. Jesus commands baptism, based on faith and repentance, in His plan of salvation for the Christian faith (Matthew 28:18–19; Mark 16:15–16).

Immediately, when Jesus is baptized, God gives His approval. Again, we notice the activity of the Holy Spirit in the life and ministry of Jesus, reinforcing the aspect of divine intervention. On this occasion the Holy Spirit descends on Jesus like a dove, giving visual manifestation of His presence. Following that, a loud voice proclaims that Jesus is the Son of God, and that God is pleased with Him. Divine approval. We see two Old Testament passages brought together at this point, Isaiah 42:1 (Jesus as God's servant) and Psalm 2:7 (Jesus as God's Son), tying Jesus into the line of God's saving activity from the Old Testament to the present. In Judaism, the term *Son of God* had already become a phrase associated with the Messiah. (This same voice would again affirm Jesus in Matthew 17:5 at His transfiguration.)

Jesus' baptism plays a significant role in affirming Jesus' Sonship.

📖 **4:1–11**

JESUS' TEMPTATION

Though the record in Mark is only two verses, the temptation of Jesus is found in all three synoptic Gospels (Matthew 4:1–11; Mark 1:12–13; Luke 4:1–13), indicating the significant role of the event. Matthew and Luke make more of this event than Mark does, and their records differ in order:

TEMPTATIONS	MATTHEW	LUKE
First	Stones into loaves	Stones into bread
Second	Pinnacle of temple	Kingdoms of the world
Third	Kingdoms of world	Pinnacle of temple

Luke's order for the temptations ends at the temple, a place that plays a central role in Luke's narrative. Matthew's order ends on the mountain, and mountain revelations play a major role in Matthew's narrative (for instance, the Sermon on the Mount).

Matthew's purpose for recording the temptations is more theological than chronological or historical. This should not be taken to mean that the temptations did not occur; it simply means that Matthew is making theological applications, not just reciting an event.

At a Glance: The Temptation of Christ			
TEMPTATION	NATURE OF THE TEMPTATIONS	SATAN ARGUES	JESUS ANSWERS FROM SCRIPTURES
Stones into loaves	Physical temptation: hunger	If you are the Son of God, tell these stones to become bread.	Man doesn't live on bread alone, but on every word God speaks. (Deuteronomy 8:3)
Pinnacle of temple	Physical temptation: personal safety	If you are the Son of God, throw yourself down and angels will catch you. (Psalm 91:11, 12)	Do not put God to the test. (Deuteronomy 6:16)
Kingdoms of world	Spiritual temptation: power	If you'll worship me, I'll give you all these kingdoms.	Worship the Lord God and serve Him only. (Deuteronomy 6:13)

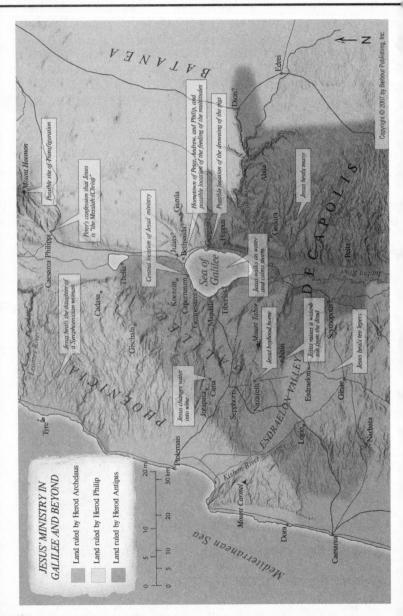

JESUS' MINISTRY IN GALILEE AND BEYOND

Land ruled by Herod Archelaus
Land ruled by Herod Philip
Land ruled by Herod Antipas

Copyright © 2007 by Rose Publishing, Inc.

Possible site of Transfiguration

Peter's confession that Jesus is "the Messiah (Christ)"

Central location of Jesus' ministry

Homeland of Peter, Andrew, and Philip, and possible location of the feeding of the multitudes

Possible location of the drowning of the pigs

Jesus heals many

Jesus heals the daughter of a Syrophoenician woman

Jesus walks on water and calms storm

Jesus changes water into wine

Jesus raises a widow's son from the dead

Jesus heals ten lepers

BATANEA
PHOENICIA
GALILEE
DECAPOLIS
ESDRAELON VALLEY

Mount Hermon
Caesarea Philippi
Leontes River
Tyre
Cadasa
Gischala
Thella
Konezin
Capernaum
Gennesaret
Magdala
Tiberias
Sea of Galilee
Bethsaida?
Julias?
Gamla
Gergesa
Hippus
Caedura
Abila
Pella
Dion?
Edrei
Jordan River
Mount Tabor
Nain
Jotapata
Cana
Sepphoris
Nazareth
Legio
Scythopolis
Esdraelon
Ginae
Nabata
Ptolemais
Kishon River
Mount Carmel
Dora
Caesarea
Mediterranean Sea

N

20 mi
30 km
0 5 10 20
0 10 20

28

Take It Home

There is a strong connection here between Israel's ancient story and Jesus' story. Jesus' forty days in the wilderness are analogous to Israel's forty years wandering in the wilderness. The three Old Testament passages Jesus cites are all from Israel's wilderness wanderings. When put to the test, Jesus succeeds where Israel had failed. This seems to be the central analogy in the temptation account.

There are several applications for us in the story of Jesus' temptation or testing in the wilderness.

1) Jesus is prepared for the temptation. He has been taken there by the Spirit, and He has fasted.

2) Jesus is identified as the Son of God. Satan himself recognizes that fact.

3) Jesus does not use His divine power to defeat Satan. He becomes a man, is tempted as a man, and dies as a man.

4) As a man, Jesus turns to God and His Word for strength and deliverance from temptation.

We can follow Jesus' pattern by practicing spiritual disciplines that will prepare us for temptation and by turning to God's Word for the strength and guidance we need to stay strong. Jesus came here to face the life we live so that He could show us how to better live (1 Corinthians 10:13).

📄 4:12–17

THE BEGINNING OF JESUS' GALILEAN MINISTRY

The return to Galilee at the news of John's imprisonment is the first of several retreats Jesus makes. While Matthew mentions John's imprisonment here, it is not until Matthew 14:3 that he explains the reason: John had preached against Herod's marrying Herodias, his brother Philip's wife. John's arrest must have been a politically tense topic in Judea because he was popular with the community, having preached successfully in the wilderness and baptized many (Matthew 3:5 states all the region went out to hear him).

After visiting Nazareth, Jesus goes to Capernaum. From this point on, Capernaum becomes Jesus' home base. (All four Gospels inform us that Jesus moves to Capernaum at this point.) John adds that during the journey, Jesus spends a few days in Samaria, where He speaks to the woman at the well about living water (John 4:1–42).

Matthew introduces this narrative by referring to his fifth fulfillment passage, an application of Isaiah 9:1–2. In Isaiah, this prophecy pertained to the promised restoration of Israel. While the cities mentioned seem to be the tie-in for this prophecy, there is more. For so many years, particularly in captivity, Israel remained in a national and spiritual darkness, always with the hope of the light-bearing Messiah who would usher in God's salvation. Matthew is applying this hope to the beginning of Jesus' ministry. With this comment, Matthew adds that Jesus begins to preach. His message is that of John's—"Repent, for the kingdom of heaven is at hand" (NIV).

Critical Observation

Matthew 4:17 and 16:21 are key verses identifying a topical outline for Jesus' ministry. These two texts form pivotal points in the ministry of Jesus, separating or defining the periods of public and private ministry:

Matthew 1:1–4:16	Preparation for Ministry
Matthew 4:17–16:20	Public Ministry: Jesus' ministry to the Jews primarily in Galilee and Judea. He teaches as He performs miracles and clashes with the Jewish leadership.
Matthew 16:21–28:20	Private Ministry: Jesus' ministry to His disciples in the last week of His life prepares them for His trial, death, burial, and resurrection.

▤ 4:18–25

THE CALL OF THE DISCIPLES: PETER AND ANDREW, JAMES AND JOHN

All four of the New Testament Gospels describe the calling of the first disciples. The accounts of Matthew and Mark (Mark 1:16–20) are shorter than those of Luke (Luke 5:1–11) and John (John 1:35–42).

Peter and Andrew were brothers, as were James and John. They worked as partners in the fishing business. When Jesus calls the two groups of brothers, they immediately leave their fishing boats and their families and follow Jesus. The emphasis on *immediately* stresses the radical nature of discipleship to which they are called by Jesus.

The radical nature of discipleship will become a major theme in Matthew's Gospel. Luke recounts that henceforth the disciples will be catching people, not fish (Luke 5:10).

After the call of the first disciples, Jesus travels throughout Galilee and the Roman province of Syria, which included the Decapolis (a ten-city federation) and Judea. He teaches in the synagogues, local Jewish teaching centers, preaching the gospel of the kingdom and healing every disease and infirmity of the people, as well as casting out demons. Jesus' ministry, in all its aspects, is a fulfillment of His mission as Messiah (Matthew 11:2–6; 12:28; Luke 4:16–21).

MATTHEW 5:1–7:29

DISCOURSE 1: THE SERMON ON THE MOUNT

Setting Up the Section

To fully understand The Sermon on the Mount, it's best to know the context of the theology of Matthew and the discourse that grows out of his first narrative (Matthew 2–4). Matthew's theology is that Jesus is the Messiah, the King of God's kingdom, that He does the works of the Messiah, and that He calls disciples to follow Him and make disciples of all nations.

At the conclusion of the first narrative, Jesus has called disciples to follow Him. In Matthew 4:17 Jesus passes from His preparation for ministry into His public ministry.

The Sermon on the Mount picks up from the calling of the disciples and offers the called disciples information about what kind of person a disciple must be—character development. A key thought is that disciples are different in righteousness, piety, and ambition from the scribes and Pharisees (Jewish religious leaders), and from the Gentiles (non-Jews).

The Sermon can be broken down into seven sections:

- **Matthew 5:1–12 The Disciples' Character: The Beatitudes**
- **Matthew 5:13–16 <u>The Disciples' Influence:</u> Salt and Light**
- **Matthew 5:17–48 The Disciples' Righteousness: To Exceed That of the Scribes and Pharisees**
- **Matthew 6:1–18 The Disciples' Piety: Deeds of Righteousness**
- **Matthew 6:19–34 The Disciples' Ambition**
- **Matthew 7:1–27 The Disciples' Pitfalls**

📖 **5:1–12**

THE DISCIPLES' CHARACTER: THE BEATITUDES (INTRODUCTION)

The word *Beatitudes* derives from the Latin *beatitudo* (supreme blessed, happy). The popular use of the term *beatitude* and its meaning of happiness derived from its Latin background lead to the unfortunate concept that these verses have to do with some form of happiness.

Actually, the Beatitudes teach what kind of person Jesus expects His disciples to be. They address the desired character of the disciples, but are given in the form of a blessing to those who manifest this character.

The term *blessed* carries with it the sense of deep spiritual richness. The Greek term that Matthew uses in chapter 5 is drawn from the Old Testament concept of blessedness that is found in the Wisdom Literature, especially the Psalms (Psalms 1:1; 2:12; 32:1) and in other Old Testament passages such as Isaiah 56:2; Jeremiah 17:7; and Daniel 12:12. When interpreting the word in Matthew 5, be careful to keep the meaning within this context.

Critical Observation

An interesting factor in the study of the Sermon on the Mount is a comparison of Matthew's account of the sermon to Luke's (for instance, Luke records fewer Beatitudes and in a different order than Matthew). Scholars are somewhat divided as to whether the sermons are the same sermon or whether both Matthew and Luke created their sermon from sayings delivered by Jesus on different occasions.

It's important to remember that each Gospel writer reported Jesus' sermon in a manner that suited his purpose and his particular audience. The sermons, however, have the same historical roots—they are true and reliable accounts of Jesus and His ministry.

To understand this passage, we need to understand it from two different perspectives. First, we should hear it from the perspective of Jesus' original listeners. He was addressing Jews who were longing for God to restore His kingdom to Israel.

Then we must understand it in terms of Matthew's original audience in the late first century. Matthew

CONTINUED

was writing for Jewish Christians who were struggling to understand the Messiah's role in light of the recent destruction of Jerusalem. They may have hoped for the Messiah to bring a political triumph for Jerusalem, but if so, it was obvious when the temple was destroyed that this triumph had not come about. So they had to sort through what Jesus' ministry and message meant, rather than what they had expected it to mean.

📖 5:1-2

THE BEATITUDES: ON THE MOUNTAIN

The region north of the Sea of Galilee is mountainous. Several important events take place on mountains—Jesus' temptation (4:8); Jesus praying (14:23); healing (15:29); and the Transfiguration (17:1).

Jesus assumed the authority of a rabbi with His teaching style and pose:

- He sat down, the customary position for teaching rabbis in Palestine.
- He opened His mouth, a Semitic idiom for public address.
- He began to teach.

📖 5:3

THE BEATITUDES: THE POOR IN SPIRIT

Poor in spirit means spiritually destitute without God. There are two Greek words for poor. The one used here means not simply "poor," but "abject poverty." It is only when the disciple understands that he is destitute without God that he can truly be blessed and filled by God.

Kingdom of heaven, the inheritance of the poor in spirit, is the same as kingdom of God. (See the discussion of this in Matthew 3:2.) *Kingdom* means the reign of God from heaven, or the reign of Christ. The kingdom or reign of God demands complete surrender to God. Only the poor in spirit, those who recognize that without God they are spiritually destitute, can surrender completely to the reign of God.

📖 5:4

THE BEATITUDES: THOSE WHO MOURN

Only those who mourn truly understand the need for comfort.

The background to this Beatitude is Isaiah 61:2-3. This passage is in the context of God's promise of restoration for those who repent. This is also the text that Jesus uses to introduce His ministry at Nazareth (Luke 4:18). Although this Beatitude carries the concept of mourning in general, within the context of Jesus' ministry the mourning is specifically for personal sin and estrangement from God.

📖 5:5

THE BEATITUDES: THE MEEK

The Greek word translated "meek" means gentle, humble, considerate, and unassuming. Jesus did not simply have in mind those who were gentle and kind, but rather those who were humble and downtrodden and oppressed. These will be the true heirs of God's promise and covenant with Abraham.

5:6

THE BEATITUDES: THOSE WHO HUNGER AND THIRST FOR RIGHTEOUSNESS

Those who hunger and thirst after righteousness are the poor, downtrodden, and oppressed, who are longing for the relief promised by God to His people. The term *righteousness* is a popular religious concept in both the Old and New Testaments. In the context of the Beatitudes (poor, downtrodden, grieving) it is best understood as justice. In this instance, it is best to understand righteousness as not just personal moral righteousness, but societal righteousness, or justice.

5:7

THE BEATITUDES: THE MERCIFUL

Justice and mercy were significant themes of the Old Testament prophets. On several occasions Jesus challenges the Pharisees and religious leaders of His day with the idea that God wants their mercy, more than their sacrifice. Jesus has in mind passages such as Hosea 6:6 and Micah 6:6–8. Mercy is obviously a fundamental characteristic of a disciple of Jesus.

5:8

THE BEATITUDES: THE PURE IN HEART

To see God is a Hebrew saying for standing before God (Psalm 11:7), or having fellowship with God in His kingdom. It is only those with a pure heart who are able to stand before God. This Beatitude recalls the thrust of several psalms such as Psalm 24:3–4.

5:9

THE BEATITUDES: THE PEACEMAKERS

The term translated as "peacemakers" is only found twice in the New Testament, here and in Colossians 1:20. The reason for this Beatitude lies most likely in the turbulent days of Israel under Roman rule. The violence came to a head for Judea and Jerusalem in the late 60s AD and the destruction of Jerusalem in AD 70.

Late in Jesus' ministry (according to John 13:35), He encourages the apostles to understand that the world will know that they are His disciples because they love one another. Here in Matthew He adds that it is those who are peacemakers who will be called children of God. The stress on peace, and following after things that make for peace, becomes a significant motif for disciples in the New Testament (Romans 12:16–18; 14:19; Hebrews 12:14; James 3:18; 1 Peter 3:11).

5:10

THE BEATITUDES: THOSE WHO ARE PERSECUTED FOR RIGHTEOUSNESS' SAKE

Righteousness in the Jewish sense had to do with a person's relationship with God. The righteous were in a right relationship with God. Because of that relationship, disciples would be persecuted. Persecution was synonymous with discipleship in the first three centuries of the Christian faith.

Jesus later warns the disciples that their discipleship will lead them into opposition with their families, the authorities, and the world. Many will die for their faith. He ties the blessedness of persecution to *suffering for righteousness sake*, not merely suffering for any reason. The reward of suffering persecution faithfully is a share in the kingdom (reign) of God. This is the very message of Revelation—if you die as a martyr for your faith in Jesus, you reign with Jesus in His kingdom.

`5:11–12`

THE BEATITUDES: WHEN MEN REVILE YOU AND PERSECUTE YOU

This Beatitude is obviously an expansion on the previous one regarding persecution. Jesus warns that being a disciple will cause some people to react harshly. In Jesus' day Christianity certainly was a threat to the Pharisees, Sadducees, and others who did not see in Jesus the kind of political Messiah they hoped for.

SUMMARY OF THE BEATITUDES:

- The Beatitudes addressed the disciples' character.
- They are set in the context of Old Testament theology and Jewish expectation.
- The blessedness they promised is a deep, inner spiritual richness, not a superficial happiness.
- They stress the radical nature of Christian discipleship.

`5:13–16`

THE DISCIPLES' INFLUENCE: SALT AND LIGHT

In regard to the influence that disciples have, notice that Jesus does not say the disciples should be *like* salt and light. He says they are salt and light. Disciples are expected to be an influence on those with whom they come into contact.

With reference to salt, Jesus picks a common metaphor. Everyone listening would know about salt and its unique characteristics. Whether Jesus is focusing more on the preservative nature, the seasoning nature, or the purifying nature of salt is impossible to determine. All three have relevant applications.

The salt that loses its saltiness is likely a reference to the impure salt drawn from the Dead Sea, which contained other minerals. Normally today, salt does not lose its saltiness, but the common salt of Jesus' day may well have been known for this characteristic. Whatever the case, salt that does not produce saltiness is worthy of being discarded.

The reference to light is intriguing. Typically light is a common metaphor referring to God rather than His followers (Isaiah 60:19–20; John 8:12; 1 John 1:5). Light was often opposed to darkness as an illustration of the radical difference between God and evil.

Jesus is the light of the world; His disciples are to reflect that light. The result of lives used properly to reflect the light of the kingdom will result in praise and glory being given to God.

📄 5:17–20

THE DISCIPLES' RIGHTEOUSNESS: TO EXCEED THAT OF THE SCRIBES AND PHARISEES

The major thrust of this section is that the disciples' righteousness must exceed that of the scribes and Pharisees—the Jewish religious leaders of the day. Also, the disciples' righteousness must be the right kind of righteousness. Here Jesus is pointing out that it's not *how* one becomes righteous, but rather the *nature* of that righteousness. At this time, the scribes and Pharisees held that righteousness could only be possible if one obeyed every minutia of the law as taught by the Jewish system and the traditions associated with it.

Jesus begins by stressing that His purpose is not to destroy the Law, but to establish its real purpose. In doing this, He addresses the scribes' and Pharisees' attitudes through six opposing conceptions or antitheses. Jesus wants the attitude of a disciple to address the deeper matters, the root issues for which the Law was intended, those which the scribes and Pharisees had missed.

The fact that Jesus intends to fulfill Jewish Law is vitally important to His ministry. In fact, He repeats the saying twice in a parallel form. But what exactly does Jesus mean by *fulfill*? The word translated "fulfill" can mean to accomplish, to complete, to finish, to bring to an end, to validate, to confirm, to establish, to uphold, or to bring out the intended meaning.

To emphasize His conviction that He has no intention of destroying the Law, Jesus adds that heaven and earth will pass away before He removes one *jot* (smallest letter, comma) or *dot* (period, tittle, little stroke) from the Law. The jot is a translation of *iota*, the letter "i" in English and the smallest letter in the Greek alphabet or the *yod*, one of the smallest letters in the Hebrew alphabet. The dot is one of the minute markings of a written text.

Matthew 5:20 is the clinching statement, or what this section is all about. It is possibly the key and pivotal statement to what follows in the Six Antitheses, and in Jesus' understanding of righteousness. His point: Kingdom righteousness is different from that of the established scribes and Pharisees. Jesus does not deny that the scribes and Pharisees have some form of righteousness. However, He stresses that their righteousness is not adequate for kingdom righteousness.

Critical Observation: Matthew's Understanding of Righteousness

Although the word *righteousness* is not often found in Matthew, the concept of righteousness is fundamental to Jesus' and Matthew's teaching. We can summarize Matthew's use of righteousness as:

1) the right relationship to God and His will, and

2) the right conduct that flows from that relationship to God.

In the Sermon on the Mount (here at 5:20, but also at 6:1 and 6:33), the point Jesus makes is that the behavior that flows from the disciples' relationship with God must be deeper and more extensive than that of the scribes and Pharisees, whose concept of righteousness was limited to superficial deeds in accordance with their interpretations of the Law.

THE SIX ANTITHESES (INTRODUCTION)

The expression "you have heard that it was said. . ." (NIV) is repeated in five of the antitheses and is included in similar form in the third antithesis. The use of this phrase was a typical device by which the teaching rabbis demurred from pitting their views against scripture, or even readily commenting on scripture. It was their custom to refer back to the teachings and conclusions of previous rabbis with the expression, "you have heard that it was said," contrasting their views with the rabbinic tradition rather than scripture.

Jesus sets His teaching against the rabbinic tradition with this same traditional saying but then draws His conclusions from scripture, correcting the rabbinic tradition. Jesus' teaching, therefore, carries a much stronger scriptural authority. It is no wonder that at the end of the Sermon on the Mount, the crowds are astonished because He teaches with authority (7:29).

ANTITHESIS ONE—MURDER

In Jesus' mind, the rabbinic teaching "You shall not kill; and whosoever kills shall be liable to judgment" misses the meaning and purpose of the sixth commandment (Exodus 20:13). The quotation of the commandment is precisely as stated in Exodus 20:13 and Deuteronomy 5:17; the concluding comment regarding judgment is an interpretation of the commandment.

It is difficult to determine with any certainty what was meant in the rabbinic tradition by *judgment*. In all probability, it referenced the judgment and death penalty of the Jewish Sanhedrin. If we move from that Jewish understanding, and remember that Jesus and Matthew are speaking to Jews, then we should interpret Jesus' teaching from within that Jewish context. The Jewish court system was similar to our present day court system, ranging from local county courts to state courts up to state supreme courts and the national supreme court. The Jewish system had a local Sanhedrin comprised of twenty-three male members, and then the Jerusalem Sanhedrin was comprised of seventy-one male members. Cases would move from the local court to the Jerusalem Sanhedrin.

The mention of "the fire of hell" certainly has eschatological (end times) judgment overtones. The phrase is from a Hebrew word meaning Valley of Hinnom, a valley which lay just outside the city of Jerusalem to the south. This was a smelly, smoky place where the city refuse was burned. In earlier pagan days it had been the place of human sacrifice. This valley became a suitable Jewish metaphor for the final judgment.

Jesus goes right to the heart of murder, addressing anger that grows to insult and finally into open denigration, which often lies at the heart of murder. The strict adherence to the sixth and other commandments was admirable, but fell short of the divine intent of the commandments.

In Matthew 22:36–40 Jesus observes that to love God and one's neighbor is the sum of the commandments, and in Matthew 19:16–22 Jesus tells the rich young man that there is more to eternal life than merely keeping the letter of the commandments. Jesus is teaching that there is more to the sixth commandment than mere murder.

The next verses (5:23–26), regarding making things right with your brother before taking an offering to the altar of sacrifice, drive home the point that God wants more than mere sacrifice. He wants love, mercy, and righteousness. This reinforces Jesus' message that love comes before the strict literal performance of the commandments. This does not diminish the need to respect and keep the commandments. It does, however, demand the correct understanding of the meaning of the commandments.

📖 5:27–30

ANTITHESIS TWO—ADULTERY

This quotation of the seventh commandment is verbatim from Exodus 20:14 and Deuteronomy 5:18. The word translated "adultery" is the normal word for the breaking of the marriage covenant in extramarital sexual intercourse.

Like the previous teaching of Jesus on murder, this teaching goes straight to the heart of the commandment—not the mere commission of the act, but the inner thought and being of the person. Jesus describes the heart of the sin—the lust of the eye and mind, the desiring or imagining a sexual relationship. From Jesus' perspective, this lustful desire of the eye and heart is the same as committing adultery, only this adultery is perhaps more serious than the act itself, for it speaks of the heart of man rather than merely his actions.

The plucking out of the offending right eye and right hand is a Hebrew idiom or hyperbole stressing the seriousness of the action or offense. This antithesis on adultery leads straight into the third antithesis on divorce.

📖 5:31–32

ANTITHESIS THREE—DIVORCE

Unlike the previous two antitheses, this one is not based on one of the commandments, but arises out of the command against adultery. Jesus will again comment on divorce in Matthew 19:3–12, where He is tested by the Pharisees on Deuteronomy 24. The debate on Deuteronomy 24 was obviously one that engaged the scribes and Pharisees considerably.

Although Jesus comments briefly on divorce and remarriage in this section, He does so because of the previous discussion on adultery. Jesus does not get involved in a lengthy discussion on divorce, but uses the occasion to address the problem of divorce. The proximity of this teaching to adultery leads one to believe that adultery and divorce both arise in the lustful heart of men. Whatever Jesus says about divorce and remarriage must be seen in the context of what He has most recently been discussing—adultery.

The current teaching was that all a man had to do was to give his wife a certificate of divorce in accordance with Moses' instruction (Deuteronomy 24). Jesus' response challenges the superficiality of that practice. In the discussion among the rabbis on divorce and remarriage in Jesus' day, two opinions held sway, that of Rabbi Hillel and that of Rabbi Shammai. Rabbi Hillel interpreted Deuteronomy 24 loosely so that divorce was granted for almost any reason. Rabbi Shammai interpreted Deuteronomy 24 narrowly so that divorce was granted only in cases of unchastity or sexual immorality. (See Demystifying Mark," page 180.)

Again, as in the case of the previous two antitheses, Jesus takes the more difficult road that challenges the inner heart of a person rather than the superficial nature. In this third antithesis Jesus takes the narrower view of divorce indicating that kingdom ethics on the matter of marriage and divorce are different from the laissez-faire ethic of much of the current attitude of His day. In Jesus' radical view of discipleship, more is expected of in the kingdom than is manifest in the practice of the day. (In Matthew 19:10, Jesus' attitude is so narrow that even the disciples have problems with it.)

📄 5:33–37

ANTITHESIS FOUR—OATHS

In this case Jesus is not taking issue with how the scribes and Pharisees treated a commandment, but rather against the lax rabbinic rationalization in the treatment of oaths. Jesus is addressing a crystallization of several teachings (Leviticus 19:12; Numbers 30:2; Deuteronomy 23:21–23; and possibly Exodus 20:7).

In this day and time oaths were used to assure the truth of the one making a promise, similar to a witness swearing to tell the whole truth with his or her hand on the Bible. Oaths could be sworn on many things. Swearing by heaven, the temple, earth (the footstool of God), Jerusalem, or one's head were typical examples of how rabbinic thinking shifted the oath to a lesser one which was not as binding as an oath before God.

Jesus teaches that kingdom ethics demand absolute integrity rather than the easy way out offered by lesser oaths. Kingdom ethics demand that the disciples' word be binding regardless of an oath. Jesus is not teaching against oaths taken, but against the attitude that lesser oaths are not binding. Nor is Jesus teaching against taking oaths, since Jesus takes an oath in Matthew 26:63–64 and God swears by His promise and His person (Luke 1:73; Acts 2:30; Hebrews 6:16–18).

📄 5:38–42

ANTITHESIS FIVE—RETALIATION

Rabbinic practice in response to the law that permitted recompense for loss (Exodus 21:24; Leviticus 24:20; Deuteronomy 19:21) permitted equal recompense for loss by one's neighbor. A legalistic response to personal loss was not what this original law was intended to accomplish. Jesus' understanding of these laws is that they were intended to restrict *excessive* retaliation rather than empower retaliation. Jesus' teaching runs in opposition to the current practice and normal human reactions. In broad sweeping terms, He teaches that kingdom ethics elicit no retaliation at all. Illustrating the extent of kingdom ethics, Jesus encourages the disciples when taken to court over a coat (inner garment) to surrender a cloak (outer garment) as well.

📄 5:43–48

ANTITHESIS SIX—LOVE

The command to love your neighbor is drawn directly from Leviticus 19:18, and later Jesus will teach that this is the second most important commandment. The second part of rabbinic teaching, to hate your enemy, is not commanded or taught directly, but may be a summary drawn from such passages as Psalm 139:21–22; 26:5; or Deuteronomy 7:2 and 30:7. Following centuries of aggression against Israel's enemies in the occupation of Canaan and Palestine, it is natural that Jews would see hating one's enemy as a legitimate attitude.

Jesus' response is a radical departure from current Jewish attitudes toward enemies, and the Jews had many enemies among the Roman occupation armies. In contrast to hating, Jesus teaches love for one's enemies, and prayers for those persecuting the disciple. Since persecution is to be a major part of discipleship for several centuries, this teaching will be a critical aspect of future kingdom ethics and behavior.

📖 6:1–18

THE DISCIPLES' PIETY: DEEDS OF RIGHTEOUSNESS (INTRODUCTION)

Setting Up the Section

In this section on the disciple's piety we find three important emphases:

1) **Almsgiving**
2) **Prayer**
3) **Fasting**

These three elements were important religious practices of Jewish religious lives.

📖 6:1–4

THE DISCIPLES' PIETY: ALMSGIVING

The main thrust of this section is that the disciple's piety, almsgiving, and prayer are not to be like that of the hypocrites who did their righteous deeds to be seen and admired by others. The disciple's prayer is also to be different from that of the Gentiles.

Although disciples are to let their lives shine as light (5:14), they are not to do so in order to be seen and admired by others. The reward of a public display of deeds is the public acclamation of others. The reward of righteous piety is the reward from the Father in heaven. Jesus is reacting to the public performance of piety practiced by many of the Jewish leaders of His time.

Matthew appropriately connects piety with the practice of almsgiving (6:2). The practice of giving money to the poor was common among the Jews. We have already noticed Jesus' concern for the poor in Matthew (5:3).

This was a Jewish problem of considerable concern to Jesus, as can be seen in His strong language. The English word *hypocrite* comes from a word that originally referred to one who performs in front of others, an actor. This is Jesus' opinion of the righteousness of the scribes and Pharisees. He sees in the Jewish leaders of the day an insincerity that is not befitting of the kingdom.

The expression, "do not let your left hand know what your right hand is doing. . ." (NIV) is a Hebrew idiom indicating the discretion needed in the process of doing benevolent works.

THE DISCIPLES' PIETY: PRAYER

Public prayer can be a challenge, especially to the one leading the prayer. There is the danger of it being said to impress others rather than being addressed to God. Here Jesus takes exception to the prayers of both the Jews and the Gentiles.

Apparently some people prayed in public to be seen by others. Jesus again observes that those who pray to be seen by others have their human reward in the acclamation of others, but those who pray unobtrusively will be seen by God.

In regard to the Gentiles, the empty phrases (babbling, rambling, repeating) are apparently attempts to manipulate God into fulfilling some desire of the petitioner by repeating a supposed magic formula, not merely the repetition of words. From Jesus' instruction and His own religious lifestyle, prayer should be an important aspect of the disciple's righteousness.

What follows is commonly referred to as the Lord's Prayer. Some take exception to this name and prefer to call this the Model Prayer. Certainly this is intended to be a model prayer—Jesus' words opening Matthew 6:9 indicate this clearly—but in contrast to model prayers taught by others (John the Baptist to his disciples) this is Jesus' model prayer, so it can legitimately be referred to as the Lord's Prayer.

Luke records that in this prayer, or at least on a similar occasion, Jesus' disciples ask Him to teach them to pray "as John taught his disciples. . ." (Luke 11:1 NIV).

From what we know of Judaism in Jesus' day, His model prayer is shaped by the prayer tradition and pattern of the synagogue. The primary concern is a redemptive theme, not concern for mundane, earthly matters.

Note the remarkable structure of the opening of this prayer. All three of these parallel clauses are modified by the last clause of the petition: on earth as it is in heaven. What this means is that disciples are to pray that:

> God's name would be holy. . .as it is in heaven, so on earth;
>
> God's kingdom would come. . .as it is in heaven, so on earth;
>
> God's will would be done. . .as it is in heaven, so on earth.

This is not a prayer that God's kingdom would come sometime in the near future, but a prayer that God's kingdom would be presently on earth just as it is in heaven. How? By His name being holy and His will being done.

The second petition of the Lord's Prayer (6:11) looks simple on the surface, but just what does Jesus mean by His request for daily bread? The Greek reads, "The bread of ours for tomorrow give us today." If this is a simple prayer for physical food, then it is the only emphasis on the physical in The Lord's Prayer. All the other petitions are for spiritual concerns. While there may be several interpretations, Jesus is not simply concerned for the mundane physical food (although this would fit well into the prayer for daily sustenance), but also for the spiritual food that sustains us for the future.

The next petition for forgiveness (6:12) is a prayer for the forgiveness of sins or, perhaps better put, shortcomings. The point in this petition is that disciples should pray to God on a regular basis for the forgiveness of their sins, but also that disciples must be forgiving like their Father in heaven.

The final petition (6:13) relates to temptation. First, the word often translated as "temptation" can mean both temptation and testing. While James 1:13 informs us that God does not tempt His children, God does allow His children to be tested. This is one of the secondary lessons we learn from the Old Testament book of Job.

However, this petition cannot be fully understood until put in context with the request for deliverance from evil. Perhaps it is better to translate *evil* as "the evil one." This petition is a plea to God that He deliver, rescue, guard, and protect those facing trials.

The final verses of this section (6:14–15) repeat the warning and encouragement to forgive one another as the Father forgives the disciple. However, here the statement is in a conditional form—if you forgive. . .your Father will forgive your trespasses.

📖 6:16–18

THE DISCIPLES' PIETY: FASTING

Again, Jesus contrasts the disciple's righteous behavior with that of the Jewish leaders whose fasting had become a performance of righteousness.

Fasting is an interesting subject. This is a Jewish practice that is more traditional than biblical in the sense that fasting was not commanded but practiced. We read of people in scripture fasting, but nowhere does it seem that it is commanded. Rabbinic tradition informs us that the stricter Jews fasted regularly on special days such as Monday and Thursdays.

From what we learn in the Gospels, Jesus is neither proposing that disciples fast nor condemning the practice of fasting. He simply speaks out against hypocritical fasting, which had as its goal to be noticed. Some fasting Jews disfigured their faces, didn't keep their hair tidy, or smeared ashes on their faces. It was this ostentation that Jesus speaks out against. Anointing the head (with oil) and washing the face, which Jesus suggests, has the opposite effect of the facial disfiguration or the smeared ashes.

Though fasting is less in the forefront today, the principles Jesus gives are still relevant. If a disciple chooses to fast as an occasion of deep spiritual mourning or commitment, this is admirable and to be commended. However, it should be a private matter and not become a spectacle. Demanding others fast or indirectly communicating that fasting is a sign of one's spiritual superiority over another is an abuse of this fine practice.

📖 6:19–34

THE DISCIPLES' AMBITION (INTRODUCTION)

Setting Up the Section

The general thrust of this section is this: The disciple's ambition should be toward being rich in God, not in worldly things. The key to this passage relates to the problem we all have with anxiety over the things of this life. Disciples must know that their hope and comfort lie not in Jerusalem or this world but in the future prepared by God for His people.

THE DISCIPLES' AMBITION: TRUE RICHES

This passage serves as a key to the upcoming discussion on anxiety. It was common in the Jewish tradition to see good works as being the treasures that one lays up in heaven—not good works as merit, but good works as serving. The result of true discipleship (loving service, good works) is a treasure waiting in heaven. Jesus promises a treasure in heaven to those who give to the poor (19:21).

THE DISCIPLES' AMBITION: TWO PARABLES

Jesus reinforces His point with two parables, one regarding the problem of covetousness and lust, the other the problem of serving two masters.

The good (single, clear, unclouded) eye is contrasted with the bad (evil, diseased) eye. In both instances, Jesus is speaking figuratively of covetousness and lust. The thought carries over from the previous discussion on treasure—what a person covets or lusts after shapes his or her life.

The second parable of two masters is clearly understood in a culture familiar with slavery. The term *mammon* (money, wealth, property) illustrates the anxiety of physical earthly matters as opposed to spiritual heavenly matters. In Luke 16:9–11, Luke adds the term *unrighteous* mammon (tainted, dishonest, worldly), contrasting this focus in life with true righteousness that derives from a right relationship with God.

The expression of hating the one and loving the other (6:24) was a common Jewish idiom that stressed the contrast between absolute and partial commitment. The love-hate terminology found in both Judaism and Jesus' teaching should not be taken literally, but should be understood as an idiom stressing the absolute priority of certain matters over others.

THE DISCIPLES' AMBITION: TRUST AND ANXIETY

This section is also found in almost the same content in Luke 12:22–31, although some of the terms used by Luke differ from those used by Matthew. Both Matthew and Luke find this teaching of Jesus to be fundamental to their teaching, stressing the proper focus and commitment of discipleship.

Jesus reminds the disciples that life is full of matters more necessary than food and clothing. As important as physical concerns may be, they must never dominate the disciples' dedication. Jesus' illustration of the birds and flowers is most meaningful and beautiful. The God who is able to take care of and provide for His natural creation can surely take care of and provide for His ultimate and spiritual creation—mankind.

In contrast to this, Jesus encourages disciples to seek other goals and priorities in life that hold better and more lasting hope. This is the climactic teaching of the whole section, and perhaps of the entire Sermon on the Mount—seek first His kingdom, and everything else will follow (6:33). Perhaps these words are some of the best known of all Jesus' teachings. But what do they mean?

The first priority of the disciple is to seek the reign of God in one's own life. This whole section is an encouragement to refocus one's life, and a warning against anxieties that interfere with ultimate matters such as God's reign and a right relationship with God.

The admonition to not be anxious about tomorrow (6:34) is similar to the prayer of Matthew 6:11 for daily bread. The disciple should be more concerned for the present today than for what might happen tomorrow, over which we have no control. Do not be anxious of tomorrow or the future. Leave that to God; He will provide.

📖 7:1–20

THE DISCIPLES' PITFALLS (INTRODUCTION)

Setting Up the Section

In this section the disciples are warned of the pitfall of constantly judging one another (as was the practice of the Pharisees), and are encouraged to treat one another as they would like to be treated (the Golden Rule). Finally, Matthew includes admonitions by Jesus to be alert to false teachers, and a call to commitment to the teachings of Jesus and the will of God.

📖 7:1–6

THE DISCIPLES' PITFALLS: JUDGING ONE ANOTHER

Apparently the tendency to judge one another was widespread in the first century and has been common in religious groups throughout history.

Although Christianity should be an exception to this weakness (the basic ethical foundation to the Christian faith is that disciples, being children of God, should love one another since love is the fulfillment of the law, and God is love [see John 13:34, 35; 1 John 3:11; 4:7]), but human nature still leaves Christians open to this sin.

When Jesus says, "Judge not...," He is not saying that believers should not be discerning or should never point out sin. Jesus is not implying that disciples should never make personality or relational decisions, sometimes even judgments, but that they should beware that this does not become habitual. There are certainly times when disciples must make fellowship decisions (1 Corinthians 5:9–13; 2 Thessalonians 3:6–13), and other times when disciples must simply decide that they cannot share in the lifestyle of others. But the warning is against becoming judgmental and continually pointing to the faults of others, instead of loving them and looking out for their best interests.

Jesus' amusing story of a man with a log in his eye, trying to take a speck out of another's eye, is one of the most powerful and telling illustrations of human foolishness manifest in many of our judgmental situations. If we took our own imperfections seriously, we would have little time for judging others. Jesus' warning is punctuated by the harsh term *hypocrite*, which, as before, implies a play actor. Those who make a habit of judging others are playacting in the Christian faith.

The next short section has raised several problems for interpretation. The parable in itself is not difficult. One should not give to the unclean (dogs and swine) that which is clean or holy.

However, does *the unclean* refer to Gentiles, or simply to the undeserving? Does it perhaps refer to the hypocrite of 7:5? It is difficult to determine what holy thing Jesus is referring to at this point as it relates to the previous admonition against judging. It may be in the larger picture that in the kingdom, disciples who love one another should not destroy the harmony of the kingdom by their sinful tendency to constantly be judging one another. The nature of a disciple's life in the kingdom, or the nature of the harmony of the kingdom, is that which is holy.

📄 7:7–12

THE DISCIPLES' PITFALLS: PRAYER, FAITH, AND THE GOLDEN RULE

The next pitfall disciples face is the loss of faith (7:7–12). Jesus encourages His disciples to keep on asking, seeking, and knocking, for true faith never loses heart and quits.

Again, Matthew follows this encouragement of Jesus with a saying that seems to be detached, the Golden Rule, but it does have some connection to the previous admonitions of Jesus. Disciples are to be like their heavenly Father. They are to love one another and be constant in their faith.

The Golden Rule, as this saying is commonly known, is not unique to Jesus or Christianity, for it is found in most religions in some form. In Judaism it is found in the negative form. Rabbi Hillel summarized it as follows: "What is hateful to yourself, do to no other." The Christian form as given by Jesus is, however, more positive and powerful than the negative form, which does not deny the good intention of the negative form. Again, this proverbial saying is simply another way of expressing the fundamental kingdom ethic of loving one another. The Golden Rule, expressing the law of love, is what the law and prophets were all about (7:12).

📄 7:13–20

THE DISCIPLES' PITFALLS: FALSE TEACHERS

The following three admonitions, all demonstrating pitfalls the disciple faces, are related. They address the problem of false teachers and commitment to the teachings of Jesus.

We are again introduced to the Jewish idiom of two opposing ways—here, one is the narrow way, the other way broad. The narrow way is the more difficult. Jesus knows that the road ahead for disciples will call for opposition and even serious persecution. Faced by such choices, disciples will be tempted to choose the easier way, perhaps that of retaining their Jewish religion based on law rather than following God in freedom.

The New Testament is replete with warnings against false teachers, indicating the seriousness of the problem faced by the early church. However, false teachings in the New Testament do not refer to differences of biblical interpretation or church doctrines. In the New Testament the truth or sound doctrine refers to teachings regarding the nature of Jesus as the Son of God, the Messiah. Apostasy is a denial of the divinity of Jesus and His death, burial, and resurrection. False teaching is that which denies the all-sufficiency of Jesus and the gospel of grace through faith that was preached by the apostles.

📖 7:21–27

COMMITMENT TO JESUS AND TO THE WILL OF GOD

Jesus is fully aware that many will follow Him, but on their own terms or when it is convenient. Obedience to the will of God will be the hallmark of true discipleship. In the context of the Sermon, with its heavy emphasis on righteousness as the right relationship with God and His will, it is not surprising the Jesus closes with this teaching. Failure to submit to and do the will of God will result in Jesus' denial of the disciple.

Jesus refers to entering the kingdom in the future (7:21). The verb in the future tense indicates that Jesus has in mind the future eschatological kingdom that one will enter after the judgment day—not the present reality of the inaugurated kingdom we currently enjoy. This is also supported by the words *on that day* (7:22). This is a common Jewish reference to the judgment day and is found in many instances in both the Old and New Testaments (Isaiah 2:20; Amos 8:9; 9:11; Zephaniah 1:10, 14; Zechariah 14:4; 2 Thessalonians 1:10; 2 Timothy 4:8).

The parable of the two builders (7:24–27) provides a powerful conclusion to this section on commitment to the will of God, as well as to Jesus' emphasis on the necessity of doing the will of God.

📖 7:28–29

JESUS' AUTHORITY

When Jesus finishes teaching, the crowds are astonished at the authority with which He spoke to them. A statement like this can be found at the conclusion of each of the great discourses in Matthew. In each of these formula endings to the teachings of Jesus, Matthew draws attention to the authoritative role of Jesus:

- Matthew 5–7   He teaches the crowds (The Sermon on the Mount)
- Matthew 10   He teaches His disciples (The Limited Commission)
- Matthew 13   He teaches the disciples (The Kingdom Parables)
- Matthew 18   He teaches the disciples (The Christian Community)
- Matthew 23–25 He teaches the disciples (The Apocalyptic Discourse)

This is one of Matthew's tools that emphasizes the unique character of Jesus.

MATTHEW 8:1–9:38

NARRATIVE 2: THE AUTHORITY OF THE MESSIAH

Setting Up the Section

In this section we move from one miracle to the next as we see Jesus performing the works expected of the Messiah. The focus here is on the messianic deeds Jesus performs. Matthew follows Mark in recording a string of Jesus' miracles, with a few observations included by Matthew. As in Mark, Matthew demonstrates Jesus' power over physical illnesses of all types, the demon world, as well as His power over the physical world of nature. The miracles of restoration and healing recorded here also indicate the presence of the kingdom of God (Isaiah 29:22–24; 35:3–10).

While Jesus continues to do the powerful works expected of the Messiah, He is not accepted by the scribes and Pharisees.

📖 8:1–4

CLEANSING A LEPER

Leprosy was a common ailment in the ancient world, and one Israel had encountered throughout its history. It was a most dreaded illness. Biblical leprosy is not the same as modern leprosy (Hansen's disease). In the Bible, the word *leprosy* refers to a variety of skin ailments, some serious and some not—but all rendered its sufferer unclean. Thus, the issue of leprosy has as much to do with ritual uncleanness as great danger to health or imminent death.

Having been declared a leper, a person was considered dead. Leprosy was so serious a problem that the Mosaic Law addressed the condition of the leper and the process of being cured from this dreaded illness (Leviticus 13–14). Jesus heals this man and instructs him not to tell anyone about his healing, but to do as the Law of Moses commanded regarding cleansing from leprosy.

Jesus' instruction not to tell anyone about the cleansing is in line with His desire not to be followed because of sensationalism. Jesus simply does not wish to be followed because of mistaken understandings of His messianic role.

Jesus' instruction for the leper to show himself to the priest as proof (a witness) is interesting. The proof was in keeping with the Jewish legal requirements for a cleansed leper's return to society. Jesus' requiring this demonstrates His support of the Jewish law.

📖 8:5–13

THE CENTURION'S SERVANT HEALED

The centurion was either a Syrian or Roman, probably a Roman. He was a soldier in command of 100 soldiers. Groups of Roman soldiers were posted throughout the Empire. The encounter between Jesus and this man introduces a major theme that Matthew develops throughout his Gospel: The Jewish religious leaders who should have believed in Jesus do not, and the Gentiles, who had no real reason to believe, do (remember Herod and the Wise men of Matthew 2:1–12).

There are some questions as to whether the specific word that Matthew uses in verse 6 should be translated as "son" or "servant." Luke's parallel of this account uses a word that undoubtedly translates as "servant." Either way, Jesus' response and the significance of the account remain the same.

The relationship of Greek words in Jesus' response—I will come and heal him—is interesting. The Greek reads "I, having come, will heal him." The sentence indicates that Jesus has no hesitancy in entering the Gentile's house and healing his son or servant. The centurion realizes the problem and, sensitive to Jewish concerns, indicates his unworthiness to have Jesus in his home. Jesus is amazed at the depth of this man's faith and confidence. Thus His remark that nowhere in all Israel has He found such depth of faith.

Demystifying Matthew

The comment regarding those from the east and west (Gentiles) sitting with Abraham, Isaac, and Joseph is striking, and would be shocking to the Jewish mind. That Gentiles would sit with Jews at the eschatological banquet (Jewish eschatological expectation of the end-of-the-world banquet with God) was in keeping with Matthew's purpose in challenging his Jewish-Christian community to engage in a worldwide mission to include the Gentiles (Matthew 28:18–20). Jesus declares that those to whom the kingdom should have belonged will be thrown into outer darkness, obviously because of their refusal to accept God's Messiah.

📖 8:14–17

PETER'S MOTHER-IN-LAW HEALED

Upon entering Peter's house in Capernaum and learning that Peter's mother-in-law is ill with a fever, Jesus heals her. Many others hear of this and gather at Peter's house. Jesus heals all who are sick and demon possessed. Matthew sets this series of miracles in the context of one of the ten unique fulfillment prophecies he builds into his text. The citation is obviously of Isaiah 53:4, but is apparently a free translation by Matthew. The brevity of this section, describing the powerful miracles of Jesus, highlights the incomparable authority of Jesus as the Messiah.

📖 8:18–22

IMPULSIVE AND RELUCTANT WOULD-BE DISCIPLES

First a scribe, then another would-be disciple are challenged by Jesus to understand the radical nature of discipleship.

The scribe promises to follow Jesus wherever He goes, not realizing the true nature of the radical call to discipleship. That call means leaving all, including home and its comforts.

The second would-be disciple is a reluctant follower who likewise does not understand the commitment demanded by discipleship. Removed from the Jewish setting, this saying of Jesus is difficult to understand, but left in the Jewish context it has considerable meaning. The context is the Nazarite vow of Numbers 6:6–8 and the priestly service of Leviticus 21:11. In both cases, touching a dead body resulted in ceremonial uncleanness. Both called for a radical dedication and sanctification. Discipleship of Jesus calls for the same sanctification from the world and dedication to service. Kingdom service is total commitment to Jesus.

Take It Home

This section dramatizes the dedication demanded by messianic discipleship. The full force of the radical call to discipleship must be set in the context of Jesus' own disciples and the reaction of the Jewish leaders to Jesus, and then in the context of Matthew's community and their settlement in a new and hostile Gentile community. However, even today, the call to discipleship must be accompanied by a willingness to make a radical change in lifestyle. Following Jesus still demands a willingness to leave everything, including our "boats" and follow Jesus.

📖 8:23–27

THE STORM STILLED

The miracle of stilling the great storm is a lesson on faith, or the need for faith in seemingly impossible situations. The disciples are still struggling to understand the full nature and power of Jesus. This section also speaks clearly on the nature of discipleship. Disciples are people of deep faith, even in the face of the impossible and unbelievable.

The Sea of Galilee was surrounded by hills and was susceptible to sudden and violent storms. Matthew indicates that the sea was extremely rough and dangerous. The disciples' frantic reaction is a natural one. Jesus' response and His reference to little faith pick up on one of Matthew's themes: people of little faith who should have great faith. Jesus' response to the disciples' fear is found five times in Matthew (6:30; 8:26; 14:31; 16:8; 17:20), and is well translated "O men of little faith" as in the Revised Standard Version, or "you of little faith" in the New International Version.

The disciples marvel that Jesus can still the sea, and ask the rhetorical question, "What sort of man is this, that even the winds and sea obey Him?" (NRSV). The answer is obvious—this man is not an ordinary man, because only God can command the waves and sea and they obey the command.

Note the following psalms with which Jesus and His disciples would have been familiar, and surely Matthew's community would have known:

- Psalm 89:8–9: "O Lord God Almighty, who is like you? You are mighty, O LORD, and your faithfulness surrounds you. You rule over the surging sea; when its waves mount up, you still them" (NIV).
- Psalm 65:5–7: "You answer us with awesome deeds of righteousness, O God our Savior, the hope of all the ends of the earth and of the farthest seas, who formed the mountains by your power, having armed yourself with strength, who stilled the roaring of the seas, the roaring of their waves, and the turmoil of the nations" (NIV).

8:28–34

DEMONS CAST OUT

Crossing the Sea of Galilee to the eastern shore of the Gadarenes (Luke calls them the Gerasenes), Jesus encounters two persons possessed by demons (a common phenomenon of that day).

The exact location indicated by Matthew and Luke can't be known with complete certainty. This possibly refers to a town called Gergasa (modern Khersa or Kursi), which is among cliffs overlooking the Sea of Galilee.

Critical Observation

Another problem encountered in this section, and which we encounter on other occasions when we compare Matthew with Mark and Luke, is that Matthew's account includes two demoniacs—Mark's (Mark 5:1–20) includes one man, and Luke's includes one man (Luke 8:26–39). This should not pose a serious problem, with Matthew's predilection for truth being established by two witnesses. He includes both men rather than only describing one of them. In another event, Mark (Mark 10:46–52) describes one blind man, but Matthew (Matthew 20:29–34) describes two.

In contrast to the Jewish leaders in Matthew (scribes and Pharisees), here at least two demons recognize Jesus as the Son of God. The little expression "before the appointed time" (NIV) in verse 29 indicates the Jewish understanding of an end-time judgment. The demons recognize that in Jesus the end was already near.

In keeping with their request, Jesus casts the demons out and they enter a herd of pigs, causing them to rush over the cliff into the sea. The Gadarenes obviously do not understand and are fearful of Jesus, possibly believing Him to be a powerful magician. They ask Him to leave the area. After all, they have just lost a herd of pigs. The fact that they had a herd of pigs indicates that they were Gentiles, not Jews.

9:1–8

A PARALYTIC FORGIVEN AND HEALED

Returning to His own city (Capernaum), Jesus enters a house and a paralytic is brought to Him. Jesus does a startling thing for the man—He forgives his sins. The scribes are beside themselves because they know only God can forgive sins, and Jesus is doing just that. In their eyes this is a grievous sin—blasphemy (taking or using God's name falsely or inappropriately). Their problem is that they have not taken note of His messianic signs and will not believe that He is the Messiah.

In verse 5 Jesus asks which is easier, to say someone's sins are forgiven or to tell a paralyzed person to walk. While claiming to forgive sins is easier (Anyone can claim this, and who could disprove them?), the healing proved He had the power to forgive sins.

Demystifying Matthew

The connection of sickness and sin lay deep in the Jewish psyche and could be taken all the way back to the Fall (Genesis 3). All sickness, suffering, and death can be traced back to the Fall and God's condemnation of sin. However, the Jewish religious leaders took this to the extreme: They blamed sickness on individual sin or the sin of the parents. Jesus did not follow that line of thought, but nevertheless the connection between the Fall and sickness and death cannot be overlooked.

The cross of Jesus overshadows this section; Jesus could forgive sins for He was the Son of God. It would be much easier to heal a man than to forgive sins. The forgiveness of sins was the greater gift of the Messiah, connecting His ministry to His primary reason for coming, that is, to die on the cross for sins.

We encounter one of Jesus' early "Son of Man" sayings in this section. Jesus uses the term in the tradition of Daniel 7:13–14 to demonstrate that He has the authority to forgive.

📖 9:9–13

MATTHEW'S CALL

This is the only Gospel in which the first disciple is called Matthew. Both Mark and Luke call him Levi. Many suggestions have been given for the difference in names. The simplest and most likely is that Matthew had two names, Matthew and Levi. This was not uncommon in ancient times, especially among the Jews.

All three synoptic authors identify Matthew/Levi as a tax collector. Tax collectors were despised for their avarice, being self-serving and dishonest. Furthermore, they were the agents of the despised Roman power. They were considered by the Jews to be among the worst of sinners. In fact, Jews viewed tax collectors to be as lowly as the Gentiles. When accused by the Pharisees of fraternizing with tax collectors and sinners, Jesus responds by saying that it is the sick who need a physician, not the healthy. This did not mean that Jesus saw the Pharisees as healthy, but that He saw the tax collectors as those in need of help. He then follows this with a searing reference to Hosea 6:6, the scathing implication of which would have been clearly understood by His audience. Jesus adds furthermore that His purpose in coming is not to call those who saw themselves as righteous, but to call those who would see their need, the sinners. This passage draws attention to the growing antagonism between the Pharisees and Jewish leaders and Jesus.

📖 9:14–17

THE QUESTING ABOUT FASTING

Fasting was a cultural-religious practice with a spiritual depth almost synonymous with righteousness among the Jewish religious leaders. The Day of Atonement was the only annual national fast day set out in Jewish Law. The requirement for this fast was repentance for sin (Leviticus 16:29, 31; 23:27, 32; Numbers 29:7).

Demystifying Matthew

There are several references to personal fasts that involve smaller groups and individuals. These are likewise associated with occasions of mourning and penitence, or are associated with prayers of supplication (1 Kings 21:27; Numbers 30:13). After the Jews' return from exile, a number of annual public fasts were instituted (Ezra 8:21–23; Nehemiah 9:1). Of particular interest would be the fast at the time of Purim (Esther 4:16).

- During the period between the Old and New Testaments, fasting as a sign of spiritual devotion was associated with prayer and almsgiving.

- By New Testament times, fasting as a sign of mourning and for personal sin, as well as its association with prayer, had become synonymous with the righteous life.

- During the time of Jesus, the practice of the Pharisees was to fast twice a week, once on Monday, then again on Thursday.

- Jesus gave instruction regarding fasting in the Sermon on the Mount, warning against the hypocrisy of the scribes and Pharisees (Matthew 6:16–18).

In this section, the setting for the discussion of fasting arises from the question of why the disciples of John fasted, but Jesus' disciples do not. Fundamental to the situation was that John and his disciples were expectantly waiting for the Messiah. Jesus knows that the messianic age is breaking in through Himself. The presence of the Messiah is not an occasion of mourning, but one of rejoicing. In other words, while the Messiah is present, fasting is not called for. In the coming days, when the Messiah will no longer be with them, there will be time for fasting.

Jesus follows His answer with two proverbial sayings: the first regarding new cloth and old garments, the second regarding new wine and old wineskins. The core of these two proverbial statements is that you do not mix the old and the new. Perhaps there is an indication in Jesus' response that the old message of Torah thinking should not be mixed with the new messianic ways and that the coming of the kingdom inaugurated a new age of salvation for all people, not just a reforming of Judaism.

📖 9:18–26

THE ISSUE OF BLOOD STOPPED AND THE DEAD RAISED

Matthew's narrative that includes these miracles is much shorter than Mark's. This indicates that Matthew's purpose in recording them is different from that of Mark. Mark's emphasis is on the remarkable power of Jesus. Matthew's purpose is to demonstrate the remarkable faith in the woman and the ruler of the synagogue.

The first story regarding the ruler (Mark and Luke revealed his name as Jairus, a ruler in the synagogue) is abruptly broken off for a while by the intrusion of the woman with the twelve-year hemorrhage. Matthew does not explain to his Jewish audience that the man is a ruler of the synagogue.

First, the healing of the woman. We do not know for certain the nature of her hemorrhage, but assume that it is a hemorrhaging of the womb. If this is the case, then her problem is two-fold:

1) The difficulty of a physical problem she has endured for twelve years.
2) The ceremonial uncleanness that would have been pronounced on her by Jewish custom because she is bleeding (Leviticus 15:19–23).

She is unclean, yet she reaches out and touches the fringes of Jesus' garment. Jesus evidently follows the Jewish instructions regarding the four fringes to be at the four corners of the garment (Numbers 15:38–41; Deuteronomy 22:12).

It is obvious that this story is about the simple faith of the woman. She is convinced that if she can only touch the fringes of His garment, she will be healed. Jesus acknowledges her faith and encourages her to take heart, for her faith has made her well. Instantly she is healed.

Now to Jairus, the ruler of the synagogue, and his daughter. Jairus's faith is also the point of this section, indicating that some of the Jewish leadership believed. His confidence in Jesus is such that all Jesus has to do is reach out His hand and touch his daughter and she will be healed. (Luke's Gospel tells the story from the beginning when Jairus's daughter is dying. Matthew tells the story from the point where Jesus gets into the action, when Jairus first contacts Him.) By the time Jesus gets to Jairus's house, the girl is dead. When Jesus says the girl is not dead, the crowd laughs because they know she is dead. Jesus knows, however, that her death is not permanent, for He is about to raise her up from death.

9:27–34

THE BLIND SEE, AND A DEMON IS EXORCISED

In striking contrast to the Jewish leaders, two blind men recognize Jesus and confess their faith by calling Him the Son of David. (Notice Matthew's reference to *two* blind men. This is significant in a Jewish context because two witnesses were required for any testimony.) Jesus asks whether these men really believe He can heal them, and they confess they do. They not only demonstrate great faith, but acknowledge Him as Lord, something the Jewish leaders refused to do. Jesus immediately restores their sight. Again, Matthew demonstrates the necessity of great faith in Jesus, and the acknowledgement of His lordship.

Jesus, fearing that the crowds would acclaim Him Messiah for the wrong reason, strictly charges the two men not to tell others of their healing. This proves to be an impossible task, for soon the news of this spreads throughout the region.

Without much fanfare, Mathew recounts that Jesus also has power to cast out demons, for a demoniac is healed. The crowds marvel and observe that nothing like what Jesus is doing has been seen in Israel. In contrast to the two blind men, the demoniac, and the crowds, the Pharisees refuse to believe in Jesus, and charge that Jesus has cast out demons by Satan, the prince of demons. There's no response from Jesus listed here, but in chapter 12 a similar charge is made with a response from Jesus included.

Critical Observation

Matthew 9:35 marks the beginning of a transitional passage connecting Jesus' messianic deeds and Matthew's second discourse. Here's a review of the flow of Matthew's Gospel thus far:

- Narrative One established Jesus' right to be the Messiah, and was devoted to the preparation for His ministry. His genealogy and birth narrative emphasized the divine intervention aspect of His birth. Narrative One closed with the radical call of the disciples (Peter, Andrew, James, and John.)

- Discourse One, the Sermon on the Mount, described the character, influence, righteousness, and ambition of a disciple, and introduced the radical nature of discipleship. We learned what kind of person a disciple of Jesus should be.

- In Narrative Two Jesus performed astonishing miracles and demonstrated the ministry of the Messiah. There was a developing contrast between the Jewish leaders, who should have believed in Jesus but were blind to His ministry and messiahship, and the great faith of those who had no great reason to believe other than their need. There was also developing opposition from the Jewish leaders. The emphasis in this narrative section was on Jesus performing the powerful deeds of the Messiah.

9:35–38

THE NEED FOR WORKERS

Jesus continues to preach and teach the gospel of the kingdom in the synagogues, performing great messianic deeds. Matthew emphasizes that Jesus has compassion on the crowds because they are harassed and are without a shepherd. The Jewish leaders (scribes and Pharisees) should have been providing this leadership, but were not.

With the observation that the harvest is plentiful, Jesus means that there are many people who will believe in the gospel of the kingdom. The scribes and Pharisees should have been laboring in the kingdom, but were more interested in their religious position. Jesus' instruction is for the disciples to pray for the Lord of the harvest to send laborers into the ministry of the kingdom.

MATTHEW 10:1–42

DISCOURSE 2: THE LIMITED COMMISSION

Setting Up the Section

In the second narrative (Matthew 8–9), Matthew paralleled Mark's basic narrative of Jesus' powerful messianic ministry as He went from place to place, performing the powerful works expected of the Messiah. At the conclusion of this narrative, Jesus encouraged the disciples to pray that the Lord of the harvest would send laborers.

At this point, Mathew's narrative takes a dramatic turn, for the laborers sent out into the harvest turn out to be the disciples themselves. Here, Matthew discusses the commissioning of the twelve apostles in greater detail than do Mark and Luke (Mark 6:7–13; Luke 9:1–6).

We call this section the limited commission because Jesus limits the scope of the effort to the Jews. The disciples are told not to preach to the Gentiles or the Samaritans at this stage, but only to Israel. Later, in Matthew 28:19–20, Jesus charges His followers to make disciples of all nations—that passage is often referred to as the Great Commission.

Mark and Luke also record this commission (Mark 6:7–13; Luke 9:1–6), but neither of them limit the commission to only Israel. Since Mark and Luke are writing to Gentile audiences, the point is not as relevant, particularly in light of the later, greater commission. However, Matthew is writing to a Jewish audience who should have been able to understand that the gospel is intended first for their nation, who were to be God's special people and a light of revelation for the Gentiles (Isaiah 49:6).

📖 10:1–4

COMMISSIONING THE DISCIPLES

In verse 1, Matthew refers to Jesus' closest followers as the twelve disciples, but then in the second verse he calls them twelve *apostles*. The term *apostle* means "one sent out," or a person commissioned to go.

The names of the twelve apostles differ in some traditions or accounts. In John 1:45, Nathaniel is listed rather than Bartholomew. In some manuscripts, Thaddaeus is known as Labbaeus, and in Luke 6:15, Simon the Cananaean (Aramaic for "zealous one") is called Simon the Zealot. Notice that Matthew groups the names into six groups of two. In similar fashion, in Luke 10:1, Luke records Jesus sending seventy disciples out in groups of two. This is significant in the Jewish culture in that two witnesses were required to affirm truthful testimony.

📖 10:5–15

THE MISSION OF THE APOSTLES

After His resurrection, Jesus will again commission the apostles (Acts 1:6–8), when He charges them to begin witnessing first to Jerusalem, then to Judea, Samaria, and finally to the end of the earth. The kingdom is to begin with Israel, but is not to be limited to Israel. On the day of Pentecost (Acts 2) Peter preaches the first gospel sermon to the Jews; in Acts 8 Philip preaches to the Samaritans; then in Acts 10 Peter preaches the first gospel sermon to the Gentiles (Cornelius and his household).

The content of the gospel to be preached by the twelve apostles in the limited commission is the same as that preached by Jesus, "The kingdom of heaven is near" (4:17 NIV). Along with this preaching, the apostles are to perform the messianic deeds of healing, identifying their message with that of the Messiah.

Jesus' instruction to take no provisions on the journey and to stay with those who welcome them is within the tradition of traveling rabbis or teachers in both the Jewish and Gentile cultures. Traveling or itinerant teachers and philosophers were common in the Jewish world, and it was expected by good Jewish communities to welcome and care for such itinerant rabbis (Romans 15:19–24; 1 Thessalonians 2; 2 John; and 3 John). In Matthew 10:15, Jesus adds a sense of finality on those who do not accept the apostles and the message they preach, comparing them to Sodom and Gomorrah.

📖 10:16–42

WARNINGS OF OPPOSITION TO THE PREACHING (INTRODUCTION)

Setting Up the Section

In four alarming paragraphs, Matthew records Jesus warning the disciples of serious opposition and persecution that will result from preaching the kingdom message.

📖 10:16–23

WARNINGS: PERSECUTION

Because of their testimony, the disciples will be hated and faced with death. The apostles are not to be overly concerned as to how to react in such circumstances, for the Holy Spirit will give them the words they need.

You can hear throughout this text not only Jesus' concern for His disciples, but also Matthew's concern for his community as they testify to their faith in a hostile Jewish and Gentile context. Persecution is sure to arise and threaten.

Jesus uses the puzzling expression that they will not go through all the cities before (or until) the Son of Man has come. This expression could refer to:

1) the transfiguration of Jesus (Matthew 16:28 and 17:1–2);
2) the destruction of Jerusalem itself (Matthew 24:30);
3) some other unusual event such as the day of Pentecost (Acts 2);
4) the coming of Jesus at any time as a demonstration of His final judgment (Revelation 1:7; 2:16; 22:7, 12);
5) Jesus' second coming at the end of the world (Matthew 24:28).

Keep in mind that Jesus' words were originally spoken *before* the destruction of the temple in Jerusalem, while Matthew's Gospel was probably written afterwards. Jesus' original listeners and Matthew's later readers encountered these ideas from differing perspectives. If the coming of the Son of Man referred to the destruction of Jerusalem, and Matthew was writing *after* the destruction of Jerusalem, it is possible that Matthew's purpose in recording this was to challenge his Jewish church community to move on to Jesus' greater commission to disciple the Gentiles, not just the Jews. Jesus obviously had a vision of a later Gentile mission beyond the cities of Israel and the destruction of Jerusalem, but at the time that He spoke these recorded words, His focus was still on the apostles and their early Jewish mission.

10:24–33

WARNINGS: THE DISCIPLE AND HIS FOLLOWERS

Jesus warns His disciples that they should expect nothing less than what He, their teacher, will receive from the Jewish leaders. Since the Jewish leaders had called Jesus "Beelzebul"—a Hebrew name for Satan (9:27–34), they would also malign Jesus' disciples. Jesus warns the apostles not to fear those who could, and would, kill them, but rather to fear the One who had the power to destroy both body and soul in hell—God Himself.

The term for "hell" is the Hebrew *Gehenna*, meaning the valley of Hinnom, or the place of destruction. It was a euphemism for the Christian concept of hell. (This is a different concept than *hades*, the place of the dead.) The apostles are encouraged not to fear persecution because God knows them and will ultimately protect them. This does not mean that they will not have to die, but it means that they do not have to fear the destruction of hell. Jesus will acknowledge before God those who faithfully testify to Him as Messiah.

10:34–39

WARNINGS: THE DISCIPLE AND THE CROSS

Jesus explains that His coming will bring suffering for those who believe in Him. Parents and family will turn against the disciple because of Jesus. The radical nature of messianic discipleship is that disciples must choose Jesus before all family allegiance. Those who will not choose Jesus over all others are not worthy disciples. Jesus adds a brief statement about disciples taking up their crosses and following Him. He will again take up this thought in Matthew 16:24–28. Taking up one's cross is a picture of being willing to die for Jesus—it means far more than accepting one's responsibilities. Those who faithfully preach the gospel will have to make this decision in the first three centuries of Christianity.

10:40–42

WARNINGS: THE DISCIPLES' MESSAGE AND REWARD

Jesus assures the apostles that whoever receives them and their message receives both the Son and the Father. Jesus follows this with a proverbial saying about the righteous receiving their just reward. Jesus' closing statement in this section sets the scene for a discussion Matthew will take up in Chapter 18, namely, that of taking care of the little ones. At first glance this might be construed as a reference to children, but Jesus will later describe these little ones as those who believe in Him (18:6). In Matthew 11:25 Jesus will comment on the Father revealing things to babes. The context here indicates that the babes are the ones who have received the Father's revelation, that is, the disciples. But why call the disciples babes and little ones? Because disciples, like little children, are vulnerable to abuse. We should remember that these comments in Matthew 10 are in the context of disciples being abused and persecuted simply because they believe in and proclaim Jesus as the Messiah.

MATTHEW 11:1–12:50
NARRATIVE 3: OPPOSITION REJECTED

Setting Up the Section

Jesus continues the powerful works expected of the Messiah but receives increasing opposition from the Jewish leaders. The events of these chapters are somewhat paralleled by those described in John's Gospel at the time when many disciples were leaving Jesus because He did not meet their expectation of a militant messiah who would lead them to freedom from Rome (John 6:60–69).

Also, there is an increasing emphasis on the kingdom of God and its glory.

📖 11:1–6

JOHN THE BAPTIST'S QUESTION

It is difficult to know exactly what is going on in John the Baptist's mind while in prison. Matthew has already informed his readers that John had been arrested by Herod (4:12). In chapter 14, Matthew records John's death. Here in chapter 11, we encounter what seems to be the troubling doubt of John regarding Jesus' messiahship. However, there may be another way of looking at John's question.

At this time John is incarcerated in the fortress of Machaerus, in the wilderness east of the Dead Sea. His future is certainly discouraging. Emotionally, he must be at a low point in his life. The kingdom he had predicted as imminent has not materialized. It would have been natural that some questions and doubts could be plaguing John.

An alternative view is that John is turning his disciples away from himself to Jesus. He may be asking questions for the benefit of his disciples.

Jesus' response to John's question draws attention to His messianic ministry. He has been doing what had been prophesied the Messiah would do (Isaiah 61:1–3; 35:5–6; Luke 4:16–19): healing the sick, blind, lame and deaf, and taking care of the poor. Jesus' messianic ministry should have been all the witness John and his disciples needed.

📖 11:7–19

JESUS' ESTIMATE OF JOHN THE BAPTIST

Jesus continues the discussion on John the Baptist by asking what kind of person the Jews had set out to see when they went to the Jordan River to witness John's baptisms. His somewhat colloquial language reflects that they had not gone out to see a weak person, but a bold prophet. Jesus cites Malachi 3:1 in support of John's ministry of preparing the way for the Messiah. Following this He pays John a great compliment—there is no one greater than John.

The last statement could be interpreted as contradictory, or at least vague. Jesus (and Matthew by his record of Jesus' words) is laying the foundation for kingdom business. John is great, yet in the kingdom, it is the humble servant that is the greatest. The kingdom of Jesus is different from all earthly kingdoms, and Jesus' and John's disciples need to know this.

Jesus continues that God did not intend to inaugurate His kingdom. Instead, it will be realized fully only through the death of the Messiah. This is a lesson that the zealous Jews (Zealots) cannot accept, and that the disciples will have trouble understanding (16:21–23).

Finally, Jesus again returns to John the Baptist and his testimony. John the Baptist is the expected Elijah who was to come and testify to God's messianic plans. However, the Jewish religious leaders of Jesus' day are like children—fickle and easily swayed. They will accept John the Baptist, but reject the Messiah he proclaims. When things get tough they will say that John has a demon, and that Jesus is only a friend of tax collectors and sinners.

📖 11:20–24

JUDGMENT ON THE UNREPENTANT

Chorazin and Bethsaida were small towns just to the north of the Sea of Galilee and the town of Capernaum. Jesus had performed powerful signs in those towns, but they refused to believe in His ministry and messiahship. If the miracles performed in these two cities had been performed in the Gentile towns of Tyre and Sidon, the Gentiles would have believed.

Because a great revelation had been made to these places, a great accountability would be leveled against them. Jesus pronounces judgment on Chorazin and Bethsaida. Then, He pronounces a worse judgment on Capernaum than on Sodom, the Old Testament city with a reputation for great sinfulness. (Genesis 18–19 records God's judgment of fire that destroyed the city of Sodom, a place where not even ten righteous men could be found.)

📖 11:25–30

THE REVELATION OF THE FATHER

In this passage, Matthew exhibits his rabbinic skill. The literary form of this text is in the genre of a Jewish revelation text, which was comprised of three sections:

1) Thanksgiving for the revelation from the Father (11:26)
   a. Thanksgiving to God for revealing the kingdom message
   b. The wise and understanding—a reference to the Jewish leaders who in their so-called wisdom did not receive the revelation regarding Jesus.
   c. The babes or little children are the disciples.

2) The revelation itself (11:27)
   a. All things or everything that had been given to Jesus related to the kingdom message regarding Jesus, the Messiah.
   b. The Son revealed the will and plan of God regarding the kingdom.

3) An invitation arising out of the revelation (11:28–30)
   a. An invitation to become a disciple of Jesus
   b. Promised rest to the poor and heavy-laden
   c. The gentle nature of the kingdom of God
   d. The promise to make the disciples' burden of sin and suffering light through the glorious kingdom message of redemption

This passage must be seen in the context of Jewish rejection of Jesus and His message. The learned ones rejected Jesus' message; the poor, needy, and humble ones believed and followed Him.

Critical Observation: The Religious Leaders

Here is a brief discussion of the makeup of the Jewish religious and political groups—the Pharisees, scribes, Sadducees, Herodians, Essenes, and Zealots.

- **Pharisees.** A variety of resources exist from which to learn about the Pharisees, and with that wealth of information there can be some confusion as to their exact identity. Some refer to them as a sect, some as a school, some as a political movement, some as a group of scholars, others as a middle class group of Jews, and on it goes. In all probability, all these concepts can be found in the term *Pharisee*. At different points in the history of the Jewish nation, the Pharisees played different roles—political, religious reformers, separatists, and social. The long history of this group's members makes it difficult to define them or their role with precision. The existence of the Pharisees can be traced back to about 134 BC. In Josephus's writings, they are often pictured in conflict with the Sadducees. Although not definitive, it is held by some that the Pharisees resisted Hellenization (adoption of Greek culture) as opposed to the Sadducees, who were more comfortable with Hellenization. When we encounter the Pharisees in the Gospels, they had formed a popular religious reformer group that included scholars of the Law. The Pharisees manifested a political messianic inclination but possessed little political power. They held to a strict observance of the Mosaic Law and interpreted the Torah in a broader sense than the Sadducees, including the

CONTINUED

remainder of the Jewish cannon as well as the vast rabbinic tradition in their legal code. They believed in a judgment for the Gentiles and the resurrection of the dead.

- **Scribes.** The term *scribe* meant those who were primarily secretaries. They were responsible for recording both the religious and legal aspects of Jewish life. Most were sympathetic to the Pharisees and some were even members of the Pharisees (Mark 2:16). As such they were the scholars on the Law upon whom the Pharisees depended for their interpretation of the Law. They were not so much a sect as a social or scholarly group.

- **Sadducees.** Like the Pharisees, it is difficult to define the Sadducees as a group. Sometimes they acted as a sect, at other times as a political movement. Their history is difficult to determine with precision, but like the Pharisees they can be traced in Josephus's historical writings, the New Testament, and rabbinic writings. Sociologically, they were mostly upper class and wealthy members of society. They therefore possessed greater political influence than the Pharisees. They were also more comfortable with Hellenization and social conformity than were the Pharisees. The Sadducees were often in religious conflict with the Pharisees. They only believed the Torah, the five books of Moses, to be inspired Scripture. They adopted a free will mind-set in regard to life, and rejected personal immortality and the resurrection.

- **Herodians.** The Herodians are mentioned only three times in the Gospels: Matthew 22:16; Mark 3:6; and Mark 12:13. Little is known of them other than they formed a political royalist group in support of the Herodian family. In the Gospels they aligned themselves with the Pharisees in opposition to Jesus, obviously in opposition to any kingdom He might inaugurate. Under normal conditions, the Pharisees would not have been associated with the Herodians, but they subordinated their differences to form an alliance against Jesus.

- **Essenes.** The origin of the group is uncertain. Some were monastic and some were not. There are some indications that they were opposed to the temple sacrificial system, believing that mainstream Judaism was corrupt. Remains of animal bones carefully buried indicate some possibility that they offered animal sacrifices apart from the temple. They held to the Mosaic Law and interpreted it literally, and treasured ancient literature. A strict code and ceremony of admission into the group was followed, with a strong code of communal living. It is believed that they adopted orphans from the mainstream of Jewish life. They held to a form of the afterlife. Most scholars consider the group that produced the Dead Sea Scrolls to be Essenes who lived at Qumran near the Dead Sea.

- **Zealots.** The term *zealot* derives from the concept of "zeal for God and the Law." The Zealots took pride in past heroes who had stood adamantly for God and the Law against all odds. They stood against any form of idolatry and offenses against the Law. Later they became revolutionaries against the opposing overlords, especially against Roman Imperialism. (This was not the only revolutionary group during the late Roman period. The historian Josephus lists five such groups.) The Zealots were a coalition of a lower group of priests, Jerusalem insurgents, and refugee bandit groups. During the time of Jesus, their zeal was for the overthrow of Rome. Jesus did not fit their ideal of a revolutionary king. We read little of the Zealots in the Gospels other than Simon, one of the apostles, who was a member or former member of the group (Luke 6:15).

LORD OF THE SABBATH

In a series of encounters with the Jewish leaders, Matthew 12 narrates the building controversy between Jesus and the scribes and Pharisees.

Matthew records that it is on the Sabbath that Jesus and His disciples are traveling through the grain fields. The disciples, being hungry, pluck grain to eat. To the Pharisees this was a serious violation of the Sabbath Law—resting from all work on the seventh day—as recorded in Exodus 20:10; 34:21 and Deuteronomy 5:14.

Rabbinic tradition listed at least thirty-nine classes of work the rabbis saw covered by this law. The overzealous literal application of the legal principle obviously overlooked a deeper principle to which Jesus holds the Pharisees. He corrects their understanding by referring to two examples in the Jewish writings (Torah), which were obvious exceptions to the legal application of the Law. Furthermore, He finally explains the place of the Law in God's purpose.

Jesus' opening statement, "Have you not read. . . ," is somewhat of a rebuke or reminder of what they should have known regarding David and his men eating bread of the Presence in the Tabernacle, which was bread reserved only for the priests (1 Samuel 21:1–6; Leviticus 24:5–9). When this occurred, the priest brought no condemnation against David and his men, and obviously in the mind of Jesus this occasioned no sin.

Jesus' next argument is that the priests broke the literal interpretation of the Sabbath Law every Sabbath as they served in the temple, yet the Pharisees took no offence at this. Obviously, this was another occasion when the Sabbath law should not be taken legalistically.

Jesus' next statement raises several questions. What does He mean by one who was greater? In all probability Jesus has in mind the new system of grace that had come to take over from the legal system of Law. This seems to fit, since Jesus then refers to a principle often brought up in the Torah, especially in Hosea 6:6 and Micah 6:8, God's desire for mercy rather than sacrifice.

Finally, Jesus makes the remarkable statement that the Son of Man is Lord over the Sabbath. The Gospel of Mark (Mark 2:27) records this saying of Jesus more fully to include the concept that the Sabbath was in fact made for mankind, not mankind for the Sabbath. Jesus is setting the Torah in a more mature expression or context than the Pharisees of His day did.

The Pharisees are not content with Jesus' rebuff and return to similar themes again in other settings, as in the next section.

JESUS HEALS ON THE SABBATH

Matthew's use of the expression *their synagogue* sets the synagogue of the Jews in contrast to the community of believers, namely, the church. When a man with a withered hand appears, the Pharisees take advantage of this to raise another question and accuse Jesus regarding lawful activity on the Sabbath. In this instance, Jesus knows that rabbinic practice permits the rescuing of an animal on the Sabbath (Luke 14:5). Arguing that it is far more important to heal a person than an animal, Jesus heals the man's withered hand. The Pharisees, obviously dissatisfied with Jesus, take council on how to destroy Him.

JESUS HEALS MANY

Jesus withdraws. Rather than incite the Pharisees further, Jesus seeks out quieter climes away from areas where the Pharisees frequented, but continues His healings. Matthew draws attention to one of the Servant Songs in Isaiah (Isaiah 42:1–4) to demonstrate that Jesus, as the Messiah, is involved in messianic works.

THE CHARGE OF BLASPHEMY

When a blind demoniac acknowledges Jesus as the Son of David (a term that had come to refer to the Messiah and was Matthew's favorite title for Jesus), the Pharisees take exception, charging that it is by the power of Beelzebul, the Prince of demons, that Jesus cast out demons.

Critical Observation

Be-elzebul, sometimes spelled Be-elzebub, or Ba-alzebub.

In Matthew, Mark, and Luke this term is another name for Satan. The etymology of this name has been difficult to determine with any degree of finality; the term has been thought to mean "Lord of the Flies," "Lord of Dung," "Lord of heaven" (a star god), "Master of the House," and "Fly Lord" (flies being demons).

Whatever the case, the term as used by the Pharisees was a pejorative one, intended to be an insult to Jesus.

When the Pharisees once more charge that Jesus cast out demons by the power of Satan, Jesus responds with three basic arguments and a startling announcement:

Argument 1.   A house divided against itself will fall. If Jesus was casting out demons by the power of Satan, then Satan's house was divided.

Argument 2.   To what power did the Pharisees attribute the power of their own disciples to cast out demons?

Argument 3.   Before one can enter a house and plunder the goods of the house, one must first overpower the owner. If Jesus had entered Satan's house and plundered his goods (those people held captive by demons), this must mean Jesus had overpowered Satan.

Jesus' startling announcement is this: Since He is indeed casting out demons by the power of the Spirit of God, then the kingdom of God has come. Not that it *will* come, but the kingdom has already come and is upon them.

Jesus continues His rebuttal of the Pharisees' charge of blasphemy with another remarkable statement that has given problems to scholars and ministers—the unforgivable sin (v. 32). This section begins with the word *therefore* (12:31 NASB), which connects this discussion to the previous one in which the Pharisees had attributed the work of God through His Holy Spirit as a work of Beelzebul, or Satan. To attribute the work of God through His Holy Spirit as a work of Satan is the worst kind of blasphemy possible.

While there are many differing opinions regarding the unforgivable sin, it is possible to understand the meaning in this section as it relates to the previous discussion of the Pharisees' blasphemy against the Holy Spirit. To set this section in context:

1) The Pharisees had blasphemed the Holy Spirit, charging that Jesus cast out demons by the power of Satan, whereas He claimed to cast them out by the power of the Holy Spirit.

2) To deny, or blaspheme, the work of the Holy Spirit is to blaspheme the Holy Spirit Himself and to deny the very process of new birth, regeneration, and sanctification.

3) To deny the work of the Holy Spirit is to remove oneself from the process of forgiveness and to place oneself outside the process of God's atonement, and to undercut the very possibility of experiencing the reality of God's salvation.

4) To oppose the Holy Spirit is the same as opposing the very mission of Jesus Himself.

5) Although rejecting Jesus' divine ministry has catastrophic consequences, Jesus Himself stressed that the denial or blasphemy of the Holy Spirit has ultimate, unforgivable results.

To summarize: The blasphemy against the Holy Spirit that is unforgivable is a denial of the working of the Holy Spirit in God's system of atonement. Jesus considered this blasphemy even worse than blasphemy against Himself. To reject the saving power and work of the Holy Spirit is ultimately to reject God's working His salvation in the individual.

Jesus closes this encounter with the Pharisees with a pronouncement of judgment on them for the careless words they had just uttered. In their haste to deny Jesus, they had in fact blasphemed the very working of God through His Holy Spirit. Their words, uttered in the heat of their hatred, were not thought about, and through their cavalier treatment of Jesus and the Holy Spirit, they had brought judgment on themselves.

📖 12:38–45

THE SCRIBES AND PHARISEES SEEK A SIGN FROM JESUS

Joining the Pharisees, the scribes ask Jesus for a sign. There is nothing wrong in seeking a sign, as long as the seeker is sincere. It is apparent that the scribes and Pharisees are not sincere, for they have already witnessed many miracles of Jesus and still refuse to believe. In fact, as in the previous section, they attribute the power of His miracles to Satan.

In a striking analogy, Jesus makes reference to the sign of Jonah, the prophet. Unlike the people of Nineveh, the scribes and Pharisees would not believe and repent. The sign of Jonah here is the analogy between Jonah in the belly of the large fish and Jesus' burial and resurrection. Jesus knows that the scribes and Pharisees will not even believe in His resurrection as a sign. So Jesus reprimands and condemns them for their unbelief. (In Matthew 16:4 the sign of Jonah is used to refer to the unbelief of the Jews in general.) Twice in the Gospels, both times in Matthew in the context of the sign of Jonah, Jesus refers to these religious leaders as evil and spiritually adulterous.

Jesus concludes this encounter with a parable of an unclean spirit leaving a man and returning to find his house clean. The spirit returns with seven more spirits and moves into the house. Jesus compares the generation of the scribes and Pharisees with this spirit. Those who do not respond will find in the end their situation is worse off than it was in the beginning. Obviously, Jesus has in mind that by refusing His message, the scribes and Pharisees face certain judgment. Did Jesus have in mind the eschatological judgment at the end of the world, or the impending judgment of the destruction of Jerusalem? Possibly Jesus and Matthew had both in mind.

📄 12:46–50

JESUS' TRUE FAMILY

This is the first reference to Jesus' family in Matthew. The last reference to Mary was in Matthew 2. The next reference to family will be in Matthew 13:55–56, where the Jews attempt to find Jesus' significance in His family of origin by asking if He's the carpenter's son, if His mother is Mary, and if His brothers are James, Joseph, Simon, and Judas.

In this encounter with His family, Jesus is not rejecting them, but demonstrating that kingdom relationships take precedence over physical relationships. The section serves as a transitional passage, as Matthew moves on to the third discourse and the teachings on the kingdom.

MATTHEW 13:1–58
DISCOURSE 3: THE TRUE NATURE OF THE KINGDOM

Setting Up the Section

The previous narrative was about the opposition and controversy to Jesus' identity and message. The events described came approximately at the same time as the events described in John 6, when many of the disciples were leaving Jesus, disappointed with His claims of messiahship. They did not understand the nature of the kingdom of God and had anticipated more of a political physical kingdom, whereas Jesus' kingdom was a spiritual relationship with God. Jesus asks His closest disciples whether they, too, are about to leave Him. Peter has answered that there is nowhere else to go because Jesus alone has the words of eternal life (John 6:68).

13:1–9, 18–23

THE PARABLE OF THE SOWER

This is not a parable about sowing—it is a parable about hearing. Mark begins his version with a call to listen (Mark 4:3). Luke ends his version with the call to his readers to be careful how they listen to the message (Luke 8:18). To his version, Matthew adds the Jewish proverbial saying that whoever has ears, should listen well (Matthew 13:9). The parable—the simple analogy of a farmer sowing seed in Palestine—is about how a person hears and understands the message of the kingdom.

PARABLE AT A GLANCE

The soil	The seed	The application
The path	The birds ate them.	Those who hear don't understand, and so Satan snatches them away.
Rocky or stony places	They developed no roots so were scorched by the sun and withered.	Those who hear receive with joy, but fall away when faced with persecution.
Among the thorns	They were choked out by the growing thorns.	There are those who hear, but worries and wealth prevent the seeds from bearing fruit.
Rich, fertile soil	They produced a great crop.	Those who hear and understand produce the crop God intended.

The point is that in order for the message of the kingdom to germinate and flourish, the mind has to be prepared for hearing and understanding the kingdom. A stubborn and rebellious heart cannot receive the Word.

This parable had borne itself out with those who heard the message of the kingdom (John the Baptist's and Jesus' preaching): some were snatched away, others fell away when discipleship became difficult, some heard the truth but could not sacrifice their own lives to follow, others heard and followed and brought others. Those disciples who had been willing to hear, who had prepared their minds and hearts and believed and repented, were able to understand the message that had brought forth fruit in their faith and lives.

Take It Home

The significant lesson for us today from the parable of the sower and the soils is that we must pre-pare our minds and hearts for the Word of God before it can take root and grow. Paul commends some first-century Christians in Thessalonica in the same way, thanking God that they received God's Word, not as the teaching of humans, but for what it really is—the Word of God (1 Thessalonians 2:13).

The message for Jesus' disciples (and for us) is simply this: Some will never receive the Word, some will begin and fall away, some will keep on growing. The difference will be in how they hear and under-stand. Do not expect the same from everyone because not everyone is willing to hear and understand.

📄 13:10–17

WHY DID JESUS TEACH IN PARABLES?

Parable teaching was a favored rabbinic teaching style. The Jews were familiar with parable teaching. Also, Jesus explains that the crowds surrounding Him are expecting some teaching, though they are not ready for the deeper matters of the kingdom, or willing to understand the true spiritual nature of the kingdom. Jesus is well aware that the crowds are willing to hear Him but are not willing to hear His message. His understanding of the mysteries of the kingdom is not in step with theirs.

The next proverbial statement—that those who have will receive more and those who have not will lose even what they have—was well known in rabbinic Judaism. It implies that if one does not take the opportunities presented, the opportunities will be denied. Since the Jewish leadership refuse to believe in Jesus, even the opportunities to believe will be denied.

Jesus' reference to Isaiah 6:9–10 must be seen in relation to the calling and commissioning of Isaiah. Isaiah was to preach to the rebellious Israel even though many would not repent and believe His message. One must be sensitive to the poetic form of Isaiah 6 to understand the message it conveys. Israel cannot in its unfaithful heart see and hear. In this condition, for Israel to turn to God for healing is ludicrous.

In contrast to the stubborn Jewish leaders, the disciples believe. To them the secret things of the kingdom will make sense. For this reason, Jesus teaches in parables. The Jewish leaders who are looking for the wrong kind of kingdom will still find some message in Jesus' teachings in parables, but the disciples who believe will be in a position to receive and accept the deeper spiritual nature of the kingdom.

Critical Observation

There are two fundamental principles in interpreting a parable:

1) Determine the context of the parable in the light of its origin and setting in the overall text. How does the parable fit into the full story or narrative that it is intended to enlighten? What was going on historically when the parable was told?

CONTINUED

2) Determine the central truth or lesson the parable is intended to illustrate or teach. While you may apply a parable in a variety of ways, it had only one central lesson or principle when it was originally used. Maintain the interpretation within that principle or lesson. Remember that a parable is an earthly story with a central spiritual truth or lesson.

It is not difficult to determine the nature of the parables in Matthew 13, for in each instance Jesus either relates the parable to the kingdom, or says "the kingdom of heaven is like. . ." (13:24 NIV). These are parables about the kingdom.

What is the historical setting for the parables in Matthew 13? Jesus is running into increasing opposition from the scribes and Pharisees. Many of the disciples are leaving Jesus because they do not understand the nature of His messianic reign or kingdom (spiritual rather than a physical). Thus, He teaches them about the kingdom.

13:24–30

THE PARABLE OF WHEAT AND TARES

This parable, like the sower, receives additional attention and explanation by Jesus (13:36–43). The parable is also similar to the kingdom parable of the dragnet (13:47–52).

The parable of wheat and tares explains that in the kingdom of God one can expect a mixed crop. This is first because of human fallibility and weakness. But also, Satan is busy working on human minds. He plants seeds, sometimes of false teaching, sometimes of doubt. Whatever the case, a mixed crop is the result.

The temptation for the disciples is to intervene and attempt to pluck out what they consider to be the bad seed. Disciples must refrain from this since they are not in a position to determine all of the circumstances involved. The parable emphasizes that the judgment of crops (a person's faith) is beyond the disciples and must be left to the reaper himself (Jesus). Jesus explains in Matthew 13:36–43 that it will be the Son of Man and His angels who will do the reaping and judging. Even the well-meaning can judge a person too soon.

13:31–32

THE GRAIN OF MUSTARD SEED

In this time, the mustard seed was considered the smallest of seeds. The size of the mustard seed would have been well known among those hearing Jesus tell this parable. The size and slow growth of the mustard seed is an excellent metaphor for the humble beginnings of the kingdom. The Jews expect a triumphant arrival of the kingdom and expulsion of the Gentile enemy, but that is not how the kingdom of God is going to work. The Messiah came not to a princely house, but to the house of a lowly carpenter. The beginnings of the kingdom are in fact small—12 apostles and about 120 other believers (Acts 1:13–15).

Despite its humble beginnings, the kingdom slowly matures and grows significantly. The mysterious growth of the kingdom is the working of God's grace and power in human lives, not the result of human intervention and work.

The meaning of the parable for Jesus' disciples is simple. The kingdom begins small, but given time will grow into something significant. Do not expect too much too soon. The lesson for the church today is likewise one of encouragement and warning—give the seed of the kingdom time, give people time to grow, give God time to work in people's lives.

There is also a significant lesson and warning for the church today regarding triumphalism (expecting the church to burst in and be great by human standards). The church will always be made up of humans who are not yet "there." We experience the work of God in our lives and grow, but it is only when we reach the end, the eschatological goal of the Christian age, when we will be fully triumphant. We experience many wonderful victories over Satan and the world, but there remain yet many battles to be fought and much weakness to be revealed. However, the final victory has been secured by Jesus' death and resurrection. It will be fully revealed at the end.

Matthew's church needed to hear this message as keenly as did Jesus' disciples in those early days of the kingdom. But so do we today, 2,000 years later.

13:33–35

THE PARABLE OF THE LEAVEN

This brief parable, whose images are well-known to the disciples and Jesus' audience that day, repeats much of the same message as the mustard seed. Baking bread was an everyday experience in ancient days, especially among the Jews. It is widely known that leaven spreads throughout the loaf, but the maturing of the leaven and its leavening power take time. Hurry the process and you end up with a lump of hard bread that is useless and inedible. Give the leaven time and it produces a wonderful loaf of bread.

So it is with the message of the kingdom. Do not expect too much too soon. Interfere with the process of slow leavening and growth and you end up with a catastrophe. Give the power of God time to work in people, and do not expect too much too soon.

13:36–43

THE WHEAT AND THE TARES EXPLAINED

This section continues to develop as the parable of the wheat and tares. The message is simple—judging is not the role of the disciple. The mission of discipleship is planting, not reaping. Jesus will take care of the reaping and do a far better job than humanly possible.

The message is especially meaningful to the disciples who must have been disappointed that many did not believe and receive Jesus, and that many were leaving. Likewise, the message must be meaningful to Matthew's disciples who now find themselves in a Gentile and hostile world that deserves judgment. Perhaps the meaning is just as powerful today in church life, when members are prone to judge others and in many cases even write them off.

13:44–46

THE HIDDEN TREASURE AND PEARL OF GREAT PRICE

These two parables are similar in meaning and application. The kingdom is of inestimable value, and those who find it are greatly enriched. However, the richness of the kingdom is not out on the surface to be seen by all. It takes a discerning (believing) eye to understand and find the richness of the kingdom. Furthermore, these parables teach that one must search to find the mystery and richness of the kingdom.

Perhaps the most significant message of these parables is that when one finds the richness of the kingdom, one must be prepared to give up everything to attain it. Matthew will develop this point later when he narrates Jesus' encounter with the rich young ruler (19:16–30). These parables also fit in with the theme of radical discipleship—the willingness to give up everything for the sake of gaining the kingdom. Many of the disciples in Jesus' day were not willing to pay this price, so when they learned the radical nature of the kingdom, they left.

📄 13:47–51

THE DRAGNET

This parable is reminiscent of the parable of the wheat and tares, for it emphasizes judgment. The kingdom of God involves judgment. It is for this reason that John the Baptist and Jesus demanded repentance in view of the arrival or breaking in of the kingdom.

Jesus sets this parable in the context of the end of the age by emphasizing that the angels will come to separate the evil from the righteous and throw the evil into the fire of judgment (typical Jewish and rabbinic images of the final judgment). It is a sobering thought that one's attitude toward Jesus and His kingdom involves final judgment.

📄 13:52–58

THE CONCLUSION TO THE KINGDOM PARABLES

This little section is thought of by some to be an eighth parable. However, it is best seen as a concluding statement to all the preceding Kingdom Parables.

The thought is in the form of a proverbial saying. The scribes, the learned scholars of the Law, should have been trained for the purpose of revealing all the mysteries of the kingdom. However, the scribes of Jesus' day are blinded by their reaction to Jesus and the nature of His message and kingdom.

Jesus has revealed the richness and mysteries of the kingdom—both the old thoughts of the kingdom and the new ideas and thoughts of the kingdom. His disciples, by learning from Him about the kingdom, can bring together the promise of the old covenant with the fulfillment of the new.

As in each of the other four blocks of discourse or teaching material, Matthew concludes the discourse with a transition into the next section. In this discourse, the focus has been on the true nature of the kingdom and matters that disciples should know regarding the kingdom.

When Jesus finishes teaching these parables, He goes away from that place and comes to Nazareth, where the people are amazed at His teaching but are reluctant to follow Him because they feel they know Him too well. After all, was this not the carpenter's son? Because of their lack of faith, Jesus does few of His miracles in Nazareth. It was not because they simply did not believe; it was because they would not believe. Sometimes prejudice obscures faith.

1) These Kingdom Parables came to their original audience at a crucial point in Jesus' ministry. Many disciples were turning back because the kingdom offered by Jesus did not meet their expectations and desires. The radical call to discipleship and the radical nature of the spiritual kingdom were too much for them.

2) These parables were also of extreme importance for Matthew's church, since his readers had just given up all for the kingdom and needed encouragement that their decision was worthwhile. They needed reminding also that it was not their prerogative to begin judging their Gentile neighbors, for God could also work His power in the life of the Gentiles and bring them into His kingdom. Making disciples by teaching the message of the kingdom is the ministry of disciples; judging belongs to the Son of Man and His angels.

3) Growth in the kingdom is by the power of God, and not human endeavor. Disciples need to give the seed of the kingdom time and space to mature. The kingdom begins small in human hearts, but nurtured and sustained by God's power and grace, matures slowly into something beautiful and useful.

4) The kingdom involves radical commitment with the promise of accountability to God. One cannot escape the kingdom and its message by walking away. There will be a judgment, and Jesus' followers will be judged by their reaction to the message, the kingdom, and the King.

Take It Home

In Matthew's description of Jesus commissioning His disciples, there was a challenging message for Matthew's original audience, as well as for us today. When we pray earnestly that the Lord will send laborers into the harvest, it might be that we turn out to be the laborers that the Lord of the harvest has in mind.

MATTHEW 14:1–17:27

NARRATIVE 4: FINAL DAYS OF PREPARATION OF DISCIPLES

Setting Up the Section

A report of John's death is found in all three synoptic Gospels (Matthew, Mark, and Luke), but briefer in Luke. Luke gives none of the details described in Matthew and Mark. Mark includes the sending out of the twelve disciples, which Matthew has included earlier in his Gospel (Mark 6:7–13).

While John's death is described here, chronologically his death actually occurred earlier on the time line. His imprisonment is mentioned in Matthew 4:12. The details given here are in light of the connection made by Herod about the possible return of John the Baptist. It was a common perception that some of the prophets would return to introduce the end of the age.

📖 14:1–12

THE DEATH OF JOHN THE BAPTIST

"At that time. . ." (NIV) is a favorite transition for Matthew. In this instance it merely highlights Herod's reaction to Jesus and introduces the section on John the Baptist's death. The description of John's death is a flashback, prompted by Herod's speculation that Jesus might be John the Baptist raised from the dead.

This Herod is Herod Antipas, one of the sons of Herod the Great. He is identified by Matthew as the tetrarch, and by Mark as the king. Herod had divorced his first wife and married his brother Philip's wife, Herodias. John the Baptist had repeatedly warned him of this sin. Herod, frustrated with John and in an attempt to silence him, had imprisoned him in the fortress of Machaerus, eventually executing him as a result of the schemes of Herodias and her daughter (Salome).

Herod evidently feels guilty for beheading John, and so when he hears of another prophet (Jesus), he superstitiously wonders whether John has come back from the dead.

Matthew mentions this for two reasons:

1) To narrate the events of John the Baptist's death
2) To focus attention on the importance of Jesus' ministry and the concerns this raised for Herod Antipas, the ruler of Jesus' home region

Critical Observation: The Herodian Dynasty

Herod the Great (37 BC–4 BC) was the great builder of the temple, palaces, and fortresses. He had many children by several marriages. Three of his sons ruled after him: Antipas, Philip, and Archelaus. The Herodian dynasty can be confusing, because of rulers who shared common names and because of much intermarriage. The Philip mentioned here in Matthew 14:3 (Mark 6:17) is a fourth son of Herod the Great.

- Herod Antipas (4 BC–AD 39) was the tetrarch (ruler over a fourth of the kingdom). He ruled over Galilee (Jesus' home province) and Perea. He married Herodias, his brother Philip's wife. He also murdered John the Baptist.

- Herod Philip (4 BC–AD 34) was tetrarch of Iturea and Traconitis (Luke 3:1). He was the son of Herod the Great and Cleopatra of Jerusalem.

- Herod Archelaus (4 BC–AD 39) ruled over the province of Judea. He was titled an ethnarch (ruler of the people).

- This Philip is not well attested in history. He was apparently the first husband of Herodias and the father of Salome—facts we discover through information regarding Antipas.

📄 14:13–21

FEEDING THE FIVE THOUSAND

This is the only miracle of Jesus recorded in all four Gospels. The section begins a series of situations focused on the need for faith and the failure of the disciples and others to have adequate faith.

The narrative of the miracle of the feeding of more than five thousand people has more than historical significance. It drives home the point that Jesus, as the Messiah, could take care of His people. The feeding of the five thousand has an obvious connection to God feeding the children of Israel with manna in the wilderness after they left Egypt. It also has insights into the messianic banquet at the end of time when God's redeemed will sit at God's banquet table and be sustained.

The miracle itself is simple. Taking five loaves and two fish and multiplying them into food enough for more than five thousand is no test to God's sovereign power. The power of this miracle lies in two points:

1) The disciples' failure to have faith in Jesus' ability to feed them
2) The illustration of Jesus' ability to take care of every need His disciples might have, with an emphasis on the spiritual food symbolized by the Old Testament manna and the New Testament loaves and fish

The spiritual significance of this miracle is extremely important to Matthew's late first-century community, which needs to understand that the Messiah can take care of its spiritual needs apart from Jerusalem and the temple (which had been destroyed).

14:22-36

JESUS WALKS ON THE SEA

This is one of two miracles common to all four Gospels, the other being the feeding of the five thousand. Several items stand out in this striking section.

1) The sea. To the Hebrew mind the sea was sinister and a symbol of evil.
2) Jesus' power over nature. Jesus had previously calmed a tempestuous sea (8:23-26).
3) The distress and lack of faith in the disciples
4) The recognition of those in the boat that Jesus was the Son of God

This miracle is not as much about the natural elements, other than Jesus' power over them, but is more about Peter and the disciples' faith. The situation surrounding Jesus' ministry required Him to have time to Himself for prayer and spiritual strength. He compels His disciples to get in a boat and set out to sea. A storm arises in the middle of the night (the fourth watch, between 3:00 a.m. and 6:00 a.m.), and the disciples are struggling with the waves. They are about a mile out at sea (a *stadia* [NASB], being about 200 yards). They see Jesus walking on the water and think He is a ghost.

Jesus calls out to them not to fear. An expression similar to this is found eight times in Matthew, indicating that having faith in Jesus drives away fear. He also tells them to take heart, for "it is I" (NIV) or "it's me." The Greek phrase that is translated here may be an allusion to the divine name of God, who is the great "I am" (Exodus 3:14). In the context of a Jewish gospel and a Jewish community, this certainly would carry the significance of a symbol of the presence of God in Jesus. The recognition of the disciples that Jesus is the Son of God supports this thought.

The narrative indicates that Peter initially steps out in faith, but that his faith wavers, resulting in his sinking into the sea. But Jesus saves him. It is easy to find fault in Peter for his wavering faith, but where were the other disciples? Still in the boat. Jesus gently rebukes the disciples for being men with little faith.

The striking thing about this event following immediately after the feeding of the five thousand is that the disciples still have a lot to learn about faith and trusting Jesus. Faith is something that needs time and experience to develop.

15:1-20

CEREMONIAL AND REAL DEFILEMENT— WASHING HANDS

Once again, the Pharisees and scribes accuse Jesus of desecrating the Jewish tradition of the elders, this time because His disciples do not wash their hands before eating. The Pharisees were experts in interpreting the tradition of the elders, but that was not the same as the actual Torah (Genesis, Exodus, Leviticus, Numbers, and Deuteronomy). Translating this into contemporary contexts, human interpretations are opinions, and not the law or doctrine itself. These traditions in themselves are good, but when they are put on the same level as God's Law, then mankind's opinion has been set on the same level as God's Word. This is the mistake the religious leaders have made.

In this instance, the Pharisees have not only put their interpretation on the level of God's Torah, but in fact have put one of their traditions above God's Law. Jesus focuses His answer on this. The problem is their interpretation of Corban (also Qorban or Korban), a vow permitted by a righteous Jew to maintain a sacred offering to fund the temple. Korban was not a command of God, but was a practice of the day. In this case, the Pharisees allow a person to offer this monetary gift to the temple rather than use it to support their parents—a fulfillment of God's command to honor one's parents (Exodus 20:12). The Pharisees are setting their tradition above the direct command of God.

There is another sense in which the Pharisees are speaking out of turn. They charge that the disciples are transgressing the tradition of the elders by not washing their hands before eating. In this case, though, they are applying instructions given for the sake of ceremonial purity (the priests carrying out sacrifices) to the normal household matters of eating. These two things were not the same (Exodus 30:17–21; Leviticus 15:11).

Jesus' condemnation of the Pharisees is scathing. He likens them to the Jews in Isaiah's day who honored God with their lips but whose hearts were far away from God (Isaiah 29:13). The Jews in Isaiah's day had taught their own opinion and thoughts on an equal level with the sacred scriptures. The Pharisees were blind guides leading blind men, resulting in everyone falling into a pit. It is not what goes into the mouth that defiles people, but instead what proceeds out of their hearts and mouths.

Take It Home

Understanding the mistake of the religious leaders of Jesus' day offers the modern church an opportunity to examine its own heart. Do we honor our beloved traditions above the greatest commandments—loving God and loving our neighbors? Are we sometimes blinded to what God is doing in the world around us because we are so focused on our religious customs that, while based on our understanding of the Bible, are not scripture themselves?

Just as Jesus called the scribes and Pharisees to open their eyes and look beyond their own religious structure to see what unexpected thing God was doing—so He calls to the church today.

📖 15:21–28

THE CANAANITE WOMAN AND TYRE AND SIDON

This section continues the story of the need for faith, and the lack of faith, on the part of the Jewish leaders.

Jesus leaves Capernaum and travels west into the Gentile region of Tyre and Sidon, where He is met by a Canaanite woman whose daughter is possessed by a demon. In her plea to Jesus she acknowledges that Jesus is the Lord and messianic king, crying out "Have mercy on me, Lord, Son of David" (NRSV). Because she was a Gentile, the disciples would have sent her away, but Jesus simply remarks that His ministry is to the Jews, not the Gentiles. She remains persistent, so Jesus offers a proverbial statement that His ministry is not for the unclean (dogs), but for the children of God. Her response indicates that she understands His remark, but observes that even dogs (a derogatory term commonly used by the Jews to refer to Gentiles) eat food from the Master's table. Jesus commends her for her great faith and heals her daughter.

The point of this narrative is this: The Jews, who should have accepted Jesus and believed in Him, did not, but this Gentile woman, who had no reason to believe in Jesus, did. Jesus finds great faith where no one would have expected it, but no faith where it should have been. The lesson for the members of Matthew's community is that they, too, should not ignore the Gentiles among whom they now lived, for one can find faith also among the Gentiles.

📖 **15:29–39**

THE FEEDING OF THE FOUR THOUSAND

Jesus returns from the region of Tyre and Sidon to the Sea of Galilee. Sitting with a large crowd on the mountainside, He performs many miracles. Again, Jesus wants to feed the crowd. The disciples, seemingly with a short memory, ask where they can get enough food to feed the crowd. After Jesus takes the seven loaves and few small fish and feeds more than four thousand people, there are more than seven baskets of food left over.

The point of this narrative is, again, that Jesus can take care of the needs of His people, no matter how little they have and how great the need. A secondary lesson is that the disciples' faith still needs much maturing.

The location of Magadan (and in Mark's account, Dalmanutha) is unknown in both cases. This is the only mention of Magadan and Dalmanutha in ancient literature.

📖 **16:1–4**

THE PHARISEES AND SADDUCEES DEMAND A SIGN FROM HEAVEN

The Pharisees are now joined by the Sadducees to continue the attack on Jesus. These two theological and political enemies join together in their opposition to Jesus, illustrating their frustration and desperation. We have not heard of the Sadducees since Matthew 3:7 and will hear of them in Matthew only seven times (four times in Matthew 16, and twice in Matthew 22).

The request for a sign (from heaven, which also meant from God) is intended to trap Jesus and provide evidence that they might use against Him. Jesus' response draws attention to the fact that they already have all the signs they need. His comment about their ability to read natural signs indicates the duplicity of their request.

Jesus' strident rebuke likens them to an adulterous generation, which has all the evidence it needs yet still rebels against God. Therefore, they are guilty of committing spiritual adultery. This is the second time Jesus refers to the sign of Jonah. The first was in Matthew 12:40. In both cases Jesus is referencing His resurrection from the dead. Jonah was in the belly of the fish for three days and nights, and Jesus will be in the grave for the same period.

📖 **16:5–12**

THE LEAVEN OF THE PHARISEES AND SADDUCEES

Jesus warns the disciples to beware of the leaven (yeast) of the Pharisees and Sadducees. The disciples associate this with physical bread, which they have forgotten to bring with them. Reminding them of His miracles with the five thousand and four thousand, Jesus warns them again. Finally, the disciples understand Jesus' warning regarding the Pharisees' and Sadducees' teaching and refusal to believe, and the need they have for faith. Since the disciples continued to display little faith (17:20), this warning is entirely appropriate.

CAESAREA PHILIPPI AND PETER'S CONFESSION

The confession of Peter is a crucial turning point in the Gospels of Matthew, Mark, and John. It is only here in Matthew, though, that the high status in the church is assigned to Peter at the end of the passage. In fact, this section is one of the central texts in the Gospel of Matthew, and it is certainly central for the existence of the church as the messianic community.

The discussion begins with the seemingly neutral questioning of the disciples by Jesus, regarding who people think He, the Son of Man, is. The response is mixed—John the Baptist, Elijah, or one of the prophets (a sign of the end times and God's imminent judgment).

When Jesus asks more specifically who the disciples think He is, Peter responds with the famous confession, "You are the Christ, the Son of the living God" (NIV).

Jesus' response recognizes that Peter's understanding is the result of the revelation of God. This does not necessarily mean that at that instance God had revealed this to Peter. It most likely means that human ingenuity could not have full credit for Peter's conclusion. The hand of the Father can be seen in the process that has led to Peter's understanding. God has been working His plan, attested to by both prophetic utterance and the powerful miracles of Jesus.

Critical Observation

Jesus' response to Peter—calling Peter a rock on whom Jesus will build His church—opens the door to much speculation and debate.

The Greek word for Peter is *petros*. The Greek word for rock is *petra*. Both petros (masculine) and petra (feminine) mean rock. But in the original conversation, Jesus may have been speaking Aramaic. In that language there is only one word, *kepha*, which means rock. Whether you consider the language Jesus is probably speaking in or the language that Matthew is writing in, Jesus is making a play on words.

While looking back through Protestant-Catholic history, there have been many discussions about the connection between this passage and the role of Peter as Pope. But keep in mind that this was not an issue for Matthew. It's important to look at this text as it was meaningful to those for whom it was written.

It is possible that the rock-like confession of Peter is the play on words Jesus is making, and that it is on the confession of the divinity of Jesus that He will build His messianic community. It is in this manner that thinkers such as Calvin, Zwingli, and John Locke understood the expression. The focus of the discussion can be seen in the parallelism between Peter's confession and Jesus' confession.

CONTINUED

This section clearly states that Peter's confession and apostolic office are the bedrock of the messianic community Jesus claimed He would build—the church.

The word *church* appears here, then again in Matthew 18:17. Elsewhere the reference to the messianic community is to the kingdom of heaven or kingdom of God. The Aramaic word underlying the Greek is normally translated as "synagogue." In most instances in the New Testament, *church* is the favored word, although *synagogue* is occasionally used in references to the church.

It is interesting that Jesus distances His messianic community from the Jewish synagogue, and that Matthew makes this distinction for the sake of his community that had just been uprooted from the temple. It could no longer identify with the Jewish synagogue, for the Jewish synagogue was not the messianic community of Jesus.

The word used here that some versions of the Bible translate as "hell" actually references another place—Hades—the realm of the dead or the underworld. Jesus is stating that not even death or the realm of the dead will prevail against this establishment of the church. This probably refers to His own imminent death (the next section in Matthew develops this), but some would include in His meaning the fact that death and martyrdom will not hinder the establishment and growth of the church.

The keys of the kingdom that Jesus offers Peter represent authority. Historically, it is Peter who preaches the first gospel sermon that leads to the salvation of the first Jewish converts to Christianity after the resurrection of Jesus (Acts 2:17–40), which then leads to the first Gentile converts to Christianity (Acts 10–11).

Binding and *loosing* were rabbinic expressions found in many places in the Jewish tradition that had a variety of usages. Fundamentally it involved including and excluding people from the community, and setting the rules for behavior in the community. It is to the apostles, beginning with Peter, that the responsibility is given to establish the church and the community life within. In Matthew 16 this has reference to Peter, but later this authority is expressed in regard to all of the apostles (18:18). It is to the apostles that, through their preaching, authority is given to shape the New Testament church.

16:21–23

JESUS FORETELLS HIS DEATH, BURIAL, AND RESURRECTION

Matthew 16:21 marks a dramatic turning point in Jesus' ministry. From this point on He turns away from the crowds and to His disciples in a personal ministry intended to prepare them for His imminent suffering and death. Although there have been some allusions to Jesus' coming suffering and death (9:15; 12:40), this is the first real announcement by Jesus.

Mathew's Gospel continues to narrate accounts of Jesus' powerful healings, but these are no longer the main focus of the narrative. From this point on, Matthew will develop the necessity and inevitability of Jesus' suffering and death. This is the first of four predictions by Jesus of His death, burial, and resurrection, the others being Matthew 17:22–23; 20:17–19;

and 26:2. The focus will also shift to the development of the radical nature of the call to discipleship, and the central meaning of the Gospels—Jesus' sacrifice and resurrection.

Matthew records that Jesus begins to show His disciples that He has to go to Jerusalem. In doing so, He demonstrates that His suffering and death are not accidents, but part of God's will, purpose, and plan. It is necessary by God's will and purpose for Jesus to do four things:

1) Go to Jerusalem
2) Suffer at the hands of the ruling power of the Jews
3) Be put to death
4) Then be brought back to life on the third day

This passion statement (*passion* is used here as a technical term for Jesus' death, burial, and resurrection) becomes the central theme of the gospel message (1 Corinthians 15:1–4). It is certainly the central theme of Peter's preaching on Pentecost (Acts 2) and to Cornelius (Acts 10:34–43).

Peter's comment "God, forbid it, Lord" (16:22 NRSV) may be better translated as "far be it from. . ." or "may God be gracious to you and forbid this. . . ." Peter still does not understand the full implication of Jesus' messianic ministry as the suffering servant described by Isaiah (Isaiah 53), and of God's purpose for and in Jesus. But who would have understood this fully at that time?

Jesus' response is a strident and harsh rebuke. A paraphrase of Jesus' response might read "Peter, you are a hindrance to God's purpose for me. You are functioning under the influence of Satan."

A major lesson we learn from this exchange is again the radical nature of Jesus' ministry and our discipleship. Jesus' purpose, contrary to human tendencies, was not to take the easy solution to the problem. Our discipleship is radical because our Master is radical.

📖 16:24–27

RADICAL DISCIPLESHIP

The unsettling and radical thrust of Jesus' passion pronouncement is followed by an equally unsettling and radical revelation from Jesus on the cost of discipleship—true discipleship must entail a willingness to die for one's faith. Discipleship must be modeled on Jesus' pattern of being the suffering servant of God—denying one's self and taking up one's cross just as Jesus did. In other words, do as I do, follow My example.

Taking up our crosses for Jesus can have a lot of contemporary applications, as we sacrifice in order to follow Him closely. However, in the context of Jesus' discussion and Matthew's community's needs, coupled together with what Jesus has taught His disciples in Matthew 10:16–39, and especially verses 34–39, we should understand this as a radical call to discipleship and if necessary, martyrdom.

This understanding comes from the discussion that follows, in which Jesus elaborates and it seems to best fit the context of martyrdom. Martyrdom was a very present reality to Christians in the first century. In fact, by the second century of Christianity, discipleship held the threat of martyrdom for many.

Jesus speaks of losing one's life for His sake. The word translated "life" here can also be translated as "soul" (16:26 NIV). Reading the entire passage, "life" fits the context better in this instance.

In the Greek school of thought (Plato), a person was merely a physical body in which a spirit dwells. Not so in the Jewish view of humanity. In the Jewish view, a person was seen as an integrated spiritual being, not merely the housing of a spirit. The Jewish view did not separate the physical and spiritual life, but conceived them to be a unit. Thus, as written in the book of Romans, death is the consequence of sin (Romans 6:23), implying both physical and spiritual death. Considering this, it is appropriate to understand *life* in this passage to include the soul, which represents the whole being of mankind, both physical and spiritual.

Life is valuable and we treasure it, but by seeking to save one's life (not being willing to die for Jesus) one does in fact lose it. Notice the irony of Jesus' statement. What we treasure so much, we lose by trying to keep it.

Earlier in Matthew, Satan had sought to tempt Jesus by offering Him the kingdoms of the world (4:1–10). If Jesus had accepted Satan's offer, He would not have had to die on the cross. He could have saved His life, but in saving His life He would have lost everything.

Jesus' next statement adds a dramatic note to the discussion. Those who seek to save their lives by denying Jesus will be judged by this at the end of the age.

16:28

THE SON OF MAN COMING IN HIS KINGDOM

As in Matthew 10:23, Jesus uses the puzzling expression that something will not be completed before (or until, or till) the Son of Man comes. This expression could refer to:

1) the transfiguration of Jesus (Matthew 16:28 and 17:1–2);
2) the destruction of Jerusalem itself (Matthew 24:30);
3) some unusual event such as the destruction of Jerusalem (Matthew 24) or the day of Pentecost (Acts 2);
4) the coming of Jesus in judgment at any time as a demonstration of His final judgment (Revelation 1:7; 2:16; 22:7, 12);
5) Jesus' second coming at the end of the world (Matthew 24:27–28).

Within the Judeo-Christian understanding of eschatology (end times), any event in the eschatological age (from the coming of the Messiah to the final end of the age) is referred to as an eschatological event, and is an act of the Messiah coming in some form of dramatic action. Thus the destruction of Jerusalem is an expression of the coming of the Son of Man in power or in an eschatological act of judgment. And Jesus coming in judgment on one of the seven churches in Asia (Revelation 2, 3) can be spoken of as a coming of the Son of Man in judgment.

17:1–13

THE TRANSFIGURATION

Matthew's mention of six days having passed is interesting in that Luke mentions eight days having passed. This indicates that the precise timing is not the central point of this section. The central point is the glory of Jesus and God's acknowledgement of His divine role.

The fact that this section appears in all three Gospels immediately after Jesus' prediction of His death is striking. The passion prediction must have left a dark cloud over the disciples. They needed encouragement and hope. The Transfiguration and God's approving statement regarding

Jesus provide a ray of light and encouragement for the immediate circle of disciples (Peter, James, and John), and for Matthew's readers, too.

Jesus, taking only Peter, James, and John with Him onto the mountain, indicates His need to maintain a sense of secrecy and quietness in the matter of His messianic glory. Throughout the Gospel accounts of Jesus' ministry, He has tried to keep the crowds away to avoid sensationalism. Jesus later takes these same three men with Him into the Garden of Gethsemane to pray (26:37). We have no real indication why it is these three that seemingly formed the inner circle among the disciples.

The miracle of the Transfiguration is one of the truly great experiences of the story of Jesus. He is transformed. The shining of His face like the sun and the brightness of His garments are reminiscent of the Shekinah Glory of God that shone from Moses after his encounters with God on Mt. Sinai (Exodus 34:29–35).

The proposal by Peter that they build three tents has prompted much speculation as to what Peter had in mind. It is doubtful the tents were intended to be three shrines for worship because in Israel the booths were not for that purpose. Booths of branches were built for shelter on pilgrimages to Jerusalem, not worship. The simplest conclusion here is that Peter is proposing they spend more time in this transformed state with Jesus, Moses, and Elijah.

While Peter is still speaking, a bright cloud surrounds them (again an indication of the presence of God and God's involvement in this experience) and the great voice of God speaks in recognition of Jesus. This is the same message heard at the baptism of Jesus (3:17) with its inherent allusions to Psalm 2:7 and Isaiah 42:1. However, on this occasion God adds an allusion to Deuteronomy 18:15, the admonishment for those present to listen to Jesus. Most likely Moses represents the Torah Law given at Sinai, and Elijah represents the prophets, but now the authority to speak for God is transferred by God Himself to Jesus. Moses and Elijah had been the voice of God and the interpreters of the Torah, but from now on it will be Jesus who will interpret.

Following what was a magnificent experience—and frightening for Peter, James, and John—Jesus warns them not to tell others of this experience until after His resurrection.

The disciples are still confused about the expectation of the return of Elijah during the end times and question Jesus in this regard. Jesus explains that Elijah had returned in John the Baptist, but people were not ready to receive John and his message. In a similar vein, neither are they willing to receive the Son of Man and His message, and because of this, the Son of Man has to suffer at the hands of the Jewish leaders.

📖 17:14–21

HEALING OF THE EPILEPTIC BOY

The disciples are not able to heal this epileptic boy of his demon possession. The boy's father pleads with Jesus to heal the boy, which Jesus does. The healing is not the striking point of this section, since we already know that Jesus could, and did, heal many. Neither is the faith of the father the central point. It is the lack of faith, or weak faith, of the disciples that is at issue. Jesus is again working to build the faith of His disciples. His comment that faith can move mountains is a Hebrew proverb that meant faith can move immovable obstacles. The emphasis is not on the literal moving of mountains, but on the insurmountable problems that the disciples and all Christians face in life. John will write later that it is faith that is the victory that overcomes the world (1 John 5:4).

Matthew 17:21, the statement that prayer and fasting are required for this kind of feat, is missing in the more reliable ancient manuscripts. The verse appears in Mark's parallel (9:29) and was likely added by a later copyist to harmonize the two accounts.

📖 17:22–23

JESUS AGAIN FORETELLS HIS DEATH AND RESURRECTION

For some reason, possibly because the disciples are still struggling over Jesus' statement at Caesarea Philippi regarding His passion, Jesus again tells His disciples that He must be delivered into the hands of men and be killed, and then be raised by the power of God. Matthew reveals that the disciples are greatly distressed. Mark records that they don't understand but are afraid to ask (Mark 9:32). Luke records that it is hidden from them and they don't understand (Luke 9:45). These parallels reinforce the fact that the disciples are still struggling with the fate of the Messiah.

This section reinforces that Jesus' ministry falls within the will and purpose of God. The people of Matthew's community may have still been struggling with this and similar questions regarding Jesus' death, and their own subsequent suffering. They need to be assured that God is in control, that He is working His purpose, and that they are part of the plan of God.

📖 17:24–27

THE SHEKEL IN THE FISH'S MOUTH AND THE TEMPLE TAX

It is not surprising that Matthew is the only recorder of this experience, since it involves Jesus' attitude toward the temple. This would not be that important to either Mark's or Luke's audience. It is important to Matthew's community, which is struggling with the destruction of the temple. It is only the servants of the temple who need to pay the temple tax, and Jesus as the Son of God does not need to pay this tax, for sons are free of taxation. But to show His regard for the temple and for all it really stood, Jesus pays the tax anyway. However, the disciples and Matthew's community need to know that Jesus is greater than the temple, and whereas before His death the temple had been a focal point of Jewish faith, now it is Jesus who is the center of faith.

MATTHEW 18:1–35

DISCOURSE 4: COMMUNITY—HUMILTY AND FORGIVENESS

Setting Up the Section

This discourse covers several topics vital to successful church community life. It is introduced by the topic of the previous narrative in which Jesus focuses His attention on the disciples, preparing them for His death and resurrection. In this discourse Matthew takes the preparation of the disciples one step beyond the Resurrection, namely, on how they will live in a Christian community after Jesus is gone.

This discourse would have been essential for Matthew's readers in the late first century. They, as a community, had established themselves in new territory. In the same way, this discourse is also essential for churches today.

18:1–9

HUMILITY

Still struggling with the true nature of the kingdom, the disciples are concerned with who will be greatest in the kingdom. Jesus' answers in the following verses demonstrate that the disciples are struggling with matters of position, power, and authority. His response that the disciples should be like little children indicates that greatness in the kingdom has nothing to do with power and position, but everything to do with one's attitude toward self and others. Jesus has already noted that true greatness has to do with serving (11:11). He will return to this theme again when the mother of James and John seeks a high position for her sons (20:20–21). Luke 22:25–27 also drives this point home.

Jesus' response to the disciples that they must *turn* (convert, change) indicates a radical turn. The word translated as "turn" is a word commonly used to imply a moral turning or repenting. Jesus admonishes the disciples to make a radical turn in their mind-set regarding greatness in the kingdom. They need to become like little children. The point is that disciples need to be humble servants. However, we learn from the discussion that follows there is also the sense that, as humble servants, the disciples will be vulnerable to abuse. Humble disciples open themselves to abuse from others outside of the community of believers. Yet, Jesus explains, unless a disciple is willing to turn and be humble, he or she will not become a member of the kingdom, let alone be great in it (18:3).

Jesus continues by observing that to receive (welcome, accept) a disciple in the name of Jesus is the same as receiving Jesus Himself. However, to reject a vulnerable disciple (little one) is tantamount to leading the disciple to stumble or sin. The Greek word translated "stumble" or "sin" has the connotation of a snare or trap. In the religious or biblical sense, to stumble is equated with falling into sin or losing one's faith.

The discussion on humility is developed by Jesus to reflect on how disciples treat one another and influence other disciples. To cause a vulnerable disciple to stumble or lose his or her faith in Jesus is a serious matter, one in which judgment is compared by Jesus to having a millstone tied around one's neck and being cast into the depths of the sea and drowned. It seems from other references (Revelation 18:21) that this figure of speech may have been an idiom in Judaism for severe condemnation. Jesus closes this point with the interesting analogy of cutting off one's bodily members if they cause one to stumble (to lose faith and thus the kingdom).

Take It Home

What does it mean for the disciple to be humble? Unless one is willing to deny self and give up all for Christ, placing other disciples before self, one is not able to understand the kingdom. Faith and humility go hand in hand. Without both, the kingdom is impossible, for the kingdom is permitting God through Christ to reign in one's heart and life.

Consider Jesus' answer to the disciples' question regarding who is greatest in the kingdom. The one who humbles him- or herself like a little child is greatest in the kingdom, for as Jesus had previously taught, it is the servant who is greatest.

🕮 18:10–14

FINDING THE LOST SHEEP

To demonstrate further the importance of vulnerable disciples (all disciples are vulnerable), Jesus uses the illustration of the man who had 100 sheep, of which one got lost. Jesus concludes that this analogy reflects the love and concern of the Father in heaven for any one lost sheep.

Disciples are vulnerable to stumble and be lost. Disciples must be concerned for the vulnerable and lost and be sensitive to the needs of fellow disciples. Pride and seeking for greatness are not fitting for the kingdom. Having concern for fellow disciples, those who are vulnerable and easily lost, is key to kingdom understanding.

🕮 18:15–20

SOLVING PERSONAL AND COMMUNITY PROBLEMS

Hardly is there a passage that has more implications for Christians living in the kingdom than this one. In most English translations verse 15 opens with, "If your brother sins against you. . ." (NIV). Some very reliable manuscripts, from which these English versions of the Bible are translated, omit "against you." (The parallel passage in Luke 17:3 omits this.)

After reading verse 15 with the "against you" included, some have concluded that this passage refers *only* to a private sin. This is probably not the case, particularly considering the fact that the context of this section is community life and concern for disciples in general. The mention of the church later in this section (18:17–18) sets these verses firmly within the action of community life and discipline. Personal concerns do have a significant impact on congregational life, so the truth of this passage relates to both sin that is personal and private as well as sin that impacts the life of the church community.

The principles laid down by Jesus in this section are essential to resolving ruptured personal relationships, and mediating conflict. The instruction on how to handle such matters is firmly set in the threefold procedure established in Deuteronomy 19:15–21:

1) The process begins first on the personal level.
2) Then it proceeds to the second level of two witnesses.
3) The third level is bringing the matter before the community of believers.

In Deuteronomy 19:17, the final community level is considered the same as being in the presence of the Lord. Note Jesus' teaching in Matthew 18:20 that where this process is followed in His name, there He is present.

An interesting construction is evident in verses 15–17. Each initial clause in these statements of Jesus begins with "If." The careful construction of these verses indicates that Matthew has taken the time to set the verses up in a parallel structure styled in the form of a church discipline saying. The "if" clauses indicate the strong possibility, even probability, that in community life such occasions will occur and will require the appropriate corrective practice, which Jesus sets out.

1) Speak to the individual in person without publicizing the problem.
2) If an appropriate response is not forthcoming, take another person with you (at the mouth of two persons truth is established [Deuteronomy 19:15]).
3) As a last resort, bring the matter before the appropriate persons in the church community (possibly recognized leaders, elders, or even if necessary, the whole congregation). If no repentance is forthcoming, and no forgiveness requested, then the sinful person should be treated as a pagan (Gentile), meaning that the community should have no further fellowship in a brotherly sense with the sinful person.

There are other instances where instruction is given to the church on how to handle such matters. For instance, Galatians 6:1 relates closely with this section. On at least two other occasions, Paul instructs churches on matters of church discipline (1 Corinthians 5:1–13; 6:1–6; 2 Thessalonians 3:6–15).

In Matthew 18:15–20, Jesus concludes His instruction with the remarkable observation that action taken by the community in good Christian order is sanctioned in heaven and in fact becomes His own action.

The emphatic expression "truly" (v. 18 NASB) translates the Greek *amen* and adds a note of sincerity and genuineness to the saying that follows. Whatever is decided by the community in regard to settling community problems, when carried out in the appropriate manner, is accepted in heaven. The word translated as "bound" was used in marriage contracts, but in the context here implies a contract that will be honored in heaven. The full saying in Matthew 18:18 is in the form of a proverbial or idiomatic saying inferring that heaven acknowledges the decisions of the Christian community action.

The comment regarding two agreeing and two or three gathering in Jesus' name adheres to the Jewish belief that two witnesses settle a matter. The gathering together has no reference to a small gathering of the church on the Lord's Day for worship, which has become a partial excuse for a small assembly, but is a euphemism in reference to the group or community gathering in proper order to resolve problems. The community is reminded that Jesus is always present when His community gathers in His name, or under His will and lordship.

"In My name" (18:20 NIV) is a Hebrew euphemism for "in the person of Jesus" or "under His will."

📖 18:21–35

CHRISTIAN FORGIVENESS

The principles of Christian forgiveness are as essential to successful church community life as are the ones for resolving conflicts involving sin, as depicted in the previous section. Whereas the previous section initially presupposed a lack of repentance and focused on the other party, this section focuses on the first person, or the self. It asks not what the other person should have done, but what should *I* be doing?

This section begins with Peter asking how often he should forgive another person. Peter recognizes that forgiveness is vital to the process of church discipline and resolving broken relationships. His suggestion of forgiving seven times is generous. Rabbinic teaching suggested three times as the standard. Peter has chosen a favored Jewish number for completeness, but Jesus responds with a greater number—seventy times seven—indicating that there is no limit to the number of times one should be willing to forgive.

The fascinating and powerful parable that Jesus teaches drives home the need for Christians to learn how to forgive. The parable is set in the context of the kingdom, emphasizing Matthew's interest and concern for kingdom matters. When Jesus is reigning in disciples' lives and the kingdom is something real in their experience, more is expected than passive membership or church-going.

In the parable, the first servant owes the king an unpayable debt, 10,000 talents, estimated by some to be in the high millions or even billions of dollars in present-day currency. In 4 BC the total taxes for all of Judea, Samaria, and Idumea was only 600 talents. The king is merciful and forgives the first servant completely. Then there is a sudden change of events. The first servant is owed 100 denarii by another, about 100 days' wages (there were 6,000 denarii in one talent) and a payable debt. The first servant shows no mercy and no forgiveness. When the king hears, he throws the first servant in jail until he pays the full 10,000 talent (unpayable) debt. The application of this parable is timeless, applying to the first disciples, Matthew's community, and all Christians today.

We are reminded that this discourse begins with the disciples inquiring about who is greatest in the kingdom, which indicates a faulty understanding of kingdom life. Jesus' answer challenges the disciples to understand humble service in the kingdom. The discourse moves on to the need for all disciples to be concerned for all disciples, since disciples are vulnerable to sin and loss of faith. The value of one lost disciple is driven home by Jesus' teaching on the lost sheep. Jesus then moves on to community behavior and the need for disciples to resolve problems in the appropriate manner. Finally, the need for mercy and forgiveness is driven home by the powerful kingdom parable of the king and the two servants.

MATTHEW 19:1–22:46
NARRATIVE 5: TOWARD JERUSALEM—THE FINAL WEEK

Setting Up the Section

In the final week of Jesus' ministry, He continues to prepare His disciples for His death. His conflict with the Jewish leaders sharpens, leading up to exasperation and judgment on the scribes and Pharisees and on Jerusalem and the temple.

📖 19:1–12

JESUS ANSWERS THE PHARISEES ON MARRIAGE AND DIVORCE

As in Jesus' previous discussion of the divorce and remarriage issue, this discussion is set in the context of the Pharisees attempting to test and trap Jesus. This discourse on divorce and remarriage is not the final testament on the issue, but a serious answer to a trap by the Pharisees. Certainly, Jesus touches on several major issues in the debate on divorce and remarriage, but only within the context of the Pharisees' question.

The test question posed by the Pharisees is one that had troubled the rabbis for generations, in fact, since Moses had spoken to the issue in Deuteronomy 24:1. The question that arose from Moses' declaration was how to interpret the kind of indecency that would justify a man divorcing his wife. The issue placed before Jesus is not simply one on divorce, but relates to the justifiable grounds for divorce.

Two rabbinic schools of thought prevailed at the time the Pharisees posed this question:

• Rabbi Shammai interpreted the word *indecency* as unchastity or sexual immorality.
• Rabbi Hillel interpreted this loosely as any form of uncleanness on trivial grounds.

Jesus' response moves the argument back beyond Moses' permission for divorce to God's ideal for marriage. Marriage is to be for life, and what God has joined, man is not to break apart (Genesis 2:24).

Since Moses permitted divorce under the limited condition of unchastity (Deuteronomy 24:1, Shammai), we are introduced to a significant point that must impact our understanding of this perplexing dilemma: We have God's original instruction on His ideal for marriage. We have in Moses' permission the limited practical application of God's ideal.

The Pharisees' return argument is that Jesus has spoken in opposition to Moses. Jesus corrects them by showing that what Moses had done was not a command but permission. The Pharisees had attempted to place Jesus in opposition to Moses and the Law. Jesus again, as in the Sermon on the Mount, demonstrates that the Pharisaic interpretation of the Law does not take into consideration the real spirit of purpose of the Law. Moses' permission was purely because of human hardness of heart. By adding the except-for-unchastity clause, Jesus is reminding the Pharisees of the narrowness of God's permission. The narrowness of Jesus' response disturbs the disciples, indicating how lax Jewish attitudes had become in regard to marriage and divorce. Their observation is that it might be better for one not to marry if Jesus' interpretation is correct.

Jesus' response speaks of three groups of eunuchs—two literal, one metaphorical.

1) Those born impotent and therefore eunuchs
2) Those made eunuchs by others such as in the case of the Ethiopian eunuch of Acts 8, sometimes occurring in slavery
3) Those who chose to live celibate lives for the kingdom as in the case of the apostle Paul

Jesus' response to the disciples' concern again illustrates the radical nature of discipleship in the kingdom. Disciples are to live by God's ideals rather than permissiveness resulting from sinful weakness.

Although this is not the place for a full discussion of the marriage and divorce issue, note that Paul takes the argument beyond the narrow confines of Judaism and Israel as the covenant people of God into a discussion of marriages involving non-believers. Perhaps Paul's discussion is more relevant for contemporary issues and may be parallel to Moses' permission. Disciples in the kingdom should be shaped, however, more by kingdom issues and God's ideals than by permissiveness.

📖 19:13–15

JESUS BLESSES LITTLE CHILDREN

This little section in which the disciples seek to drive children away provides Jesus with another occasion to remind the disciples that the kingdom belongs to those who have learned to be humble like children. It is not uncommon for disciples to bring worldly standards of greatness into the kingdom. Followers of Jesus throughout the centuries have struggled with the principle of humble servant leadership, with many seeking positions in the church for the wrong reasons—personal importance rather than humble service.

📖 19:16–30

THE RICH YOUNG RULER

The narrative regarding the rich young ruler focuses again on radical discipleship and the true nature of the kingdom. Matthew does not identify the young man as a ruler, but Luke does so in his parallel narrative in Luke 18:18–27. Obviously the young man is not only rich, but also a person of position, possibly a ruler in the synagogue. On this occasion the rich young man addresses Jesus regarding eternal life, asking what good thing he must do to inherit eternal life (referring to the afterlife, not an eternal earthly life).

Jesus' question about the man's meaning of *good* is interesting. Rabbinic tradition defined the Torah as the good. Jesus explains that it is by keeping the commandments that one will experience eternal life. When the young man explains that he has done this, Jesus accepts his claim. One can be righteous through keeping the law, for Paul claims such (Philippians 3:6). Maintaining righteousness should not be equated here with being sinless, but instead seen as merely a claim to having maintained a right relationship with God through observing the Torah.

Jesus' instruction to the young man gets to the heart of his problem—riches. When he learns that discipleship in the kingdom involves placing kingdom matters and discipleship above personal possessions, the young man goes away sad, for the cost of discipleship is too high. His reaction reminds us of Jesus' teaching in the Sermon on the Mount, that your heart will be where your treasure is (6:21).

Jesus continues the discussion begun by the young man. He does not say it is impossible for a rich person to enter heaven, but only that it is difficult. (This Greek word for *difficult* is found in the New Testament only on this occasion in Matthew, Mark, and Luke.) Illustrating how difficult it would be for a rich person to enter the kingdom, Jesus uses the analogy of a camel going through the eye of a needle. Attempts to soften this by interpreting *camel* and *eye of a needle* in a more reasonable way fail to grasp the irony of Jesus' statement. He is using exaggeration to make a point. The reason some attempt to soften this saying is that it seems to make it impossible for a rich person to be saved. The disciples catch this and are amazed and ask who can be saved. This is when Jesus gets to the point—salvation is not the work of humanity, but of God. Even though it would be difficult for a rich person to be saved, it is not impossible for God, but it would necessitate the rich person turning away from this world and to God for His saving grace. No one can be saved by human effort. It is only through the grace and working of God that all people can be saved.

When Peter, troubled by Jesus' seemingly harsh statement, asks what will happen to them for they have given up all for the kingdom, Jesus responds that in the new world they will sit on thrones with Jesus and judge the world with Him. All who give up everything for Jesus and the kingdom's sake will inherit eternal life.

Jesus' reference to the new world (the regeneration, the renewal of all things, when the Son of Man sits on His throne) uses a Greek word that means rebirth or regeneration. The word is found in the New Testament only twice, here and in Titus 3:5, but has a rich heritage in historical writings and the Jewish rabbinic tradition. In most cases, it references a future age or occasion of renewal, rebirth, or restoration. Here Jesus links it to the time when the Son of Man will sit on His throne and reign over the kingdom. The apostles who have given up all will then sit with Him and judge Israel with Him. This is supported in Revelation, where John writes that those who have died as martyrs sit with Jesus on thrones (Revelation 2:26–28; 20:4–6).

Jesus concludes this discussion with the proverbial statement that the first will be last. Given the context of the rich young man, one must assume that the first must be in reference to the rich who believe that because of their position in life they should be privileged. In the kingdom this is not the case, for as we have already learned, it is the humble who benefit from the kingdom, not the proud (5:1–12), and it is the humble servants who are greatest in the kingdom (18:1–4).

📖 **20:1–16**

THE PARABLE OF THE HOUSEHOLDER

This parable connects back to the closing statement of Matthew 19:30 and illustrates the principle of the first being last, and the last being first. It is a parable that speaks to behavior in the kingdom. But it is also an illustration of the great kingdom principle of grace.

The householder (who represents God) hires a series of workers at different times of the day. He promises the first a day's wages (a denarius). At the close of the day he pays all the workers the same wage, but those who were hired first are upset that they'd worked longer for the same pay as those that were hired on late. The householder's closing remarks demonstrate a great principle of grace: Can't I do what I want with what belongs to me? Do you resent my generosity toward others?

Jesus closes the parable by returning to the proverb, but in this case reverses the order—the last will be first.

📄 20:17–19

JESUS AGAIN FORETELLS HIS DEATH AND RESURRECTION

As Jesus draws near to Jerusalem, He again instructs the twelve regarding His death, burial, and resurrection. This time, though, He elaborates briefly on several other things: His suffering, condemnation by the Jewish leadership, trial before the Gentiles, and the mocking and scourging He will receive.

📄 20:20–28

THE SON OF MAN CAME TO SERVE, NOT BE SERVED

We see again in this section the difficulty the disciples have understanding the true nature of discipleship and the kingdom. On this occasion the mother of James and John asks Jesus for positions of honor for her sons in the kingdom. We should not think too poorly of this mother, or of the other disciples for being indignant over her request. The temptation to see leadership positions as power rather than opportunities to serve still exists today in the church.

Jesus asks the two disciples whether they are willing to drink the cup that He is about to drink, and they respond that they are. The metaphor of drinking the cup is in reference to His suffering and death, which He has just talked about (20:17–19). The background for the use of a cup in reference to suffering can also be found in the Old Testament in passages such as Psalm 75:8 and Isaiah 51:17, 22. The immediate response of the two disciples seems to indicate they do not fully understand the implications of Jesus' remark.

Jesus follows His comments with a clear, real-life analogy. In this world the greatest are served while the least do the serving. The kingdom of God works in the reverse. The greatest are those who serve. Jesus uses a reference to Himself as the Son of Man to illustrate this. As the Son of Man, He deserves being served by others, but this is not His purpose. He came to be a servant. Luke records similar words from Jesus (Luke 22:25–27). Paul also writes of Jesus' humble service (Philippians 2:5–11).

📄 20:29–34

HEALING TWO BLIND MEN NEAR JERICHO

As Jesus and the disciples are passing through Jericho they see two blind men.

The synoptic Gospels—Matthew, Mark, and Luke—record different details. In Luke's Gospel Jesus and His disciples are coming into Jericho, as opposed to Matthew's record that they are leaving. Mark and Luke refer to one man, while Matthew, making the story more reliable to a Jewish audience, records two men. Mark includes the name of the man, Bartimaeus. But these details are not contradictory. Each writer brings out the details that serve his purpose best in the retelling.

The two blind men call out to Jesus, referring to Him as the Son of David and begging Him to heal them, which He does. The narrative draws attention to the fact that even the blind recognize Jesus as the Messiah, yet the seeing—Pharisees, scribes, and Sadducees—do not recognize the Messiah. This narrative fits in well with the preceding discussion of the greatest being last and the least being first.

📖 21:1–11

THE TRIUMPHANT ENTRY INTO JERUSALEM

This event and narrative is shared by all four Gospels (Mark 11:1–11; Luke 19:29–44; John 12:12–19).

Bethphage was a small village, possibly on the Mount of Olives near Bethany, but we do not know its exact location. The name means "house of unripe figs." We read of Bethphage only in this account in Matthew, Mark, and Luke.

Jesus' entry into Jerusalem is a turning point in the Gospel narrative. It ends His Galilean ministry and journey to Jerusalem and begins the tragic passion narrative. It is an event marked by the capriciousness of the people and manifests a mixture of truth and irony. The truth is that Jesus really is the Messiah. The irony is that His very identity as the Messiah is the reason He is rejected by the Jews, particularly the Jewish leadership. When He enters Jerusalem He is welcomed as the Son of David, but is almost immediately rejected as the Messiah and mocked by the people. When Jesus shows that He is a different kind of Messiah than they expected, He is rejected.

Jesus deliberately stages His ride into Jerusalem to fulfill Zechariah 9:9, an Old Testament passage that was interpreted with reference to the Messiah by the rabbis. Matthew's use of Zechariah 9:9 is one of the ten fulfillment passages unique to his Gospel. He combines Zechariah 9:9 with Isaiah 62:11.

Mark, Luke, and John record one animal, an ass or donkey, while Matthew records an ass that had a colt with her. Some commentators think that Matthew has misunderstood the poetic parallelism in Zechariah 9:9 to refer to two animals instead of one. But this is not necessary. Matthew's account makes sense when we recognize that—as Mark tells us—Jesus is riding on a colt on which no one has previously sat. The mother animal is therefore brought along to calm the colt as Jesus rides on it.

The crowd welcomes Jesus jubilantly, spreading their garments on the road for Him to ride into Jerusalem in kingly style, and crying "Hosanna to the Son of David" (21:9 NASB) followed by a blessing from Psalm 118:26. The term *Hosanna* in Aramaic means "O save" or "God save," but had come to be a simple term of praise. The people praise Jesus as their king, their Messiah. Yet, they also recognize Him merely as the prophet from Nazareth.

CLEANSING THE TEMPLE

The cleansing of the temple narrative is found here at the close of Jesus' ministry in Matthew, Mark, and Luke, but in John's Gospel it appears at the beginning of His ministry. There is also a difference in the order of the event in Matthew and Mark. Matthew has the cleansing of the temple immediately, or on the same day that Jesus enters Jerusalem. Mark has it on the following day and inserts the narrative of the barren fig tree between the Jerusalem entry and the cleansing of the temple. The fact that John places this cleansing early in Jesus' ministry, and that Mark places it on the second day after Jesus enters the city, indicates that chronological exactness is not of prime importance to the Gospel writers, and takes a secondary role to theological interests.

Matthew has the cleansing on the same day that Jesus is acknowledged as king, indicating that the cleansing is a messianic duty. John places it at the beginning of Jesus' ministry indicating that Jesus truly is the Son of God. Theological interests are primary to Matthew and John rather than historical or chronological concerns. It is a stretch of imagination to suggest two cleansings of the temple, since such a dramatic action would have been too remarkable for any of the writers not to mention a second one.

The authority Jesus claims for cleansing the temple is to cite scripture. "It is written" (21:13 NIV) was a recognized rabbinic expression. He quotes Isaiah 56:7 as His authority for overturning the tables of the moneychangers and the seats of the pigeon sellers. Consideration of the verses surrounding Isaiah 56:1–7 adds to the significance of Jesus' actions. Particularly notable is the fact that Isaiah 56 refers to the Gentile inclusion in God's kingdom.

There in the temple, Jesus continues His ministry of healing the blind and the lame. However, when the chief priests see the wonderful miracles of Jesus, and hear the children acclaiming Jesus as the Son of David, they are indignant and rebuke Jesus. Jesus responds by referring to Psalm 8:2, with His declaration that perfect praise can come from the mouths of babes or children.

Leaving the temple, Jesus goes to stay in Mary and Martha's home in Bethany.

The cleansing of the temple sets Jesus in open conflict with the Jewish leaders and is the first of a series of confrontations which culminates in His condemnation of the scribes and Pharisees (Matthew 23) and judgment on the temple and Jerusalem (Matthew 24). It is not surprising that Matthew places the cleansing of the temple immediately after His entry into Jerusalem and follows it with the narrative of the barren fig tree, an event which amounts to condemnation of the Jewish leaders.

THE BARREN FIG TREE

Mark's account of this event is in two narratives separated by the cleansing of the temple and is in greater detail than Matthew's.

The barren fig tree is a lesson on faith. However, it is also a lesson on the absence of faith. The point is that Jesus expects fruit on the fig tree. Fig trees in Palestine, as many places elsewhere, bore two crops of fruit, an early crop known to Palestinians as *taqsh*, and a later crop of fully formed figs. The presence of leaves indicates that the early fruit of the fig should have been present, but Jesus finds none. The harshness of His condemnation is symbolic of His condemnation of the Jewish leaders for their lack of faith. Faith should have been the trademark of the Jewish religious leaders, but had not been a typical response from them.

Jesus' statement regarding faith moving mountains is a Hebrew type of expression indicating that with faith great things can be achieved.

📖 21:23–27

CHIEF PRIESTS CHALLENGE JESUS' AUTHORITY

Upon entering the temple again, Jesus is confronted by the chief priests and elders who challenge His authority. Jesus responds with a challenge regarding the baptism of John the Baptist—was it from heaven or from men? This backs the Jewish leaders into a corner, for if they claim John's baptism was from heaven, they will blacken their own eyes that they hadn't believed John. If they answer that his baptism was from men, the crowds who followed John could turn on them. Stymied, they simply respond that they do not know. In similar fashion, Jesus answers that He will not tell them by what authority He acts. This exchange illustrates well the growing tension and opposition from the Jewish leadership and Jesus' firm response.

📖 21:28–32

THE PARABLE OF TWO SONS

The next parable involved two sons—one initially refuses to work but then works, another initially agrees to work, but never goes. The first son references the tax collectors, prostitutes, and general sinners who turn away from God but then repent. The second represents the Jewish leaders who claim to be righteous but do not repent. Those who should inherit the kingdom will not, but those who do not deserve the kingdom receive its benefits. Jesus gets very personal in Matthew 21:32 by speaking directly to the Jewish religious leaders. He confronts them on their character assassination of Him and John the Baptist as well as their refusal to repent.

📖 21:33–46

THE PARABLE OF THE WICKED TENANTS

The parable of the wicked tenants is again a reference to the religious leaders who should take care of the master's vineyard, but do not. When the master sends servants, the tenants kill the servants, and then go on to kill the heir of the master who comes in the master's name.

When asked by Jesus what should happen to the wicked tenants, the chief priests and Pharisees rightly respond that the wicked tenants deserve death. What they do not see is that Jesus is referencing them in the parable. These religious leaders had rejected the prophets and now they are rejecting the heir of the master, the Son of God. Jesus challenges the chief priests and Pharisees from Psalm 118:22–23. They are rejecting the chief cornerstone to the building of God—the true holy temple, which is the people of God—and do not recognize the error of their ways.

Jesus' next comment is a scathing rebuke—the Jews will lose the kingdom of God and the Gentiles will receive it. Finally, the chief priests and Pharisees see that Jesus is speaking about them. If not for their fear of the crowds who follow Jesus, they would arrest Him.

📖 22:1–14

THE PARABLE OF THE MARRIAGE FEAST

Chapter 22 continues Jesus' condemnation of the Jewish leaders with the parable of the marriage feast. It also includes further discussion with the Pharisees and Sadducees which leads into Jesus' scathing condemnation of the scribes and Pharisees in Matthew 23.

Demonstrating Matthew's end-times perspective, this parable is addressed as a parable of the kingdom of heaven and draws heavily on the Jewish concept of a final banquet to which those who are righteous and worthy are invited. The book of Revelation likewise draws on this concept (Revelation 19).

There might have been a sense that those who refused to come were the Jewish leaders, but by this point in Jesus' ministry the rejection had spread beyond the leaders and into the general populace. Possibly those who are invited but refuse to come are those who think they are righteous—but are not. The second group invited from the thoroughfares is both bad and good. It is interesting that Jesus mentions the bad before the good, emphasizing that it is not the righteous that come, but the sinners. The righteous do not see the need to respond.

Some say that the king sending out his army to punish the offenders might be a reference to the judgment and destruction of the scribes, Pharisees, and Jerusalem that are described in greater detail in Matthew 23–25. This might not be the case since the figure of kings sending soldiers out to punish offenders was a common one in ancient parables and narratives.

Of the many that do respond to the invitation, one man is present who is not wearing a wedding garment. Questions exist among scholars as to whether the king had provided the wedding garments for his guests, and whether this was a common practice. These details are not mentioned in the parable. It is, after all, simply a parable rather than a historical account. Not all the details are necessary to the story, nor are they pertinent to the lesson of the parable. What is pertinent to the lesson is that the man is not properly attired for a wedding and is thrown out.

The significant question is the exact meaning of the wedding garment. In the context of the parables and events in Jesus' life at this point, it is apparent that wearing the appropriate wedding garment represents being clothed by faith and righteousness, both of which are absent in the chief priests and Pharisees who are attempting to be part of the messianic kingdom on their own terms, not the terms of the king.

The final verse of this parable gets to the heart of things—many are called (invited), but few are chosen. All are called, but only those characterized by faith and righteousness are the chosen.

📖 22:15–22

THE MESSIAH, TAXES, AND CAESAR

The question of the Pharisees places Jesus between the horns of a dilemma. Whichever way He answers the question, He will be in trouble with some group of leadership. If He answers that it is permissible to pay taxes to Rome, He will meet with opposition from the crowds as well as the Pharisees—the Roman tax was despised by the Jewish nation. If He answers that tax should not be paid to the Romans, He will meet with opposition from the Herodians and the Romans themselves.

Seeking for means to entrap Jesus, the Pharisees joined forces with the Herodians (the Jewish party in support of the ruling Herod family) and hypocritically questioned Jesus regarding the Roman tax system. What is significant about this event is the apparent collusion between the Pharisees and Herodians, who under normal situations would not have had anything to do with one another. Since the Herodians were political supporters of the Herodian rulers, they were not favored by the religiously inclined populace and Pharisees who rejected the Herodian monarchy. In this case though, the Pharisees compromise by sending their disciples with the Herodians to trap Jesus. By adopting this stance, the Pharisees kept a bit of distance yet allied themselves with a group that was more politically astute.

Jesus understands the entrapment. His answer serves to give neither group grounds for uprising or arrest. Stumped again by Jesus, they leave Him and go away—for a time.

📖 22:23–33

THE SADDUCEES AND THE RESURRECTION

Next, it is the Sadducees' turn at trapping Jesus. The Sadducees were the more traditional or conservative among the Jewish sects, holding that it was only the first five books of scripture that were authoritative and comprised the Torah of God. Because of this, they rejected anything not addressed in Genesis through Deuteronomy. The resurrection of the dead was not explicitly taught there and was thus rejected by the Sadducees, along with belief in angels. The Sadducees also differed with the Pharisees on matters of ceremonial purity and civil law.

Like the Pharisees in the previous section, the Sadducees, seeking to discredit Jesus, address Him as teacher as they question Him in regard to His interpretation of the Torah. It's easy to suspect that the address "teacher" is less than sincere.

The setting of the Sadducees' question is the Mosaic Levirate law of Deuteronomy 25:5–10. According to this law, if a woman's husband dies before she bears a son to carry on the family inheritance, then a brother of the deceased husband takes the widow as his wife. The son that she bears by this man is considered the son of her dead husband, thus that man's inheritance is kept intact. Potentially, as this woman loses husbands in death, she could continue to marry the next brother in the hopes of producing an heir.

The problem the Sadducees are addressing is who then would the woman belong to in the resurrection. This poses no problem for the Sadducees if the resurrection does not exist. However, if the resurrection does exist, this poses a serious problem to them.

Jesus' answer is both direct and stern—the Sadducees' problem is that they know neither the scriptures (a serious challenge and insult) nor the power of God (which addresses the core of the Sadducees' problem with the resurrection). Jesus' challenge to the Sadducees regarding their lack of knowledge comes directly from a scripture the Sadducees have to accept—Exodus 3:6, 15. Since these verses are in the present tense, the implication is that at the time God was speaking these words to Moses, Abraham, Isaac, and Jacob, they were alive, even though centuries had passed since their deaths were recorded in Genesis. This could be possible only if the resurrection were real and true. Jesus' point, then, is that to deny the resurrection is to misunderstand scripture. This is quite a challenge to a group that defines itself by its attention to scripture.

Rather than undermine Jesus' standing as a teacher, the Sadducees reinforce it, for the crowds are astonished by Jesus' teaching.

Take It Home

We, like the Sadducees, might not have a full understanding of what life will be like in the resurrection (afterlife), but unlike the Sadducees, we believe in the power of God and leave the uncertainties to later fulfillment and understanding. Somewhat like Paul, we now see in a mirror dimly, but we'll one day see face-to-face. We know in part for now, but then we'll understand fully (1 Corinthians 13:12).

📖 22:34–40

WHICH IS THE GREATEST COMMANDMENT?

The fact that Jesus has stood up against both the Pharisees and Sadducees does not cause the Pharisees to back off from challenging Him. Their next challenge is a concerted group effort. They come together and, through a scribe (a lawyer, or expert in the Torah), the Pharisees pose a serious legal test question—which is the greatest commandment? Jesus' answer to this question will place Him either among the fringes of Jewish teachers, or within the mainstream of Jewish legal interpretation.

One wonders what must have motivated this particular question. Perhaps it was Jesus' previous teaching which seemed to go contrary to the scribes interpretation of the Torah (5:17–48). Jesus' answer, though, gets to the heart of the law by way of an orthodox path. He quotes part of the Shema (Deuteronomy 6:4–9), a passage that was quoted twice every day by all serious Jews: "Love the Lord your God with all your heart and with all your soul and with all your strength" (6:5 NIV). Jesus then follows this with a quotation from Leviticus 19:18: "Love your neighbor as yourself" (NIV).

A close examination of the Ten Commandments reveals that loving God and one's neighbor is what the Ten Commandments and the Torah are all about. Jesus' final comment that the Law and the prophets depend on these two commandments leaves the scribe silent. Neither the Pharisees nor the scribe have a response.

📖 22:41–46

JESUS' UNANSWERABLE QUESTION TO THE PHARISEES

While the Pharisees are still together, Jesus takes the initiative and asks them whose son the Messiah is. They answer, "The son of David" (22:42 NIV). This was a typical rabbinic answer of the day, for it was held and stated that the Messiah would be a descendant of King David. In fact, the term had become synonymous with the Messiah.

Jesus' question is not simply one designed as a clever trap for the Pharisees, but is one with serious implications for His own identity and calling as the Messiah. The question does, however, pose a serious interpretive problem for the Pharisees. How could David call the Messiah his Lord (Psalm 110:1) when the Messiah was to be a human descendant of his?

The core of Jesus' question addresses the issue of a human being (a son of David) being the divine messianic Lord (which is what Psalm 110:1 implied). This question and how it is answered lies at the very core of Matthew's Gospel and theology. Disciples must believe that Jesus (a human being) is at the same time a divine being (this is what the virgin birth narrative demonstrates), and the divine Messiah.

This question from Jesus, and the Pharisees' inability to answer it, closes this series of challenges in this major narrative section. However, the Pharisees' inherent denial of Jesus' messiahship, and their inability to answer His final question, set the scene for the final major discourse in Matthew, in which Jesus condemns the scribes and Pharisees and pronounces judgment on Jerusalem and the temple.

MATTHEW 23:1–25:46
DISCOURSE 5: THE APOCALYPTIC DISCOURSE

Setting Up the Section

There are four components to this discourse:

1. Jesus' Condemnation of the Scribes and Pharisees

2. The Destruction of Jerusalem Predicted by Jesus

3. Comments Regarding the End of the Age, or the End of the World

4. Warnings to Be Prepared for the Final End

📄 23:1–36

JESUS' CONDEMNATION OF THE SCRIBES AND PHARISEES

Jesus begins this significant judgment by acknowledging the scribes and Pharisees as teachers of the Torah, but warns the disciples not to imitate their actions. The problem is that the scribes and Pharisees make their interpretation of keeping the Torah a matter so strict that no one can bear the burden of their interpretation. Furthermore, the Pharisees make a show of their position and righteousness in contrast to drawing people's attention to their God and His laws.

The point Jesus is stressing in this passage is that the disciples have only one true interpreter and teacher of the Torah—Jesus—not the scribes and Pharisees. Likewise, the disciples have only one spiritual Father and that is God Himself. The scribes and Pharisees are not to be seen as the spiritual fathers of the disciples.

Jesus' seven judgments on the religious leadership—absolute in their condemnation—begin with verse 13. He refers to these leaders as

- Blind guides
- Blind fools
- Hypocrites
- Murderers
- Serpents
- Vipers
- Whitewashed tombs

The fact that Matthew clusters the judgments of Jesus against the scribes and Pharisees into seven woes is both significant and vital to this final discourse. Matthew's intention is to demonstrate that Jesus' condemnation of the scribes and Pharisees has final judgment implications. The unique structure around the seven woes sets the tone for the following two chapters (24 and 25).

Demystifying Matthew

The King James Version of the Bible has eight woes in this section, but that may be a stretch. There are sometimes a variety of ancient manuscripts to consult when translating a version of the Bible. Careful consideration of the differing manuscripts for this text indicates that the most reliable manuscripts contain only seven woes. Most other English translations either omit verse 14 or set it apart in some way (italics, parentheses, as a note rather than text). The opinion of text critics is that verse 14 is a later insertion and not original to Matthew.

There is a sense of parallelism in the content and structure of these seven woes.

1) Each begins similarly with a woe. This is a classic prophetic expression pronouncing judgment.
2) Six of the woes are pronounced against the scribes and Pharisees, the rabbinic teachers of Jesus' day who rejected both His identity as the Messiah and His interpretation of the Torah. One of the woes, the third, refers to these leaders only as blind guides.
3) Six of the woes refer to the scribes and Pharisees as hypocrites. Since this word implies a play actor or pretender, it strikes at the insincerity of the scribes and Pharisees.

The final condemnation of the scribes and Pharisees as murderers summarizes the depth of their rejection of God, His prophets, and His messengers, and predicts the coming persecution of the Christian apostles, prophets, and evangelists.

In the sense of corporate responsibility, the scribes and Pharisees of Jesus' day are responsible for the deaths of all the righteous persons and prophets of God since the murder of righteous Abel (Genesis 4) down to the most recent murder of the prophet Zechariah. Scholars debate who this Zechariah might be. Some cite the prophet Zechariah of 2 Chronicles 24:20, since 2 Chronicles was the last book of the Jewish canon, but this Zechariah was identified as the son of a priest name Jehoida while the Zechariah mentioned by Jesus is the son of Barachiah. We might not be able to identify this Zechariah, but he must have been a recognizable person of historical significance for Jesus to mention him as He does here.

Jesus' closing condemnation adds even more gravity to the woes. His inclusion of the whole generation brings the Jewish populace into the condemnation, for they side with the scribes and Pharisees in the events leading up to Jesus' crucifixion.

📖 23:37–39

THE LAMENT OVER JERUSALEM

This section is one of the saddest exclamations that can be made, and ranks with the one made by the disciple John when he states that Jesus comes to His own, but they do not accept Him (John 1:11).

The personification of Jerusalem adds to the tragedy of Jesus' denunciation of the great city, which in both the past and the present has rejected God's servants and stoned and killed them (and will do the same in the imminent future).

The desolation (abandonment, desertion) of Jerusalem's house draws on Old Testament language and situations in which Jerusalem had been judged by God and destroyed (Jeremiah 22:5; 12:7 for example).

However, no matter how drastic and complete Jesus' condemnation of the scribes, Pharisees, and Jerusalem, He does not give up hope. He instead pronounces redemption for those who believe in Him and surrender their lives to Him. He offers future hope in the midst of tragedy.

This brief section sets the scene for the next two chapters (24–25), including Jesus' prediction of the destruction of the temple and the city of Jerusalem, as well as the disciples' question regarding the end of the age.

📖 24:1–35

JESUS' JUDGMENT OF THE TEMPLE AND JERUSALEM (INTRODUCTION)

Setting Up the Section

This discourse, as with all the other materials in this Gospel, must be understood within the context of Matthew's Gospel and the Jewish context of Jesus' ministry. Jesus is addressing the scribes and Pharisees and pronouncing judgment on Jerusalem.

Critical Observation

In order to be able to follow the flow of thought and the shifts in emphasis in this section, here are several factors vital to understanding this discourse:

1) We have already noticed that Jesus begins this discourse in an apocalyptic context (the end-times connotations contained in the seven woes). He continues by keeping His discussion in an apocalyptic kind of language.

2) Any judgment on Jerusalem and the temple, and any destruction of Jerusalem and the temple, would be interpreted by a Jew as the end of the age or world. To a Jew, nothing could be worse than a judgment on Jerusalem and the Jewish religious system.

3) The disciples are so shocked by Jesus' denunciation of the Jewish religious leaders, the temple, Jerusalem, and that generation that they ask Jesus two questions, although they see them as one question: When will this be, and what are the signs of Jesus' coming?

4) Jesus responds, treating their questions as two events, not one. He separates the destruction of Jerusalem as one event and His coming and the end of the age as a separate event.

5) Jesus first discusses erroneous views or predictions of His coming (theologically, we refer to this as His second coming). He then draws on the imagery of Daniel 9:27 to describe the desecration of the temple and a great final crisis and warns the disciples to flee the city. These signs can be clearly seen and understood.

6) He draws on clearly understood apocalyptic imagery (Matthew 24:29–31) to demonstrate that this is a political enemy, and that the destroying enemy is an agent of God. (This is the genius of the unique apocalyptic genre adopted by Jesus.)

7) He makes it clear that these events will come upon the generation He is addressing.

8) Then Jesus turns to discuss the second question asked (What will be the sign of His coming and the end of the age?) and responds that there will be no sign. He warns His disciples to be alert and watchful, for no one will be able to predict when the Son of Man will come again.

9) Matthew 25 and the three parables illustrate how the disciples must be alert, watchful, and prepared for the sudden and unannounced coming of the Son of Man.

24:1–14

JUDGMENT: THE DISCIPLES' QUESTION

The disciples are so shocked by Jesus' condemnation of Jerusalem, that as they are near the temple—the bastion of Judaism—they draw Jesus' attention to the temple. Jesus responds in a manner intended to help the disciples see that the temple, however important it was to Judaism, is not to play a part in the messianic kingdom and ministry. The temple is to be destroyed.

To a Jew, and the disciples are Jews, this is inconceivable and unbelievable—the temple to be destroyed? When will such a significant event take place? Surely such an event has to be the end of the age. What will be the sign of Jesus' coming, or the end of the age?

Jesus warns that many will falsely predict His coming, but before such an event the gospel has to be preached throughout the world. Jesus encourages His disciples to not be misled by wars, earthquakes, and other such events, which false prophets will use to lure followers away. He encourages His disciples to endure such catastrophes and persecutions; those who endure will be saved in the end (He is speaking of final, eternal salvation, not the present salvation we enjoy in the Christian life).

The point Jesus is making to the disciples in this section is that they should not be lead astray by false predictions or claims that Jesus has come or is about to come. They are not to confuse the destruction of Jerusalem and the temple with the end of the world or the coming of the Son of Man.

📖 24:15–28

JUDGMENT: THE DESTRUCTION OF JERUSALEM

Jesus begins His discussion of the destruction of Jerusalem by making reference to language and events with which all Jews were familiar, the language of Daniel 9:27 and 12:11—the abomination that causes desolation. The event prophesied by Daniel had taken place in 168 BC when Antiochus Epiphanes captured Jerusalem and desecrated the temple by erecting an altar to the god Zeus there. Jesus uses this well-known imagery to describe the events surrounding the destruction of Jerusalem in His prophecy.

Most scholars identify this event with the destruction of Jerusalem by the Romans in AD 70. The historical accounts of the Roman siege and destruction of Jerusalem fit well with the language used by Jesus in this section.

Jesus warns the disciples to immediately and hastily flee Jerusalem when they see the approaching desolation. For those pregnant and with small children, the flight will be difficult. The disciples should pray that their flight will not be necessary on the Sabbath (because of the Jewish travel restrictions on the Sabbath) and that it not be in the winter.

Eusebius, the Father of Church History, recorded that in the year AD 66, when the Christians saw the approaching Roman armies, in keeping with Jesus' admonition, they fled Jerusalem for the region that is now the nation of Jordan (Ecclesiastical History, 3.5.3).

Again, Jesus warns the disciples not to believe those who might proclaim that these events usher in His second coming. In Matthew 24:22–25 Jesus repeats His previous warning—that He will come just as the lightning strikes, suddenly and without warning.

At this point, Jesus has twice warned His disciples not to interpret world events as signs of His eschatological coming.

The last saying of this section (24:28) falls firmly within the apocalyptic tradition. Some commentators interpret the eagle as the insignia on the standards or banners of the Roman legions, but this is unlikely. The word can mean either "eagle" or "vulture" and refers to a bird that eats dead flesh. The imagery expresses that there will be much bloodshed and death when the abomination that causes desolation comes (24:15).

24:29–31

JUDGMENT: THE COMING OF THE SON OF MAN

Demystifying Matthew

This short section has generated considerable discussion among scholars through the centuries. Without question, it is a difficult passage, especially if the reader does not consider the strong apocalyptic genre in which it is so obviously couched. The terms used in the passage have a long and rich history in the Old Testament and apocalyptic literature, and must be seen in line with this tradition. Failure to understand this tradition will lead to speculation, but not necessarily the truth.

The apocalyptic genre and tradition is the literature of persecution, tribulation, and suffering. It is generally pessimistic regarding the potential of human endeavor and history to solve the suffering, but is especially optimistic regarding God's ability to provide a solution. Apocalyptic writings often describe a great and final persecution of God's people and God's intervention to destroy the wicked, save the righteous, and establish His eternal kingdom.

There is a tendency in apocalyptic writing to bring several well-known scriptures together in a collage of thoughts as a symbol of what is taking place. The story is presented as bigger than life in order to make the point that this is not merely a human story, but God's divine intervention and judgment on history and mankind.

The use of the word *immediately* (v. 29) can, at first read, make it seem that the coming of the Son of Man at the end of the age is to happen just after the destruction of Jerusalem. But historically and theologically this does not happen, and Jesus has warned against such interpretation (24:5–14).

In this case, *immediately* is a transitional term that connects the section under discussion directly and dynamically back to the previous discussion, namely, the destruction of the temple and Jerusalem. This makes the case that the destruction of the temple and Jerusalem are the direct judgment of God and the Son of Man, not merely historical occurrences.

The Christian faith is familiar with concepts that have both a now and a then nature. We experience salvation now that is only to be fully experienced in eternity. We participate now in the resurrection of Jesus, but that resurrection will only be realized at the final resurrection. Any event in the Christian age partakes of end-of-the-world significance. If you believe in Jesus now, it has end-of-the-world significance. If you deny Jesus now, this, too, has end-of-the-world significance. The point is that in apocalyptic contexts one can describe present events with end-times terminology without implying the end of the world. Unfortunately, this is the pitfall the original disciples fall into when they confuse the destruction of Jerusalem with the end of the age. Knowing that Jesus has taught the imminence of the fall of the temple, the disciples naturally assume the imminence of Jesus' second coming. In their minds the two are inseparable. They can't conceive of the fall of Jerusalem apart from the end of the age, as the question of 24:3 indicates. Nevertheless, although Jesus teaches the imminent fall of Jerusalem, He does not teach the imminence of His second coming. He leaves the latter to the undetermined future.

JUDGMENT: THE SIGN OF THE FIG TREE

The attempt to tie Matthew 24:29-31 to the Second Coming creates difficulties with this section, especially regarding how to interpret or understand the reference to the current generation (24:34). To apply this section to the second coming of Christ, for which there will be no warning signs (24:42-44), is to stretch beyond the context of this section.

Typically, the pronouns *this* and *these* refer to what is closest at hand in time or in space. Note that in Matthew 24:36 Jesus speaks of *that* day or hour. The pronoun *that* indicates something further away in time or space. In Matthew 24:32-35 the signs are for what is closer or nearer. The context of the discussion and the interpretation of the warning signs point to the judgment and destruction of Jerusalem rather than the second coming of Christ.

Jesus predicts the destruction of Jerusalem and the temple. This disturbs the disciples who interpret this as the end of the age. We associate the end of the age with the second coming of Christ.

Jesus separates the destruction of Jerusalem from the Second Coming, warning the disciples to be able to interpret the signs of the coming tribulation and destruction of Jerusalem and to flee from the city before that event occurs. He warns that some will interpret the signs as indicators of His coming and clearly warns them not to be misled by such predictions. Before the final eschatological end, the gospel has to be preached to all the world.

Jesus sets the discussion of the destruction of Jerusalem in apocalyptic language to demonstrate that the destruction will not simply be the work of the Roman army, but will in fact be the work of God through the Son of Man. The Roman army will simply be God's destroying agent.

In the next section, Jesus responds to the second part of the disciples' question, and argues that there will be no sign for His second coming.

THE END OF THE AGE (INTRODUCTION)

Setting Up the Section

We saw in the last four sections (Matthew 24:4–35) that Jesus warns His disciples not to confuse the signs for the coming destruction of Jerusalem and the temple with signs of His second coming.

As this next section opens, Jesus shifts from the signs for events that can be experienced (destruction of Jerusalem) to events for which there can be no signs—the Second Coming. The first clause of Matthew 24:36 introduces a discussion of a different day from the destruction of Jerusalem, namely, the day of the Second Coming.

24:36–44

THE END OF THE AGE: THE NEED FOR WATCHFULNESS

Verse 36 introduces the idea that not even the angels of heaven or the Son of Man know when that day will be. That decision lies not in the will of the Son of Man, but solely in the will of the Father. Jesus makes a similar statement about the coming of the Holy Spirit. God sets those times by His own authority (Acts 1:7).

Since this is the case, it would be folly for the disciples and anyone else in Jesus' day to attempt to predict the second coming of the Son of Man. Likewise, today, it is the height of both folly and arrogance to predict the time or date of the second coming of Jesus or the end of the world.

In Matthew 24:38–41 Jesus introduces Noah, two men in the fields, and two women at the grinding mill. These are illustrations Jesus uses to make the point that the eschatological coming of the Son of Man will be sudden and without warning.

Matthew 24:42 gets to the heart of Jesus' teaching about the unexpected coming of the Son of Man. The disciples are to be ready, watchful, and alert, for they do not know on what day their Lord will come. As the thief does not announce in advance his coming, so the Son of Man will not announce His coming in advance. Therefore the disciples must always be ready.

24:45–51

THE END OF THE AGE: FAITHFUL AND UNFAITHFUL SERVANTS

The faithful and wise servant is the one who, when His master comes home, is busy doing what he is supposed to be doing. Jesus highlights the point by warning that the unfaithful and foolish servants are hypocrites who will be punished. This is a clear warning that eternal punishment awaits those disciples who are not ready and waiting expectantly.

Serving God involves waiting expectantly for the return of the Son of Man. How does one wait appropriately for the return of the Son of Man? In the following three parables, all part of Jesus' final apocalyptic discourse, Jesus explains how one alertly waits His eschatological return.

25:1–13

THE END OF THE AGE: THE PARABLE OF THE TEN VIRGINS

The Greek word often translated as "virgin" can also be translated as maiden, or young woman. In the context of Jesus' parable, the emphasis indicates that these are young, unmarried women—similar to today's bridesmaids.

Of the ten maidens, five are prepared and five are not. The unprepared are excluded from the marriage feast. The connection of the marriage feast with the end-times banquet anticipated by Judaism and Christianity is obvious. Disciples that are not prepared will be excluded from that banquet.

How exactly should one be prepared? Jesus answers that question in the next two parables.

Before moving on to the discussion of preparedness, think about the wise maidens who will not lend oil to the foolish maidens. That raises an important question: Why not help those in need? In response, in this case, the necessities—personal faith, repentance, baptism, personal holiness, personal service, and personal preparedness—can't be borrowed.

📄 25:14–30

THE END OF THE AGE: THE PARABLE OF THE TALENTS

In this parable the talent is an amount of money.

Critical Observation

Originally a talent was a measure of weight, but when applied to silver coinage it became an amount of money. One talent was equal to 6,000 denarii or 6,000 days' wages. Thus one talent was a considerable amount of money.

In this parable, a master leaving on a journey entrusts an amount of money to each of his three servants. The first two servants trade and double the investment. The third one, for fear of his master, buries his talent of silver and returns it to his master. The master casts this third servant into outer darkness (again, indications of the final judgment are evident in this parable). The other two servants are rewarded for their diligence.

To make His point clear, Jesus then references the proverbial saying that to those who have will be given more (because they use what they have), and to those who have not (or have little) and who do not use it, will have it taken away.

The point of the parable is that disciples must use the giftedness that they have, whatever it may be. Disciples do not all have the same giftedness, but all disciples must use what they have in service of the Master. Being involved is part of being prepared.

Is it possible that the scribes and Pharisees, who were so busy with religion, had not prepared themselves properly for the works of the Messiah, and were relying on the faith of Abraham and Moses rather than developing true faith for themselves?

📄 25:31–46

THE END OF THE AGE: THE PARABLE OF THE SHEEP AND GOATS

In this parable, the warnings of Jesus regarding watching, being alert, and being ready reach a disturbing highpoint. The reference to the final judgment is obvious and clear.

The sheep, those on the right hand, are blessed and inherit the kingdom prepared for them from the beginning of the world. The goats, on the other hand, are cursed and cast into eternal fire. But what are the criteria for this judgment? What has the one group done that the other group has not?

The goats are so busy with their religion and hypocritical worship of God that they do not take time for the poor and helpless. The sheep recognize that true worship of God involves taking care of the poor and helpless (Micah 6:6–8; Psalm 51:17; James 1:27).

It is obvious that these qualities are absent or lacking in the scribes and Pharisees who are so busy with religion that they are missing what their charge really is—to be shepherds to the lost and disenfranchised. This is the work of the Messiah that they do not understand, and for this they are judged and condemned by Jesus.

📄 Summary

This fifth and final discourse in Matthew's Gospel comes at the time when Jesus enters Jerusalem and faces rejection, first from the Jewish leaders, then from the crowds. At the root of the rejection is the nature of Jesus' messiahship. He is not the kind of Messiah the crowds are looking for, namely, a political Messiah. Furthermore, His interpretation of the Torah challenges that of the scribes and Pharisees.

Frustrated with the hypocrisy of the scribes and Pharisees, Jesus soundly and severely condemns them (Matthew 23). His condemnation of Jerusalem and the temple (personified) leads to the disciples' concern and sense of insecurity (Matthew 24).

Jesus warns the disciples to be prepared for the destruction of Jerusalem, but not to confuse this with the second coming of the Messiah, or Son of Man (Matthew 24). Before the final end, the gospel has to be preached throughout the world (Matthew 24), but the eschatological coming of the Son of Man is certain to take place, though no warning signs will be provided.

Since the Son of Man will come suddenly without warning, the disciples must be watchful, alert, and ready. Being alert and ready necessitates being prepared for the coming of the Son of Man, being involved in messianic ministry, and being concerned for the lost.

The real issue for the disciples is that their messianic hope should not be fixed in the temple and Jerusalem, nor in the scribes and Pharisees' example of no faith in Jesus. Faith should be in the Messiah Himself and in what God is doing in and through the Messiah. This would be particularly significant to Matthew's community, which has just recently experienced the destruction of Jerusalem and the temple, and is now struggling to understand the true nature of discipleship apart from the temple.

Take It Home

One of the applications of this section is that rather than predicting the day of the coming of the Messiah, the followers of Jesus should be busy doing the work of the Messiah. We must be prepared for the coming of the Messiah by living alertly and watchfully, involved with the more important aspects of faith such as serving the lost, poor, and needy.

Another application is that Christian hope must not be in human effort, in the church, or in persons, but in Jesus Himself and what God is doing through Him. Christian hope is not fixed in the ability to get doctrine all sorted out and correct. Neither is it to be based on our own ability to achieve perfect obedience. Of course, we should make every effort to understand scripture correctly and to follow sound doctrine, but our Christian hope is fixed in our faith in Jesus and what God is doing through Jesus.

MATTHEW 26:1–28:20

NARRATIVE 6: THE MESSIAH'S FINAL WEEK

Setting Up the Section

This final narrative offers the account of the final days of Jesus' life, but also the climax of the Gospel—the passion (death, burial, and resurrection) of Jesus. In fact, some have described the substance of the Gospels as this upcoming passion narrative and the preceding chapters as simply an extended introduction to this narrative.

Here you find the fulfillment of God's plan of salvation for mankind.

📖 26:1–5

THE SANHEDRIN PLOT TO KILL JESUS

Matthew's mention of the Passover is not intended to simply provide a time reference. Instead, it sets the purpose of the passion narrative in a specific theological framework. Central to the original Passover event was the lamb whose blood, smeared on the doorposts, saved the Israelites from death (Exodus 12–14). Here, in the Gospel, Jesus is the lamb prepared for the deliverance and redemption of humanity.

Critical Observation: The Passover Feast

The roots of the Passover Feast go back to Exodus 12:1–28 and the exodus of Israel from Egyptian slavery (Exodus 12–14). The feast was to be a perpetual reminder (memorial) that God had delivered Israel from Egypt and had spared the firstborn of every house that had sprinkled the two doorposts of the lintel with the blood of the sacrificial lamb. The Passover was initially to be celebrated in homes as a family celebration. During the feast the participants were dressed for travel, sandals on their feet, and staff in hand, indicating they were ready to leave home in a hurry.

The Passover feast was celebrated beginning on the fifteenth day of Nisan, which in the year of Jesus' crucifixion fell on a Saturday, or the Sabbath day. Being defined by the Jewish calendar, the fifteenth day of Nisan would have begun that year at sunset on Friday evening. The Passover meal would have been eaten on Friday evening.

The Passover was combined with another feast, the Feast of Unleavened Bread. The Feast of Unleavened Bread was a seven-day feast that began at the same time as the Passover feast, in that it began on the evening of the fourteenth day of Nisan, and lasted for seven days. During this feast no leavened food was to be eaten. In time the two feasts were combined in practice into one feast, and both became holy days.

After the initial celebration of the Passover in Egypt, the feast became an annual one, not celebrated just anywhere, but in a place determined by the Lord as the place of His presence. (See Deuteronomy 16:1–8.) In time the feast became a pilgrimage to Jerusalem for the celebration—so it was in Jesus' day.

After the destruction of the temple and Jerusalem, the Passover was celebrated in homes in local towns.

Conflicting reports have come down through the centuries as to the exact details of the feast. It seems that in later centuries successive cups of wine (either three or four) were part of the celebration as was eating the lamb and unleavened bread with bitter herbs. To these were added prayers, blessings, and reading of the Psalms, especially Psalms 113–118.

The celebration was conducted by the head of the family with the children present. The youngest boy in the family would ask, "Why are we celebrating the Passover?" This would give occasion for the head of the family to recite the history of God delivering Israel out of Egypt and nurturing them in the wilderness. The theology of the Passover was a focus on the nurture of Israel by God. It was a reminder of God's deliverance.

Demystifying Matthew: The Jewish Calendar

The Jewish calendar was based on a lunisolar or lunar system, fixed by the first appearance of the new moon. Through the centuries differing methods were used to determine the length of the months. The days of a month ranged between 29 and 30 days, depending on the cycle of the moon.

CONTINUED

Depending on how the months were calculated, there might be anywhere between 354 and 364 days in the year.

Scholars believe that the names of the Jewish calendar were influenced by both Canaanite and Babylonian names. The months of the Jewish calendar (compared to the modern calendar and seasons) and Jewish feasts are as follows:

Nisan	Passover	March–April	Spring
Iyyar	Unleavened Bread	May	
Sivan		June	
Tammuz		July	Summer
Ab		August	
Elul		September	
Tishri	Atonement, Booths	October	Fall
Marcheshvan		November	
Chislev		December	
Tebeth		January	Winter
Shebat		February	
Adar		March	

It is two days before the Passover (26:2) when Jesus again foretells His passion and crucifixion. Since in this year the Passover falls on the Sabbath (Saturday), the Passover meal will been eaten on Friday evening. Therefore, Jesus speaks these words to the disciples on Wednesday.

The chief priests and elders (most likely the ruling members of the Sanhedrin) gather in the palace of Caiaphas, the ruling high priest, to decide how to arrest Jesus and have Him killed. They are concerned that this be done with stealth for fear of rioting, which is of concern to the Roman authorities. Being such a time of heightened Jewish religious fervor, the Romans are on guard for disturbances.

26:6–13

JESUS ANOINTED BY MARY AT BETHANY

This event occurs in the home of Simon the Leper, only mentioned in the New Testament on this one occasion. The fact that Simon has been cured is implied by the fact that they are meeting in his home, something that would not have been permissible otherwise under Jewish law. Simon lived in Bethany, a small town two miles from Jerusalem on the eastern slope of the Mount of Olives.

Luke records a similar experience (Luke 7:36–39), but in his description the event happens in Simon the Pharisee's home, and the woman is identified only as a sinner. The events and discussion recorded by Luke differ from that in Matthew, Mark, and John.

A woman anoints Jesus with ointment that obviously is very expensive. John's gospel identifies the woman as Mary of Bethany, sister to Lazarus (John 11:2). Observing her actions, the indignant disciples miss the point of her action—her love for Jesus. Instead, they raise questions as to why the gift has not been spent on the poor.

Mark (14:4) merely mentions that some present were indignant, while John adds that it is

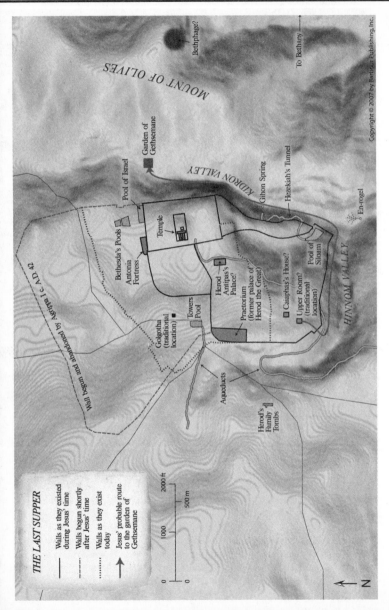

THE LAST SUPPER

—— Walls as they existed during Jesus' time
––– Walls begun shortly after Jesus' time
⋯⋯ Walls as they exist today
→ Jesus' probable route to the garden of Gethsemane

Bethphage?

MOUNT OF OLIVES

To Bethany

Copyright © 2007 by Bar-Lur Publishing, Inc.

Garden of Gethsemane

KIDRON VALLEY

Pool of Israel

Gihon Spring

Hezekiah's Tunnel

En-rogel

Bethesda's Pools

Temple

Antonia Fortress

Herod Antipas's Palace?

Caiaphas's House?

Pool of Siloam

HINNOM VALLEY

Golgotha (traditional location)

Towers Pool

Praetorium (former palace of Herod the Great)

Upper Room? (traditional location)

Wall begun and abandoned by Agrippa I c. AD. 42

Aqueducts

Herod's Family Tombs

N

0   1000   2000 ft
0   500 m

Judas who objects (John 12:4). Perhaps the objectors are beckoning to Jesus' predilection for the poor, but the Master reminds the disciples that they will always have the poor, but they will not always have Him present with them as He now is.

The theological point of this narrative is that Jesus interprets the woman's action in light of His approaching death and burial, not simply as an act of devotion. That is not to say that the woman made that connection—she has acted only out of love. Nevertheless, in the context of His imminent passion, Jesus breathes new meaning into her love.

The remarkable prediction of Jesus that her act will become a memorial to her has happened through the history in Matthew's Gospel.

📄 26:14–16

THE BARGAIN OF JUDAS

In what is perhaps one of the most tragic events in history, Judas makes plans to betray his Lord. Matthew identifies Judas by his full name—*Judas* (a form of the Hebrew *Judah*) and *Iscariot* (after the town in Judea called Kerioth). Except for Judas, the remaining disciples were from Galilee.

The sum of the betrayal agreement is thirty pieces of silver, a sum considered by scholars to be the equivalent of the price of a slave. The insubstantial sum has led some to suggest that Judas's motivation for the betrayal is not greed, but possibly disappointment in Jesus' messiahship. Some have suggested that Judas might have been motivated by the same frustrations seen in the zealots who would have been looking for a militant political messiah who would lead them in victory over their Roman overlords.

Luke identifies Satan as the motivation behind Judas's betrayal (Luke 22:3). John agrees with this conclusion (John 13:2).

📄 26:17–25

THE LAST PASSOVER SUPPER

There are some apparent variations in the Gospel accounts of the preparation and eating of the Passover. Working across four Gospels, each with its own theological purpose and each with a different audience in mind, this is not surprising. However, there are reasonable explanations for the variations.

Although we are not informed of all the details, Jesus sends His disciples to find a man in whose home Jesus intends to eat the Passover. Apparently, Jesus has made some arrangement with the man, but we are not informed regarding this. Mark and Luke add to the narrative by recording Jesus telling the disciples to follow a man carrying a water jar to the house where He intends to eat the Passover (Mark 14:13–15; Luke 22:10–12). This man would have been easily recognized since women normally carried water.

Jesus does not eat the Passover in Bethany, but in Jerusalem where the Passover should have been eaten as prescribed by the Torah. It was only after AD 70 and the destruction of Jerusalem and the temple that Jews ate the Passover in a variety of towns and villages.

Critical Observation

The term *Last Supper* is not found in scripture, but is one adopted by the Christian faith to describe this last meal, or last Passover meal, Jesus celebrated with His disciples.

The term *Lord's Supper* is not found in the synoptic Gospels, but is found in 1 Corinthians 11:20. In early post–New Testament Christianity the term *Lord's Supper* soon gave way to the term *Eucharist*, which prevailed for many centuries until the modern Protestant era. *Lord's Supper* along with the term *Communion* have become favored descriptions in many Christian circles for this memorial feast.

Jesus' Death and Resurrection

Each gospel records the events leading up to Jesus' death and resurrection. Below are the key events and where they occur in each gospel.

	Matthew	Mark	Luke	John
Jesus in Gethsemane	26:36–46	14:32–42	22:39–46	18:1
The Betrayal and Arrest	26:47–56	14:43–52	22:47–53	18:2–12
Trial Before Annas				18:13–14, 19–23
Trial Before Caiphas	26:57	14:53	22:54	18:24
Peter Denies Jesus	26:69–75	14:66–72	22:54–62	18:15–18, 25–27
Trial Before Sanhedrin	27:1	15:1	22:66–71	
The Suicide of Judas	27:3–10			
Jesus' Appearance before Pilate	27:2, 11–14	15:1–5	23:1–5	18:28–38
Jesus' Appearance before Herod			23:6–12	
Jesus' Second Appearance before Pilate	27:15–26	15:6–15	23:13–25	18:39–19:16
Crowd Asks for Barrabas	27:19–21	15:6–11	23:18	18:39–40
Jesus Whipped	27:26	15:15		19:1–5
Pilate's Judgment	27:23–25	15:14	23:20–25	19:7–16
Soldiers Mock Jesus	27:27–30	15:16–20		
Jesus Led to the Cross	27:31–34	15:20–23	23:26–33	19:16–17
Jesus on the Cross	27:35–56	15:24–41	23:33–49	19:18–37
Jesus Is Buried	27:57–66	15:42–47	23:50–56	19:38–42
The Resurrection	28:1–20	16:1–8	24:1–53	20:1–21:25

The order of the wine and bread discussed in the Passover meal by Matthew, Mark, and Luke differs somewhat, although not significantly. Matthew follows the order of the meal in Mark, but Luke differs in speaking of a cup being drunk before the bread followed by another cup. However, this is a Passover meal and three or four cups are involved. John does not discuss the Passover meal in his Gospel, leading some to question whether the meal eaten by Jesus with His disciples in John 13–17 was in fact the Passover meal.

The stern warning of Jesus regarding the one who will betray Him must have sobered both Judas and the disciples who still did not know the extent of the betrayal. Luke indicates the continuing uncertainty of the disciples over the matter of the betrayal (Luke 22:23). Jesus, however, indicates that the betrayal and consequences are according to scripture (Matthew 26:24).

📖 26:26–29

THE LORD'S SUPPER INSTITUTED

Jesus intends this institution, often referred to as the Lord's Supper, to be a way for the disciples (and later the church) to commemorate His death. As the Passover was intended to be a perpetual commemoration of God's deliverance of Israel from Egypt, so the Lord's Supper is intended to be a perpetual commemoration of Jesus' death. The eating of the Supper is intended to be a proclamation of His death as well as an interpretation of that death. The bread and wine are intended to symbolize His body and blood given for the deliverance of mankind from bondage to sin. Just as the annual Passover rite memorialized and personalized the Passover in Egypt and deliverance from Egypt, the Lord's Supper likewise not only memorializes the death of Jesus, but personalizes it as well.

The institution of the Lord's Supper is essential to the life of the church. For this reason, most Protestant churches have identified the Lord's Supper along with baptism as the two sacraments of church life. Sacraments are those religious practices that associate or identify Christians with the church, or the body of Christ. Sacraments involve a promise or commitment. Thomas of Aquinas and Augustine considered the sacraments to be signs of a holy alliance.

We are not certain at which stage of the Passover Jesus takes the bread and breaks it, but in the Passover seder (ceremony related to the Passover), breaking the bread was associated with the promise of a future redeeming Messiah.

Jesus gives the bread to the disciples and says that it is His body. Interpreting what Jesus meant by this has led to centuries of division in church doctrine relating to the Lord's Supper. The Roman Catholic tradition interprets this as "this becomes my body." This Catholic doctrine is called transubstantiation, in which the bread literally becomes the body of Christ. Protestants have objected to this, and a variety of views have surfaced.

In this context Jesus probably means that the bread symbolized His body. This is how many Protestant churches understand the expression. Jesus is implying that the bread symbolizes His whole person, His whole life, and all that His life means. By eating the bread we are reminded of all that Jesus stood for, lived for, and died for. Eating the bread is a sacrament in that it is a pledge to live the life of Jesus.

Jesus then takes the cup, the wine, and gives thanks (also used in Matthew 15:36) for it. It is because of this act of giving thanks that some Christian communities call the Lord's Supper the Eucharist.

Christian church traditions have been divided over whether the wine means grape juice or actual wine. Because of their puritan and temperance heritage, many churches insist that this can only mean grape juice. Churches from the Greek Orthodox and Eastern Orthodox traditions, and others not of the puritan temperance heritage, insist that it simply means wine.

Consider these things:

- The Greek phrase translated "fruit of the vine" in some translations (26:29) is a Hebrew euphemism for wine.
- The cups of the Passover were cups of wine, not grape juice.
- Wine drinking in the time of Christ was not socially or religiously looked down upon (though drunkenness was).
- We have several instances in the New Testament in which wine drinking is socially and religiously acceptable.
- Jesus turned water into wine at the wedding in Cana (John 2:1–11).
- Paul wrote to Timothy and encouraged him for medicinal purposes to drink a little wine for his stomach's sake (1 Timothy 5:23).

The attempt to translate or understand the drink Jesus offered as grape juice rather than wine is a modern socio-religious problem, not a biblical one. The key here is not what we use today in our traditions of celebrating the Lord's Supper, but that we do celebrate it, and when we do, we understand the purpose of that celebration.

Jesus says the wine is His blood. As in the case of the bread, this means the wine represents or symbolizes the blood of the covenant. The new covenant prophesied in Jeremiah 31 was fulfilled in the blood shed by Jesus on the cross. Those drinking the cup in the Lord's Supper, which symbolizes the blood of Jesus, are reminded of the promises of the new covenant and they participate in those promises. The fulfillment of the new covenant is described in Hebrews 8:10–12: the promise of God's people holding His Word in their hearts, of their becoming, in a unique manner, His people, and of God's mercy and grace and forgiveness of sins. It is the new covenant of deliverance empowered by Jesus' blood (through His atoning death).

The final statement of Jesus before He and the disciples sing the Hallel hymn of the Passover is an affirmation that He will drink the cup with them again, but not until He does so in His Father's kingdom (26:29). Jesus is somewhat mysterious in this comment. Does Jesus mean until He drinks it with them in the Eucharist, or does He mean until He drinks it with them in the final new-world banquet?

Possibly either or both. Not only are Christians reminded of what God did for them on the cross, but they are encouraged to look ahead to the final end and the great wedding banquet. It was for this reason that early Christians favored the term *Eucharist* (thanksgiving) to define the experience of the Lord's Supper. The Eucharist should be a celebration, not just an occasion of mourning remembering Christ's death.

📄 26:30–35

PETER'S DENIAL FORETOLD

This sad narrative stresses the tragic frailty of human effort. We don't know exactly what prompts Jesus to warn the disciples of the frailty of their faith, but His warning indicates His knowledge of their coming weakness and denial.

Jesus' statement about scattering sheep suggests He may have intended the events that followed to be seen as a fulfillment of the prophecy in Zechariah 13. Nevertheless, Jesus' warning of the falling away of the disciples obviously disturbs them. First Peter, then all the disciples, deny that they will fall away and disown Jesus. Jesus, however, forewarns Peter of his disowning Him.

The one positive element of the section is the statement that Jesus will rise and go before the disciples to Galilee. In spite of their weakness, Jesus has not given up on them. He expects to see them again in Galilee. The steadfast love of the Lord endures forever.

📄 26:36–46

JESUS IN GETHSEMANE

The Garden of Gethsemane, as it is known from John's Gospel (John 18:1, 26), was actually an olive orchard on the east side of the Kidron Valley on the lower slopes of the Mount of Olives. Matthew simply called it a plot of ground or a place rather than a garden. "Gethsemane" is the Greek equivalent of the Hebrew *gat semane* (oil press). It was a quiet place off the regular beaten pathway, a place where Jesus could be alone in prayer.

This poignant narrative stands as a monument to Jesus' agony and fear of suffering and dying as a human, but also as a monument of His willingness to submit to the will of His Father in heaven. Adding to the tragedy of this occasion is that this is the last account of Jesus spending time with His disciples before dying on the cross. At the moment that He needs them most, they fail Him miserably.

Jesus takes with Him the three disciples with whom He obviously has the closest relationship—Peter, James, and John. As a human being He needs the company of friends as He faces the most difficult time of His life and as He agonizes in prayer.

Twice He encourages (perhaps begged) the three disciples to keep watch (stay awake) with Him, and once to pray with Him. However, on both occasions they fail Him and fall asleep. Perhaps they are tired, but perhaps also they do not understand the depth of His concern and anguish. In His second encouragement to the three, He warns them not to fall into temptation (the spirit is willing, but the flesh is weak), indicating His own struggles as well as His awareness of the disciples' struggles.

Jesus' mention of the cup is a Hebrew metaphor that refers to the suffering He is about to experience. His reference to the hour at hand is not simply an indication that it is soon, but rather that it is certain and so certain that it is already upon Him. He comments that the Son of Man is betrayed in the present tense, indicating that the events are already underway.

📄 26:47–56

JUDAS BETRAYS JESUS

Judas arrives with a great crowd armed with swords and clubs as though Jesus were a robber or insurrectionist. John informs us that there were possibly temple guards and Roman soldiers in the crowd (John 18:3) as well as chief priests and elders, or the Sanhedrin.

Judas, by agreement with the mob members, kisses Jesus to identify Him as the one they are seeking. The eastern kiss was a sign of greeting. Judas adds the words, "Greetings, Rabbi" (26:49 NIV), which was a traditional eastern greeting.

One of Jesus' disciples—John informs us that it is Peter (John 18:10–11, 26)—takes a sword and cuts off the ear of the chief priest's slave. Only Luke records that Jesus heals the slave's severed ear (Luke 22:51).

📖 **26:57–68**

JESUS IS TAKEN BEFORE CAIAPHAS, THE HIGH PRIEST

Caiaphas was the high priest at that time. He was the son-in-law of Annas, who previously had been the high priest. Caiaphas had been appointed to the position by the Roman procurator, Valerius Gratus, the predecessor of Pontius Pilate. Caiaphas had been the main instigator for the arrest and trial of Jesus.

The chief priests, scribes, and elders, namely, the Sanhedrin, have gathered in anticipation of Jesus' arrest. Jesus is brought before the Sanhedrin gathered at Caiaphas's palace.

The hypocrisy for which Jesus has condemned the scribes and Pharisees comes to the forefront in the false testimony the Sanhedrin seeks against Jesus. In several attempts to gather enough testimony against Jesus to condemn Him to death, which is their purpose, they finally get two false witnesses to come forward with statements that Jesus had claimed to be able to destroy the temple and rebuild it in three days. Obviously they were taking several strands of Jesus' teachings and weaving them into ridiculous charges. When Jesus refuses to answer the charges of the high priest, the high priest places Him under oath and asks Him whether He is the Christ, the Son of God. Jesus' answer is actually a direct answer in the affirmative, a Hebrew idiom that indicates a qualified yes (Mark 14:62 records that Jesus says, "I am").

Jesus' additional comments are drawn from Daniel 7:13 and Psalm 110:1. They are so loaded with apocalyptic symbolism that the high priest immediately understands what Jesus is claiming—to be the One seated "at the right hand of Power," (26:64 NASB) and the One who will come in judgment on them. The word *power* implies God but adheres to the Jewish tradition of not saying God's name out loud.

After requesting the death penalty, those present in the Sanhedrin begin to mistreat Jesus. Their evil scheming has come to fruition. However, the Jews under Roman rule did not have the authority to carry out their condemnation of death. Only the Romans could carry out that sentence. That is why, after Matthew's description of Peter's denial of Jesus, Jesus is led bound to Pilate, the Roman governor.

📖 **26:69–75**

PETER'S DENIAL OF JESUS

Peter, we learn in Matthew 26:58, has followed the crowd that arrested Jesus, but at a distance. In the courtyard of the high priest's palace, he is confronted by a maid who recognizes him as a follower of Jesus. After his denial, Peter is again confronted with similar charges because of his Galilean accent. Again, but this time with an oath, Peter denies the charge. After a while the bystanders accuse Peter again. He begins to invoke a curse on himself and to swear that he doesn't know Jesus.

Peter's response reveals his heart. Though he failed Jesus, his own actions grieve him.

JESUS IS DELIVERED TO PILATE BY THE SANHEDRIN

Early Friday morning (still 14 Nisan which began the previous evening with the Passover meal), the Sanhedrin meets in full session to confirm the decision in Caiaphas's palace that Jesus should be put to death. It is Luke's Gospel that confirms it is a full session (Luke 22:66–71).

It is necessary for the Jewish leaders to take Jesus before the Roman authorities in order to legally put Him to death. Pilate, who is governor over Judea, is conveniently in Jerusalem at this time. The rulers of the Sanhedrin bring Jesus before Pilate, hopeful that he will confirm their judgment.

Critical Observation

Technically, Pilate's title was *prefect*. Matthew refers to him as the governor of Judea. Luke identifies him as Pontius Pilate (Luke 3:1). Pilate was governor of Judea from AD 26/27–36. His official residence was in Caesarea Maritima (beside the sea). He was perhaps visiting in Jerusalem for the Passover to maintain stability and Roman control during the feast.

JUDAS'S SUICIDE

Judas's conscience begins to work against him. When he hears that Jesus has been condemned to death, he is deeply troubled and attempts to return the thirty pieces of silver to the chief priests. He confesses he has betrayed an innocent man, but the callous chief priests will not take back the money. Matthew records that Judas is overcome with remorse (27:3).

What is ironically tragic is that the chief priests recognize earnings from betraying someone as blood money (27:6). They know they cannot put the money into the treasury since these kinds of earnings were condemned in the Torah (Deuteronomy 23:18). Yet they have knowingly provided the money for this very reason, to betray Jesus. Their duplicity apparently does not trouble them. It is no wonder Jesus condemns them as whitewashed tombs full of dead men's bones (Matthew 23:27).

Matthew merely reports that Judas goes out and hangs himself (27:5). Luke relates that he buys a field and falls dead in it (Acts 1:18–19). Some scholars see in the different descriptions of Judas's death a probable contradiction, but what we have here are merely two different accounts of what happened. Judas commits suicide for his betrayal; the field where he dies is called the field of blood since he has betrayed Jesus for blood money, and the field had been purchased with the chief priests' blood money.

Matthew clearly sets Judas's betrayal in the context of God's eternal plan. His quote combines ideas from Zechariah 11:12–13 and Jeremiah 19:1–13. For Matthew, all the scriptures come to their climax in Jesus. This is the last of the ten fulfillment passages Matthew uses in his Gospel to demonstrate that Jesus' life and death are within the eternal purpose of God.

JESUS BEFORE PILATE

Pilate asks Jesus if He is the king of the Jews. Notice he does not ask Jesus if He is king over Israel, which could seem a more politically threatening title. Pilate's political sensitivity to Roman concerns, and his ability to see that this was a Jewish matter, framed the question. Jesus' answer to Pilate, "You say so" (27:11 NRSV), implies a simple yes.

When Pilate questions Jesus further, He remains silent, reminiscent of the prophet Isaiah's description of the Messiah as a silent lamb led to slaughter (Isaiah 53:7).

At the feast, Matthew informs us, it is the governor's practice to release a Jew from prison. Although we have no external evidence for such practice other than the Gospels, this seems in accord with what the governor would have done in order to show some sort of clemency to the Jews. The person to be released would be someone meeting the crowd's request. The description of the prisoner Barrabas could be understood to mean an insurrectionist, a bandit, or murderer. Some ancient manuscripts suggest that Barabbas's first name was Jesus, a common name among Jews of the day. There may have been a play on names in Pilate's mind as he suggests two persons by the name of Jesus, hoping that the Jews will see the vast difference between Jesus, the son of Joseph, and this Jesus, the insurrectionist. Pilate knows that it is out of envy that they have condemned Jesus and want Him dead.

Romans paid much attention to warnings from divination and dreams, like the one Pilate's wife had. As Pilate attempts to remove himself from the process by symbolically washing his hands, he is indicating publicly that he does not find Jesus worthy of death. The crowds' statement that the blood of Jesus will be on their hands and those of their children was a well accepted expression from the Old Testament that spoke to full responsibility in an act (Lamentations 5:7).

The scourging with the Roman lash, which contained sharp objects for tearing the flesh, was commonly administered to those about to be crucified, possibly to so weaken them that they would not linger on the cross indefinitely. After having Jesus scourged, Pilate hands Him over to his soldiers to be crucified. Had Jesus been a Roman citizen, His death by crucifixion would have been prohibited.

THE CRUCIFIXION OF JESUS

What is striking in all of the Gospel accounts is the brevity of Jesus on the cross. We fully recognize the agony of Jesus and the suffering both emotionally and physically that He endures on the cross, but this is not played up in the Gospel accounts. In light of the Gospel theology, this death of Jesus is pictured as dramatic, but it is to be seen as a victory—the victory of God and Jesus over Satan and sin. The Gospels do not trivialize the atoning death and victory of Jesus, but simply describe it as a fact of history and God's divine plan.

After mocking Jesus in the worst manner, the Roman soldiers take Jesus out to Golgotha, the place of the skull, to crucify Him between two robbers. These men were possibly insurrectionists or bandits. Luke refers to them as criminals (Luke 23:32 NASB).

Simon, the man from Cyrene (North Africa) who carries Jesus' cross, was in all probability a Jewish pilgrim to the Passover Feast. Tradition has it that Simon later becomes a Christian.

Layers of church tradition have obscured the precise location of Golgotha, but it must have been just outside the city walls and on a well-traveled thoroughfare, for it was the practice of the Romans to carry out crucifixions in full view of people, and a road into Jerusalem would have served the Roman publicity purpose well.

The drink offered to those dying on the cross was sometimes mixed with gall, which could be a bitter, poisonous or noxious substance, which might explain why Jesus refuses to drink it when He tastes it. Most likely though, it was spoiled or bitter wine. Later, when offered vinegar on a sponge (27:48), He drinks it. The vinegar was a form of sour or cheap wine, which was known to relieve thirst better than water.

All four Gospels record that Pilate has an inscription nailed to the cross, proclaiming "THIS IS JESUS, THE KING OF THE JEWS" (27:37). John adds that it is in all three languages of the area—Hebrew, Latin, and Greek—and that the Jews object to the inscription. Pilate rejects their objection.

Matthew records that the crowds and the chief priests, elders, and scribes mock (blaspheme) Jesus as He hangs on the cross. The robbers, too, join in the mocking of Jesus. Luke records the exchange between Jesus and the two criminals dying beside Him (Luke 23:39–43), one mocking Him and the other defending Him.

It is difficult for any interpreter to fathom all that went on in the death of Jesus on the cross. It certainly was attended by supernatural occurrences and some remarkable events. The death of Jesus is not only the climax of the Gospel narrative, but more so it is the climax of the purpose of God for the person of Jesus. To die for mankind is precisely what He came to do.

From the sixth to the ninth hour (from noon to 3:00 p.m.) there is darkness over all the land, possibly meaning the region of Judea. The darkness is similar in significance to a divine judgment over the land.

Twice in Matthew's account Jesus cries out with a loud voice, once here and in verse 50. The first time He adds the words in Aramaic, but Matthew translates them for us into Greek: "My God, my God, why hast thou forsaken me?" (29:46 KJV). Scholars have been divided over exactly what Jesus meant by this expression in which He quoted Psalm 22:1, a lament psalm. (Lament psalms were characterized by a similar structure: first a complaint, then trust, then deliverance, and finally praise.) Matthew offers no explanation for Jesus' cry, but several proposals have been made:

1) Some feel it is the cry over the fact that, because of the enormity of humanity's sins, God abandoned Jesus in the moment of His death (see Isaiah 53:4, 10).

2) Others believe that Jesus felt abandoned by God in His intense suffering. However, this overlooks the nature of Psalm 22 as a psalm of lament.

3) Some feel that Jesus understood the lament meaning of Psalm 22 and used it as a prayer for God's help in His moment of anguish. In such suffering and aloneness at crucifixion, He must have felt abandoned. He was in fact abandoned by His people (Israel), the Romans, the crowds, and His disciples. While Psalm 22 is a lament psalm, it is also a psalm of confidence in God's deliverance and help. Jesus would have understood it this way. When Jesus cried this psalm out, it would have been a cry of aloneness and for help from the God in whom He trusted, not a cry of abandonment.

Some of the bystanders mistake Jesus' cry as a cry to Elijah to come and rescue Him. This is understandable from the similarity of the words *Eli* and *Elijah*.

When Jesus finally dies, Luke records that He verbally commits His spirit into God's hands (Luke 23:46).

Matthew describes the event of Jesus' death in terms of supernatural events:

- The temple curtain is torn in two.
- The earth shakes.
- Rocks are split.
- Tombs open.
- Saints are raised from the tombs and go into the city where they are seen by many.

Matthew and Mark both include the comment regarding the temple curtain being torn from top to bottom, but the remaining supernatural events are found only in Matthew.

What is strange regarding these supernatural events is that neither Matthew nor Mark explain the theological nature of the torn curtain, the earthquake, and the dead being raised. The interpretation of the events is left to the reader. But to any Christian (especially in the first century and to Matthew's community), they are loaded with significance.

Nevertheless, the meaning of the events is fairly obvious. There can be little doubt that the supernatural events support God's involvement in the death of Jesus and His approval of Jesus' atoning sacrifice. These miraculous events can happen only by God's divine intervention. The theological implication of the torn temple curtain signifies a new system of entry into the Holiest of Holies through the death of Jesus (Hebrews 9:11–14; 10:19–23). The earthquake and split rocks indicate apocalyptic judgments of God on Jerusalem, and the dead raised after the resurrection of Jesus indicates Jesus' power over death, the source of life and resurrection, and the guarantee of a future resurrection.

What is not explained or commented on by many commentators on Matthew or Mark is the historicity of the events. What complicates the problem of the historicity is that, to our knowledge, there are no Roman or Jewish records of the three-hour darkness, the temple curtain being torn, or the dead saints being seen in the city. There are some late Christian and rabbinic allusions, but since these all come much later than the destruction of Jerusalem, it is not possible to fix these allusions to the Crucifixion. They seem rather to be allusions to what happened in the temple at the destruction of the temple and Jerusalem.

The miraculous is often without scientific, empirical, or historical verification, but to deny the miraculous on such grounds is to deny the very existence of God and His Holy Spirit. There are many instances of divine intervention for which there are no reasonable empirical explanations, but they are accepted by reliable testimony. The resurrection of Jesus is in fact one such miraculous event of divine intervention that cannot be proven by empirical means, yet based on reliable testimony is believed by most to be historical.

At the root of questions regarding the historicity of certain acts of divine intervention in human affairs is the question of the miraculous. Scholars who have difficulty with the historicity of divine intervention often have questions regarding the possibility of the miraculous.

Perhaps the most important event in this section of the Gospel narrative is the comment of the Roman centurion and his companions—"Truly this man was God's Son!" (27:54 NRSV). These people saw what the Jewish leaders did not see. Luke adds the following regarding the centurion—that he praises God and claims Jesus' innocence (Luke 23:47).

Matthew records that there are women who have followed Jesus, watching from afar. Named among them are Mary Magdalene, Mary the mother of James and Joseph, and the mother of James and John, the sons of Zebedee. Neither Mary is mentioned in the Gospel prior to this occasion, but later both are witness to the risen Christ. We are uncertain who James and Joseph were as both were common names. We are not sure what Matthew means by their ministering to Jesus, but according to Luke there is a group of women, including Mary Magdalene, that has supported Jesus' ministry (Luke 8:2-3). It is surprising that Matthew mentions none of the eleven disciples as being present. Neither Matthew, Mark, nor Luke mention any of the disciples, but John in his Gospel does mention that the disciple Jesus loved (John himself) is there with the women (John 19:25-27).

John adds two other details as well.

- The request to break the legs of the three being crucified, which leads to the soldier's discovery that Jesus is already dead (John 19:31-33)
- The piercing of Jesus' side with the spear (John 19:34-37)

📖 27:57-61

THE BURIAL OF JESUS

According to Deuteronomy 21:22-23, it was a Jewish requirement that dead bodies of executed criminals not be left hanging on trees overnight. On Friday evening, just before the Sabbath begins (the other Gospels inform us that it is on the Day of Preparation, just before the Sabbath begins, for instance, Mark 15:42), Joseph, a rich man from Arimathea and a disciple of Jesus, asks Pilate for Jesus' body in order to bury Him. Pilate gives the order for Jesus' body to be given to him. We are uncertain where Arimathea is located, but it could have been a town by the name Ramathaim, a town in Judea. Joseph takes the body of Jesus, wraps it in a clean linen shroud, and lays it in his own new tomb. A great stone rock is rolled to the door of the tomb, sealing it. Mary Magdalene and the other Mary are there, sitting opposite the tomb.

📖 27:62-66

THE TOMB SEALED AND GUARDED

This narrative becomes significant in view of charges made by many against the resurrection of Jesus. It is unique to Matthew simply because it had greater significance to a Jew and Jewish Christians than it would to Gentiles (Mark, Luke, and John were written for Gentile readers). On the Sabbath, the day after the Day of Preparation (Friday) the chief priests and Pharisees request that Pilate set a guard at the tomb lest the disciples steal the body of Jesus and claim that He has risen.

The guard is to make the tomb secure. This is the Sabbath, and by now Jesus has been in the tomb all of Friday night. It is certain that the guard would have inspected the tomb. The tomb being made secure must have implied some sort of official seal.

Remember that the chief priests and Pharisees know of Jesus' prediction that He will be raised on the third day (16:21), but they do not believe it. The resurrection of Jesus was not then something unknown, unexpected, or unpredicted. The Jewish authorities knew about it, they did not believe it, and expected the disciples to make some form of effort to steal the body. Any attempt to steal the body was, therefore, rendered highly improbable.

The duplicity of the chief priests and Pharisees can be seen by what follows after the resurrection of Jesus when it is discovered that Jesus' body is no longer in the tomb. They pay the soldiers to claim the disciples stole the body while they were sleeping, promising to keep the soldiers from punishment for the dereliction of duty that their lie implies (28:11–15).

📖 28:1–10

THE EMPTY TOMB AND RESURRECTION OF JESUS

Setting Up the Section

Matthew 28 focuses chiefly on the final aspect of the Gospel narrative—the resurrection of Jesus. This is the climax of the Gospel story—Jesus' resurrection and His triumph over death and sin.

The narrative does not describe the actual resurrection of Jesus, only the results of the resurrection, namely:

1. The empty tomb and appearances of Jesus to the two women named Mary

2. The narrative of the bribing of the Roman soldiers

3. The appearance of Jesus before the disciples in Galilee and the giving of the Great Commission

There is some disagreement about the opening phrase of this section—"After the Sabbath" (28:1 NIV). The early Christians would have understood this to mean "After the Sabbath had closed and early on the first day of the week." It is because of the resurrection of Jesus on Sunday that Sunday became the holy and special day of worship for Christians. Christians, because of this, worshiped on the first day of the week (Acts 20:7; 1 Corinthians 16:2), and the day became known as the Lord's Day (Revelation 1:10).

The two women go to the tomb, most likely to mourn the death of Jesus. As in the previous chapter there is a great earthquake, signifying some divine intervention, and an angel appears and rolls back the stone, sealing the mouth of the tomb. It certainly would have been too heavy for two women to roll it back. The angel's appearance is so striking that the guards (notice, they are still there) fall down like dead men, in great fear.

Offering to show them the empty tomb, the angel encourages the two women not to be afraid, but to go quickly and tell the disciples that Jesus has risen from the tomb. They are to tell the disciples to meet Jesus at Galilee, for Jesus has gone on ahead. The words of the angel to the women are interesting, "He is not here, He is risen" (28:6 NIV).

The women leave quickly with mixed emotions—fear and great joy. Fear because remarkable and strange things have happened. Jesus has risen! An angel has appeared! There was a great earthquake! Any one of these events would cause fear in most people. But they are also filled with great joy—Jesus is not dead and He is going to meet the disciples in Galilee.

Shortly after this, Jesus greets the women. His greeting is the first words spoken by the risen Christ, and they are spoken to two women. But why first to the two women? Perhaps simply because they were there—they cared enough to be there at the tomb. The women humbly worship Jesus, and He encourages them not to be afraid and gives them the instructions for the disciples. An interesting point is that Jesus continues to call His disciples His brothers. He has done this on several occasions in Matthew (12:48–50; 25:40), and continues to do so even though they have denied and forsaken Him.

that before the close of the age or the end, there will be the need for the preaching of the gospel. Jesus' precise words are, "And this gospel of the kingdom will be preached throughout the whole world, as a testimony to all nations; and then the end will come."'

In commissioning His disciples and sending them out as apostles to make disciples of all nations, Jesus promises always to be with them. The apostles will not be alone as they preach; Jesus will be with them in power and spirit. His presence will be real.

Take It Home

We do not become disciples on our own terms. This we have learned from the Gospel of Matthew. Discipleship is a radical decision to leave self and follow Jesus. The Sermon on the Mount explained what kind of person a disciple should be. The Limited Commission explained what disciples do. The Kingdom Parables taught how to understand the life of a disciple in the kingdom. The Discourse on the Christian Community taught how Christians relate to one another in a Christian community. The Apocalyptic Discourse explains the central focus of the messianic kingdom—not Jerusalem, but the Messiah. The man who tried to enter the marriage banquet without wedding garments was cast out, indicating that one does not gate-crash the kingdom on one's own terms. As disciples, we must understand these principles about following Jesus and the kingdom of God.

Critical Observation

The fact that no one witnessed the actual resurrection of Jesus has led some critical scholars, especially during the first half of the 20th century, to question whether the Resurrection could in fact be considered historical. Since belief in the resurrection of Jesus is considered by Christians to be fundamental and essential to Christian faith, the narratives of Matthew 28 and the parallel sections in the other Gospels, as well as the testimony of other New Testament writers, are of prime importance to the gospel message.

1) None of the alternative explanations of the resurrection of Jesus—a stolen body, a Jesus who only swooned, or a mistaken tomb—is adequate to explain the total range of phenomena that must be explained historically (Matthew 27–28; Mark 15–16; Luke 23–24; John 19–20).

2) Jesus appeared after His resurrection on at least twelve different occasions:

   - Mary Magdalene (Mark 16:9; John 20:14).
   - Two disciples on the road to Emmaus (Mark 16:12; Luke 24:13–15)
   - Peter (Luke 24:34; 1 Corinthians 15:5)
   - Ten disciples in the upper room—Thomas absent (John 20:19)
   - Eleven disciples in the upper room—Thomas present, Great Commission (John 20:26; Luke 24:36; Mark 16:14)
   - The disciples at the Sea of Tiberias (Galilee) (John 21:1)
   - The eleven disciples on the mountain in Galilee—Great Commission (Matthew 28:16–20)
   - Five hundred men (1 Corinthians 15:6)
   - James (1 Corinthians 15:7)
   - All of the apostles (1 Corinthians 15:7)
   - At the Ascension (Mark 16:19; Luke 24:50; Acts 1:3)
   - Paul on the road to Damascus (Acts 9:3–8; 1 Corinthians 15:8; 1 Corinthians 9:1)

3) Paul, in 1 Corinthians 15:1–4, discusses the Resurrection as a vital and essential ingredient of the gospel message of salvation.

28:11–15

BRIBING THE SOLDIERS

It isn't surprising that the duplicitous chief priests and the Sanhedrin would have to do something to keep the guards at the tomb quiet. As they have done before, they are willing to pay a bribe to achieve their purposes. They tell the guards to say that the disciples had come during the night and stolen the body. The chief priests will take care of any concerns the governor would have that the soldiers had not adequately guarded the tomb. As a result the story of the disciples stealing the body of Jesus spread quickly. However, it is surprising that no disciple ever confesses to stealing the body of Jesus or knowing of those who did steal the body, even under dire circumstances—persecution and martyrdom.

📄 28:16–20

THE GREAT COMMISSION

This narrative of Jesus meeting His disciples in Galilee is unique to Matthew's Gospel.

Matthew 28:18–20 is a key to the whole Gospel narrative. It concerns making disciples of all nations. Matthew's Jewish community would need to know this, and that Jesus had commissioned His apostles for this purpose—including Matthew's readers.

The eleven disciples meet Jesus on a mountain in Galilee, just as Jesus had instructed them through the two women. Traditionally this mountain has been identified as Mt. Tabor, but we have no certain information on this other than tradition. Mt. Tabor is about thirteen miles west of the southern tip of the Sea of Galilee.

When the disciples see Jesus, they worship, but still some doubt (hesitate). It is not surprising they worship Him, but what does Matthew mean by the doubts? The Greek word translated by most versions of the Bible as "doubt," can also mean hesitate. It is found only two times in the New Testament, both in Matthew (28:17; 14:31). It occurs in Matthew 14:31 when Peter walks on the sea and begins to sink; Jesus asks him why he doubts.

Here in Matthew 28:17, perhaps it would be better to understand the meaning as doubt that lies in hesitancy rather than doubt that lies in disbelief. But one might ask, why uncertainty or hesitation rather than joy? Remember the trauma experienced by the disciples, as well as the guilt they felt over abandoning Jesus in His hour of trial. How will Jesus relate to them now? Matthew does not develop this point since it does not fit into the theological scheme of this last climactic paragraph of his Gospel. To learn of Jesus' reaction one should refer to John 21, where Jesus goes fishing with the disciples, encourages them, and speaks tenderly to Peter.

For Matthew's Jewish community, the point of the Great Commission focused on Jesus' messianic authority and His charge to His disciples to make other disciples of all nations. Its appearance is unique in several ways:

1) **Jesus' messianic authority.** The verb translated "give" is understood as a divine action in which God is the one who in His divine sovereignty gave Jesus the authority as the Messiah to function as the king over God's kingdom (one of the major themes of Matthew's Gospel—Jesus is the messianic king over God's kingdom). Divine authority over the kingdom is in fact divine authority over all existence, both in heaven and on earth.

2) **The charge to make disciples.** The controlling imperative of the Great Commission was the simple charge to make disciples. This is the only verb in the commission that is actually a command. It is not a surprising command since this is what we learned from the limited commission Jesus had given earlier in Matthew 10. The remainder of the words of the Great Commission explained how disciples are to be made, and of whom disciples are to be made. There are three key participles—going, baptizing, and teaching—that explain how the making of disciples was supposed to be carried out.

How does one make disciples? A disciple is a learner, one who has been instructed by a teacher and who has followed the teacher. The process of making disciples hinges around who the disciple is to follow. In the Christian case, disciples are disciples of the Messiah, or Jesus. People need to be taught about Jesus and how to follow Him.

3) **The charge to go.** Remember, the word apostle implies one sent or commissioned to go on behalf of the sender. In the context of both the eleven disciples/apostles and Matthew's community of disciples, they were to go. The tendency for a Jew would be to remain in Jerusalem or wherever he or she was in his or her community. But to carry out their messianic ministry of making disciples, the apostles were to go. In fact, this participle should be translated "you must go." This would be important to both the apostles, and especially to Matthew's community who were now living in a Gentile world. They were to leave the comfort of their own circle and go.

But where were they to go to? Jesus has already qualified this in His expression in delineating all nations. Neither the apostles nor Matthew's community were to limit their messianic ministry only to the Jews (10:6) as in the earlier limited commission. Because of this we know this commission as the Great Commission, for it was for all—the Jews and the Gentiles. For Matthew's community this would have had significant meaning, as it does today to the Christians who often are satisfied to wait for people like themselves to come to church to be converted to become even more like themselves.

4) **The charge to baptize them in the name of the Father, Son, and Holy Spirit.** Disciples become disciples of Jesus by being united with Him. In the Christian community one is united to Jesus by being baptized into Jesus (Romans 6:1–9; Galatians 3:25–29). It is obvious that before being baptized, the potential disciple must be told who to believe in—Jesus—and then how to believe. We see this in Acts 16:25–33 in the case of the Philippian jailor who first had to be informed and then was baptized.

The disciples were to be baptized in the name of the Father and of the Son and of the Holy Spirit (28:19), which probably means baptizing them as though the Father, Son, and Holy Spirit were baptizing the disciples.

5) **The charge to teach them to observe all that Jesus had commanded.** Disciples, once baptized into the fellowship of Christ and the Christian community, need to be taught. Fundamentally, they need to be taught what the life of a disciple is all about: the character of the disciple, the ministry of the disciple, the meaning of kingdom membership, how to live as disciples in a Christian community, and where to fix their hope. There are certain fundamentals of the Christian faith that new disciples need to be taught, and this teaching is an ongoing, unending process. There are always new challenges to discipleship. Disciples need to be taught the primary lesson of discipleship in Matthew's Gospel—discipleship is a radical life.

In the context of Matthew's Gospel, the expression translated "all that I have commanded you" refers to the lessons of discipleship learned from Jesus through the Gospel message.

"I am with you always, to the very end of the age" (28:20 NIV) implies an ongoing mission, especially one that reaches beyond the recent tragedy in the lives of Matthew's community, namely, the destruction of Jerusalem and/or the trauma that Jesus' disciples experienced in the Crucifixion. Through whatever lies ahead, the disciples are promised the ongoing presence of Jesus.

The expression "end of the age" is reminiscent of Matthew 24:3 and the final expression of that narrative in Matthew 24:14, "then the end will come" (NIV). The point Jesus is making is

THE GOSPEL OF
MARK

INTRODUCTION TO
MARK

The book of Mark is the shortest of the four Gospels and is considered by many to be the oldest. It may well have served as a source for the Gospels of Matthew and Luke. Numerous church leaders (Papias, Irenaeus, Clement of Alexandria, Origen, Jerome, and others) associated this Gospel with John Mark, the disciple of Peter. It was the opinion of the early church that Mark recorded the gospel that Peter preached.

AUTHOR

The writer of Mark never identifies himself, yet no serious suggestion of an author other than Mark has been put forward. John Mark was a young disciple who had traveled with Paul and Barnabas on their first missionary journey (Acts 13–14), but deserted them. His actions later caused such a rift between the two missionaries that they went their separate ways (Acts 15:36–41). Yet Mark's subsequent spiritual growth and faithfulness eventually earned Paul's trust once more (2 Timothy 4:11).

PURPOSE

Mark probably wrote from Rome to an audience primarily comprised of Gentile Christians to provide them with a defense of the gospel and encourage them in their faith. The content of the Gospel contains several indications of Mark's Roman and Gentile audience. He used ten Latin words, some of which are found nowhere else in scripture; he made a point to explain Jewish traditions; no genealogy is found for Jesus, as in Matthew and Luke; and he doesn't go into geographic or historic detail because his audience would not have been familiar with such Palestinian matters.

HISTORICAL CONTEXT

The date of Mark's writing is debated. Some people have estimated that his Gospel could have been written as early as AD 45. Most, however, agree that it was written no later than AD 60 to 70.

Not long after the death of Jesus, persecution began to intensify for His followers. For a while the Roman authorities had paid little attention, assuming Christianity was just an off-shoot of Judaism, which they had under control. But as the early church began to grow and spread out, believers experienced more and more conflicts with the Roman Empire. By the time of Mark's writing, persecution had become an ongoing concern, so he presented the life of Jesus to illustrate His willingness to suffer and sacrifice.

In the early to mid-60s (AD) the letters of Paul were beginning to circulate to the churches.

It was also the time of Nero's reign, which brought more targeted persecution to believers. A horrendous, destructive fire broke out in Rome in AD 64, suspected to have been ordered by Nero himself, and further rumored to have been blamed on the Christians as a cover-up. In the wave of persecution that followed, Peter was among those martyred for their faith (AD 64 or 67).

THEMES

Several themes and emphases can be seen in Mark's Gospel, but foremost among them are Mark's positioning of Jesus as both Son of God and Son of Man.

Son of God—Some scholars suggest that Mark 1:1 serves as a title to Mark's Gospel: "The beginning of the gospel of Jesus Christ, the Son of God" (ESV). As soon as Jesus is mentioned, He is identified as the Son of God. Throughout His life, others confirm this fact about Jesus (1:11; 3:11; 9:7; 15:39). The title alone, however, would not have meant much to a Roman audience unless Jesus also displayed the power of God. So Mark wastes no time getting to the ministry of Jesus and His performance of many amazing miracles.

Son of Man—Jesus never denied that He was the Son of God and the Messiah (Christ). However, His emphasis was not on power or politics, but on servanthood and suffering. So His preferred term of self-description was "Son of Man." Mark uses this title for Jesus fourteen times—mostly while quoting Jesus Himself.

"Son of Man" was a far less politically heated term, though certainly messianic, originating from Daniel's prophecy (Daniel 7:13–14). The Jewish people had been anticipating the arrival of a Messiah for centuries, but they were looking for a military figure to set them free from Roman domination. Throughout His ministry, Jesus slowly reinterpreted His Messianic ministry. He certainly had power, yet He refused to use His power against those in control. And His arrival did indeed bring freedom—not immediate victory over Roman rule, but spiritual triumph over fear and death available only through the suffering and sacrifice of the Son of Man. Half of Mark's Gospel (beginning with 8:31) is dedicated to Jesus' suffering, death, and resurrection.

CONTRIBUTION TO THE BIBLE

About 95 percent of Mark is found in either Matthew or Luke. Yet Mark's Gospel has a fresh and immediate tone not to be missed. His writing has a fast flow of action, moving rapidly from story to story. He records details not found in the other Gospel accounts that make the events more vivid. For example, he frequently notes the emotional reactions and gestures of Jesus. Only two discourses of Jesus are provided (4:1–32 and 13:1–37) and only four parables (Matthew recorded eighteen parables, and Luke, nineteen). Yet Mark contains eighteen of Jesus' miracles—about the same number as Matthew and Luke. So Mark's Gospel gives us a bold, concise, action-filled look at Jesus' life.

STRUCTURE

Ancient tradition considered Mark's Gospel "disorderly." Some have proposed that Mark's Gospel is best seen as a passion narrative with an extended introduction. Jesus' suffering and death is the dominant theme around which the Gospel narrative is structured. Most scholars break Mark into two main parts: 1:1–8:30 and 8:31–16:8 (with 8:27–9:1 as the transition). Some break Mark into three parts, the third beginning with Jesus' entry into Jerusalem (Mark 11:1).

While Matthew and Luke begin their Gospels with birth accounts of Jesus and genealogies to prove who He was, Mark skips the events surrounding Jesus' birth and quickly hastens into Jesus' public ministry. Mark 1:14–9:50 examines Jesus' ministry in Galilee, from His widespread popularity to His conflicts with the religious leaders to His withdrawal and preparation of His disciples. Mark 10 describes Jesus' ministry in Judea and Perea. And chapters 11–16 detail Jesus' final week, concluding with His resurrection.

OUTLINE

MARK 1:1–13

PREPARING FOR SOMETHING NEW

Setting Up the Section

Mark quickly moves from the appearance of Jesus on earth to His adult ministry. After eight verses about John the Baptist, Jesus is baptized and sets to work, calling disciples and healing.

📖 1:1

TWO TITLES

Before Mark introduces John the Baptist as the forerunner to Jesus, he provides two significant titles for Jesus that succinctly describe who He is and what He came to do. The first, *Christ*, represents what Jesus came to do. Rather than a name, the word *Christ* is a title (the Greek translation of the Hebrew for *Messiah*) that means "Anointed One." Jesus was anointed to perform the redemptive work of being prophet, priest, and king of His people. He is the divinely appointed, commissioned, and accredited Savior of humankind. (See Hebrews 5:1–4; Isaiah 11:2–4; 49:6; John 5:37; and Acts 2:22).

The second term, *Son of God*, refers to Jesus' nature rather than His office. He isn't the Son of God because of anything He has done (miraculous birth, incarnation, resurrection, etc.), but rather because of who He is. Mark uses Son of God in its messianic sense and links it closely to "Messiah."

In the ancient way of thinking, a man's life was continued in his son. A son would inherit the property of his father—and the firstborn received a double portion. A son was perceived as the extension of the father's rule and position in the house. So Jesus' title "Son of God" shows that even when He was separate from the Father, He lived to do the will of God and shared His very nature.

📖 1:2–8

JOHN THE BAPTIST

The prophets had foretold not only a Messiah to come, but also a messenger—an "Elijah"—to prepare the way. Verses 2 and 3 are quotes from Isaiah 40:3 and Malachi 3:1. Mark inserts these reminders to introduce John the Baptist. John preaches about the forgiveness of sins that would follow repentance (1:4), and he baptizes those who respond to his message.

Demystifying Mark

People of Jesus' day would expect a messenger to precede the arrival of any important person. It was the messenger's job to: (1) ensure the roads were in proper repair; (2) arrange for food, lodging, and a proper reception of the dignitary; and (3) announce the arrival of the important person. John the Baptist performed the role of messenger prior to the appearance of Jesus.

Mark's physical description of John the Baptist (1:6)—his unique diet and style of dress—creates an additional connection between the new prophet and the Old Testament Elijah (2 Kings 1:8). Even though John must have been a powerful presence, his message of repentance is based on the anticipation of "one more powerful than I" (1:7 NIV). John's comment about his own unworthiness to untie Jesus' sandals—the work of a slave—is a vivid image of the homage he pays to Jesus and the work He will do (1:7). And although John is baptizing people with water, Jesus will baptize with the Holy Spirit (1:8).

📖 1:9–13

RESISTING TEMPTATION

Even though John had proclaimed Jesus to be much greater than himself, Jesus came to be baptized by John (1:9). At this time, God makes a statement about Jesus (1:11) that He has never made about anyone after the fall of Adam. Because of the prevalence of sin, no human being can please God. Yet Jesus came to do for us what we are unable to do for ourselves.

Critical Observation

Coming out of Nazareth (1:9) didn't do much for Jesus' reputation to begin with. Nazareth was such an obscure village that it is mentioned nowhere in the Old Testament, the writings of Josephus, or rabbinic literature. While the small community was not held in high regard, archeological evidence confirms its existence.

The opening of the heavens (1:10) suggests a divine intervention and a new revelation of God after centuries of silence (Isaiah 64:1). With the advent of Jesus, we might conclude that God is becoming accessible to an extent not previously known. The descent of the Holy Spirit upon Jesus is described in a simile to symbolize the same type of beauty and majesty as a dove in flight. And God himself confirms what Mark has already told us: Jesus is indeed the Son of God who pleases His heavenly Father and is beloved (1:11). The blessing conferred on Jesus contains important allusions to Psalm 2:7 and Isaiah 42:1. Also, His empowerment with the Spirit was predicted in Isaiah 11.

Yet, immediately after this high point in Jesus' life, He goes into the wilderness where He is tempted by Satan. Matthew and Luke provide more extensive accounts of Jesus' temptation, but Mark includes additional details. We discover in verse 12 that the Holy Spirit *sends* Jesus into the desert. It was God's will for Jesus to prove Himself by resisting the temptation to sin—something no human has ever been capable of doing. Just as the Israelites went into the wilderness for forty years and failed, Jesus is in the desert for forty days and succeeds. Having triumphed over the enemy, Jesus can now go forth and call a new people who will share His spiritual inheritance.

Mark also mentions wild animals present in the wilderness (1:13). God had placed Adam in a beautiful and peaceful garden over which he had dominion, yet Adam lost that privilege due to his sin. Jesus is sent into a dangerous setting, yet overcomes physical dangers and spiritual temptations to reestablish the kingdom of God on earth—a kingdom that would be marked by peace and righteousness (Isaiah 11:6–9; 35:9). It seems clear that Jesus' spiritual temptations are severe, because angels are there to minister to Him and encourage Him (1:13).

With just thirteen verses, Mark deals with the life of Jesus prior to His public ministry. From this point onward, Jesus will be a teacher and healer, each day closer to His inevitable sacrifice on the cross.

Take It Home

It is a common experience to feel a significant letdown after a spiritual mountaintop experience. During such times, some people start to doubt and think what they felt must not have been real. But in this passage we see that even Jesus plunged from the heights of spiritual confidence at His baptism to a dark and challenging time of testing immediately afterward. What confidence should we pull from knowing that Jesus resisted where I would have succumbed? What hope can I draw from knowing that my Savior has the power to resist the devil?

MARK 1:14–45

JESUS' MINISTRY BEGINS

Setting Up the Section

As Mark begins his account of Jesus' ministry, he maintains a focus on Jesus' proclamation and demonstration of the nearness of the kingdom of God. Jesus proclaimed by teaching and preaching; He demonstrated by performing miracles. Mark wants his readers to see that Jesus is more than a prophet—He is the Messiah and the Son of God. As such, His ministry is powerful.

📖 1:14–20

THE TIME HAS COME

Jesus' ministry begins in Galilee and the surrounding regions. Mark's Gospel shows how Jesus regularly moves from place to place, which stresses the urgency of His message about the kingdom of God. Some of the travel is in Gentile territory, foreshadowing an outreach that is central to the establishment of the kingdom of God.

Jesus begins His public ministry as John the Baptist is completing his. John had been put in prison (1:14) and would not emerge alive (6:17–29). Jesus continues John's message that the kingdom of God is near, and people should repent and believe the good news (1:15; Matthew 3:1–2). The good news is twofold: (1) Because of Jesus, the kingdom of God had come to earth; and (2) Through Jesus, salvation is given to all who believe. The only way to enter God's kingdom is by believing the good news that Jesus came to take the punishment of humankind. By believing in Him, the very righteousness of God will be bestowed as a person is reconciled to God.

Critical Observation

God expects believers to repent—to turn from their sins. Yet repentance alone is not enough to save us. Repentance without faith is just self-improvement; faith without repentance is just religion. What is necessary is both repentance *and* belief in Jesus.

To help spread His message, Jesus begins to call disciples. Mark first describes the call of two pairs of brothers, all fishermen—Andrew and Simon (Peter), and James and John. Jesus promises to make them "fishers of men" (1:17). The facts that these followers would set aside their livelihoods to be in the service of Jesus and be immediately willing to follow are indications of Jesus' authority.

1:21–34

UNPRECEDENTED POWER

Jesus' authority as a teacher is authenticated by the power He displays. The first miracle Mark records is the casting out of an evil spirit from a possessed man at a synagogue in Capernaum. The crowd is already amazed at Jesus' teaching (1:22), but becomes even more astounded when He rids the troubled man of the evil spirit. Note that the demon knows exactly who Jesus is—in regard to both His humanity ("Jesus of Nazareth") and His divinity ("the Holy One of God"). And even though Jesus sternly commands the spirit to keep quiet, news about Jesus quickly spreads (1:28).

Demystifying Mark

Synagogues may have originated during the Babylonian exile when the Jewish people had no access to the temple. A synagogue was not a place for sacrifice, but rather for reading the scriptures, praying, and worshiping God. The services were led by laymen, supervised by a board of elders, and presided over by a ruler. A synagogue could be organized anywhere there were ten or more Jewish men above the age of twelve.

When Jesus and His followers leave the synagogue, they presumably go to the home of Simon and Andrew for their Sabbath meal. There they find Simon Peter's mother-in-law in bed with a fever—a very serious condition in the first century. Jesus' healing allows her to rise immediately and begin to wait on her guests—an honor for a woman during this time.

The Sabbath ended at sundown, at which time "the whole town gathered" (NIV) at the house

(1:33). And they didn't simply bring hordes of sick and demon-possessed people; they kept on bringing people for Jesus to tend to.

FIRST SOLITARY, THEN SURROUNDED

Even after the long healing session at Simon Peter's house, Jesus arises very early the next morning and finds a solitary place to pray (1:35). His solitude doesn't last long, however, because the crowds are soon looking for Him again. But Jesus opts to move on to other places. He had come to spread the Word of God, not just to heal the sick. The people Jesus healed would still die eventually. Physical healing—which was another indication of His authority—was simply proof that Jesus' message of spiritual healing should be heeded.

While traveling on through Galilee, a man with leprosy approaches Jesus, asking for healing. This man would have been considered ceremonially unclean to Jesus and His followers. Jesus seems aware that no one had been permitted contact with this man for a long time. Yet Jesus not only touches the man, but heals him, making him clean once again. The leper is expected to follow the legally prescribed course to verify healing (Leviticus 14:1–32).

Jesus warns the man not to say anything about what had happened, but the man is so overjoyed that he tells everyone he sees (1:45).

This is Mark's first mention of a pattern of Jesus' ministry that some refer to as the "Messianic Secret." He never encouraged public excitement about His healing ministry lest it create a problem with the Jews and the Romans. The Jews would want to follow Jesus only because of His power to heal and the Romans would think He was a Jewish insurrectionist trying to overthrow the government. Thus, Jesus would tell people that He had healed to keep quiet (1:44; 3:12; 5:43; 7:36–37; 8:26, 30; 9:9). In this case, as in some others, the healed man was so overjoyed that rather than keep Jesus' secret, he told everyone he saw.

From a theological standpoint, Jesus was secretive because He did not want His miracles to be seen as the central piece of His ministry. They were only meant to confirm that He was indeed who He said that He was. His miracles proved that His words should be heeded and His death and resurrection provided the power behind the promises that He made.

The tests for leprosy provided in Leviticus 13:1–46 present a symbolic picture of the problem of sin. Like sin, leprosy is beneath the surface (Leviticus 13:3); it spreads (Leviticus 13:5–8); it defiles and isolates (Leviticus 13:45–46); and it renders things fit only for the fire (Leviticus 13:52).

As word spreads about Jesus' ability to heal even leprosy, Jesus tries to avoid towns and seek out remote places. But wherever He is, the people find Him and congregate.

Take It Home

According to Mark, people were first amazed at the teachings of Jesus (1:22). Then they were even more amazed when they witnessed firsthand the power of God Jesus displayed through His miracles. In fact, the desire to see the miracles seemed to have superceded their willingness to respond to what He was saying. In your own life, to what extent do you depend on signs to confirm what you believe to be true about Jesus? Are the teachings of the Bible enough to convince you, or do you desire additional proof?

MARK 2:1–17

A MINISTRY TO THE "SICK"

Setting Up the Section

Mark has wasted no time describing the immense popularity of Jesus as He begins His public ministry. But now Jesus does something that many cannot understand: Rather than associating with only the elite of the culture, He instead chooses to hang around with the outcasts of His society. He even selects members of this group to be included among His closest companions.

`📖 2:1–12`

THE FAITH TO MOVE ROOFTOPS

Jesus returns to Capernaum, and again, huge crowds assemble to hear Him speak. This time He is in a house, and it is filled beyond capacity. Most Palestinian homes had one to four rooms, and the crowd at this one fills the house and sprawls outside.

The "word" Jesus preaches (2:2) is the good news that the kingdom of God is near (1:15). Indeed, the kingdom was arriving through His incarnation and ministry.

While Jesus is speaking, five men arrive: four carrying a fifth who is paralyzed. When they realize they can get nowhere close to Jesus, they improvise a plan to go through the roof. Many first-century homes had an outside staircase leading to a flat roof made of branches and sod. It would not be difficult to make an opening in the roof and lower their friend.

Considering the unusual entrance of the man, Jesus' first words to him are surprising (2:5). For one thing, Jesus surely knows the man has come for physical healing, not spiritual forgiveness. For another, His words trigger a negative response from the teachers of the law among the crowd.

Jesus perceives the faith of the five men (2:5), and Mark frequently associates the presence of faith with the performance of miracles by Jesus. Even though Jesus uses the passive voice in making His statement, His intent is not missed by skeptical listeners. The Jews believed that only God was capable of forgiving sin. Similar claims by anyone else were blasphemy (irreverent, profane, impious speech about God that held a sentence of death for those found guilty [Leviticus 24:16]).

Jesus knows the thoughts of the religious leaders and preempts their objections by asking a question (2:9). Clearly, the forgiveness of sin (spiritual healing) requires much more authority than performing merely a physical healing. Yet His observers know it is much easier to *say* that the man's sins are forgiven because forgiveness cannot be verified, while healing can. But to Jesus, the granting of healing and forgiveness are equally the work of God. So He heals the paralyzed man to validate His authority to forgive sins. Mark writes that as the man stands up and carries His mat out, "everyone" (NIV) is amazed, but he is probably referring to the general effect on the crowd. As we will soon see, the religious leaders are still resistant to the ministry of Jesus.

Jesus makes a very important connection here for the people watching this miracle (2:8-10). In book of Isaiah (chapters 29; 35; 61) God said when the Messiah arrived on earth that not only would God forgive sins and restore the broken hearted, but the Messiah would also bring healing to the lame. When Jesus pronounces forgiveness of sin and then backs up this declaration with a healing, He is fulfilling what the Scriptures said the Messiah would do (Isaiah 61:1).

Critical Observation

This is the first place in Mark where Jesus calls himself "the Son of Man" (2:10), although Jesus would use this term as His favorite self-designation. The vagueness of the phrase carried overtones of both humanity and deity (Daniel 7:13-14). By using it, Jesus forced people to make up their own minds about Him. If He had spoken publicly of being the Messiah (Christ), it would have quickly created problems in the politically and religiously charged culture of the time.

2:13-17

AN UNUSUAL CHOICE TO BE A DISCIPLE

Mark has already told us that Jesus had been calling disciples to follow Him (1:16-20). Simon, Andrew, James, and John seemed decent choices, even though they were simple fishermen and not among the prestigious crowd. But Jesus' choice of Levi in this passage is even more startling. (Levi is identified in Matthew's Gospel as "Matthew," but the name change is not explained in scripture.)

As usual, Jesus is surrounded by a large crowd. He is walking along and teaching them when He comes upon Levi, a tax collector sitting in his booth. Levi immediately responds to Jesus' invitation to "Follow Me" (2:14), and soon Jesus is having dinner at his house. But Jesus' willing association with tax collectors and "sinners" (2:15-16) creates instant indignation among the teachers of the law.

This is where Mark first introduces his readers to the Pharisees, a party of laymen who devoted themselves to keeping the law, especially its oral interpretation. The name probably meant "separatists," perhaps in reference to their separation from the common people—the "sinners" mentioned in this passage. The scribes, referred to by Luke as lawyers, were the official interpreters of Jewish law. The scribes and Pharisees were separate groups, though some Pharisees were also scribes.

Tax collectors were on the opposite end of the scale from the Pharisees. Roman tax collectors were despised because of their dishonesty, use of intimidation and force, and contact with Gentiles. The Jewish tax collectors appointed by King Herod weren't liked much better.

Demystifying Mark

Those who live in modern, Western society may have difficulty comprehending just how scandalous it was for Jesus to associate with tax collectors and other social outcasts. In Semitic society, table fellowship was one of the most intimate expressions of friendship. The Jewish leaders could not understand how Jesus could regard Himself as a religious person and still dine with such spiritual rebels. But Jesus defied many of the conventions of His society.

The religious leaders do not question Jesus directly (2:16). Even as they are looking down on His behavior, it seems they are still afraid to confront Him because of the power He displayed in both words and deeds. But Jesus overhears and responds directly. He clarifies that His purpose is not to affirm the good works of self-righteous people, but rather to bring healing and righteousness to those who realize their own insufficiencies. For Jesus to refuse to associate with sinners would have been as foolish as for a doctor not to associate with the sick.

Take It Home

Jesus showed love for all kinds of sinners. He took the initiative in seeking them out. He accepted them as friends, and chose to have close fellowship with them. His response to outcasts provided a new and revolutionary model for both religion and social behavior. And sadly, it might still be new and revolutionary in our own culture. Why is it hard to show love for sinners? What gets in the way of showing unconditional love? How does the love that Jesus had for sinners give us hope that we can one day love sinners?

MARK 2:18–3:6

CONFLICT INTENSIFIES

Setting Up the Section

In this section of his Gospel, Mark has collected five accounts to chronicle the growing conflict Jesus experienced with the religious leaders of Israel. We have already seen two: their reluctance to Jesus' authority to forgive the sin of the paralyzed man (2:1-12) and their disgust at his association with tax collectors and "sinners" (2:15-17). Now we look at three more conflicts and see how quickly the conflict escalated.

THE CONFLICT OVER FASTING

The Old Testament only prescribed fasting one day a year: on the Day of Atonement (Leviticus 16:29-31), although other traditional fasts had begun later (Zechariah 7:5; 8:19). But by the first century, the Pharisees made a habit of fasting every Monday and Thursday (Luke 18:12). Other occasional fasting was common following personal loss, as an expression of repentance, in preparation for prayer, or even as a meritorious act.

Jesus and His disciples did not practice the rigorous fasting of the Pharisees, or even of John the Baptist's disciples, so a group of people asked about this discrepancy. Jesus responded to their question with a question of His own—a common tactic in rabbinic debates. In essence, Jesus clarified that there were appropriate and inappropriate times to fast. His appearance on earth was a special time; He was not unlike a bridegroom at a wedding, and His disciples were like guests. For them, it was not a time to fast, but to celebrate.

In this context, Jesus' two short parables (2:21-22) make sense. The fasting of the Pharisees was not necessary because it represented an old way of doing things. With the onset of the kingdom of God on earth, certain things were going to change. The traditions of scribal Judaism were like the old garment and the old wineskin. The "old" was not inherently wrong, but its time had passed. The old ways would not smoothly merge with Jesus' new teachings; they had to be replaced with something better.

THE CONFLICT OVER PICKING GRAIN ON THE SABBATH

The Old Testament clearly forbade work on the Sabbath (Exodus 20:8-11), but the scribes had so meticulously defined "work" that they had a list of 39 different prohibitions. Third on their list was "reaping," which was their accusation against Jesus and his disciples (2:23). Since Jesus' followers were only feeding themselves, Jesus had a ready response. He referred His accusers to the story of David (1 Samuel 21:1-6) who used "consecrated bread" out of the tabernacle to feed his men. He emphasized that the Sabbath was created for people to cherish, not to enslave them with legalistic restrictions (2:27-28).

Demystifying Mark

For anyone unfamiliar with the Old Testament, Jesus' example may confuse more than clarify. Twelve loaves of bread were placed in the tabernacle every Sabbath, probably to symbolize God's presence and provision (Exodus 25:30; Leviticus 24:5-9). The bread was designated to be eaten only by the priests (Leviticus 24:9). Yet when David and his men showed up at the tabernacle, famished and with no other food available, the priest used the bread to feed them. Jesus' point was that human need should take precedence over ceremonial laws.

THE CONFLICT OVER HEALING ON THE SABBATH

For the Pharisees, Sabbath observance was one of the more important elements in Judaism and a noticeable distinction between Jews and Gentiles. When Jesus began to challenge their long-held standards, they became enraged. And when the conflict wasn't quickly resolved, they even began to plot to kill Him.

On one particular Sabbath, Jesus and His disciples were in the synagogue. So were the Pharisees. And so was a man with a shriveled hand. The Pharisees allowed healing to take place on the Sabbath—but only if a person's life was in danger, which was certainly not the case in this account. By this time, Jesus' opponents were looking for any opportunity to accuse Him, so apparently they were more interested in watching Him than in worshiping. Again, Jesus appeared to know their thoughts, so He made a public display of having the deformed man stand in front of everyone. His question (3:4) lifted the issue of Sabbath observance to a level above a list of prohibitions. His question suggested that to heal is to do good; not to heal is the equivalent of doing evil. To Jesus, merely resting on the Sabbath was not enough when the day could be used to accomplish good. And after He received no argument in response to His question, He healed the man. He then raised the analogy even higher by suggesting that failing to save a life would be equivalent to murder. The irony here is that while Jesus is doing good on the Sabbath, His opponents are plotting murder!

Critical Observations

In all of ancient literature, the Herodians are only referred to in Mark (in 3:6 and 12:13) and once in Matthew (22:16). They were a Jewish political party devoted to the Roman emperor and his deputy (Herod). Ordinarily the Pharisees would have nothing to do with such a group that submitted willingly to the government of Rome, but their common hatred of Jesus would unite these two parties at opposite ends of the political scale.

Jesus became angry that these so-called religious leaders were so hard-hearted that they would resist the healing of a person in distress. The Sabbath was created for rest and relief, yet they used it to burden people. Jesus' anger was directed at the insensitivity toward suffering as well as the entire system of legalism where the letter of the law is given more weight than the needs of the people it is supposed to help.

Mark provides this series of conflicts so we can see the tension that was developing between Jesus and His adversaries. And this certainly won't be the last of the disagreements.

Take It Home

In this account we see that Jesus got angry, so anger itself is not a sin. It was a natural response at the culmination of a long series of conflicts. Yet Jesus didn't lose control. Does your anger tend to be more in regard to offenses against God, or do you get upset more often at personal offenses? And how well do you stay in control when anger rises within you?

MARK 3:7–19

FAME AND FOLLOWERS

Enduring the Crowds   3:7–12
Calling Disciples   3:13–19

Setting Up the Section

Much of what Mark has already introduced is continued in this section. Crowds continue to vie for Jesus' attention as He continues to assemble a team of disciples to assist Him in His ministry. Yet Mark provides new bits of information with each new story.

📖 3:7–12

ENDURING THE CROWDS

Mark had just described the beginnings of a plan to have Jesus put to death. Here we read that Jesus "withdrew" to the Sea of Galilee (3:7). The word *withdrew* in this context apparently meant "flee from danger." At this point Jesus chooses to withdraw rather than debate the Pharisees because His ministry is still in the early stages, and He wants to extend it beyond the towns in Israel. In fact, several of the locations mentioned in verse 8 had large Gentile populations. It doesn't take long for Jesus' message to spread beyond the bounds of traditional Jewish locales.

The dastardly plot of the Pharisees stood in sharp contrast to how the crowds respond to Jesus. By this time, He can hardly travel anywhere without a swarm of people around Him. Many are even beginning to push and shove to get close to Him (3:10)—seemingly much more interested in being healed than in hearing what He has to say about salvation. From a similar account in 4:1 it seems likely that the boat was not intended for escape, but to provide Jesus with a podium—a buffer between Himself and the crowds.

Again, Jesus encounters evil spirits (1:23–24, 34). This time they are acknowledging Him as the "Son of God" (3:11), but He forces them to remain quiet about His identity.

This is another example of what some refer to as the Messianic Secret. Jesus often encouraged those that he helped to keep the miracle to themselves (1:44; 3:12; 5:43; 7:36-37; 8:26, 30; 9:9). While this secret kept Jesus from unwanted, untimely attention from both the Jewish leaders and the Romans, there was a more significant theological reason. Jesus did not want His miracles to be seen as the central piece of His ministry. His miracles were only meant to confirm that He was who He said that He was.

Demystifying Mark

James writes that, "Even the demons believe [that there is one God]—and shudder" (James 2:19 NRSV). Here in Mark's account, the demons are aware of who Jesus is and what He came to do. Nevertheless, they are already condemned and beyond salvation. They were not declaring Jesus' lordship as a confession of submission, but out of fear. And because it was premature for Jesus to proclaim His true identity, He had them silenced. His authority would ultimately be confirmed at the cross.

3:13–19

CALLING DISCIPLES

Mark had already written about Jesus' call of Andrew, Simon, James, and John (1:14–20), and later Levi (2:13–14). Here he provides the list of the twelve disciples chosen from the rest. They would be designated *apostles*, meaning "sent ones" (3:14), in contrast to crowds of other disciples who followed Jesus as well.

It's interesting to note the various lists of the apostles in the New Testament. There are four: Matthew 10:2–4; Luke 6:13–16; Acts 1:13; and this one in Mark. In each case, Simon Peter is always listed first, Philip fifth, James the son of Alphaeus ninth, and Judas Iscariot last.

Sometimes the names of the apostles can be a little confusing. We've seen that Matthew 3:18) is sometimes called Levi. Similarly, Bartholomew is probably the same as Nathanael, and Thaddaeus may be another name for Judas (the son of James).

These would be the twelve people Jesus would spend most of His time with, preparing them for a time when He would no longer be around to lead them. They would be the first to understand His plan of redemption and to spread the good news of that plan around the world.

Critical Observation

The number twelve recalls the tribes of Israel, God's people in the Old Testament. The twelve apostles will become the nucleus of the new, restored people of God, later to be known as the church.

Jesus retreats to a mountain to summon His twelve primary followers. The call of Jesus is always for a purpose, not just for status. The apostles are called to serve a missional purpose. Mark provides two aspects of their calling: (1) to be with Jesus (one of the most important aspects of being a disciple); and (2) to proclaim the advent of the kingdom of God by preaching and exorcising demons (3:14–15).

Mark maintains a focus on Jesus' supernatural power over both the physical world and the spiritual world. His apostles would have the privilege of sharing and using that power. Similarly, today's disciples are not expected to minister in their own strength, but to be empowered by their omnipotent Savior (2 Corinthians 12:9–10).

Take It Home

Many people find personal ministry to others fulfilling and rewarding—as long as it doesn't become too demanding. However, as we look at the ministry of Jesus we see a continual stream of people physically pressing in on Him and demanding His attention. In addition, He is getting up early to pray, making time to call and train disciples, and maintaining the important, essential aspects of ministry. How do you respond when the demands of ministry require more than the time you have allotted? What other options do you have in such situations?

MARK 3:20–35

FAMILY AND FOES

Setting Up the Section

Jesus' teachings were unlike anything the people of Israel had ever heard, and the reactions of the crowds toward Him were frequently unpredictable. Even those closest to Him didn't know what to think. In this section we see that, at times, Jesus' human family didn't respond to Him much differently than those who strongly opposed Him. Mark is here setting up his theme that while many of Jesus' own reject Him, outsiders and outcasts accept Him (John 1:11).

This is the first time Mark uses the literary device common to his Gospel called bracketing or sandwiching. In this section, Mark sandwiches one account in the middle of another. He brings two stories together to support the same point. In this case, it is to show that no one—not the religious leaders and not His own family—truly understood who Jesus was and what He came to do. Other examples of Mark's sandwiching in the Gospel are 4:1–20; 5:21–43; 6:7–29; 11:12–26; 14:1–11; 14:53–72.

▤ **3:20–21**

EVEN JESUS HAD FAMILY PROBLEMS

As we look back about 2,000 years to the ministry of Jesus, knowing what we do, it's natural to think that it would have been exciting to be there, witnessing all the newness of His power and teaching. But if we read scripture closely, we see quite a variety of responses—many of them not what we might expect.

Here we see that Jesus' own family is not only embarrassed by Him but literally thinks He is out of His mind (3:21). With all the crowds flocking to Him everywhere He goes—in this case He and His disciples are not even able to eat (3:20)—His own family does not perceive Him to be anything special.

Mark's reference to family is not a statement that Jesus' mother rejected Him, but it emphasizes that even those closest to Him did not fully understand His purpose and power. Mark will say more about Jesus' family a few verses down, but he first inserts another incident between Jesus and the scribes.

Critical Observation

Who were Jesus' "brothers"? Some people think these were children of Joseph from a previous marriage. Others believe Mary and Joseph had children after Jesus was born. Although skeptical at first, some of Jesus' brothers would eventually become church leaders and epistle writers.

▤ 3:22–30

A HARSH (AND INACCURATE) ACCUSATION

Many times in the New Testament we read of someone who "came down" from Jerusalem (3:22). The reference is geographical as well as spiritual. Jerusalem, God's holy city, was on a hill, so anyone who departed, by necessity, had to go "down."

Apparently the scribes had followed Jesus, and it didn't take them long to express their criticism. This time, however, they actually accuse Jesus of being possessed. Beelzebub (3:22) was the Greek form of a Hebrew name that meant "lord of flies," and was the name given to the prince of demons. In essence, the religious leaders are accusing Jesus of being possessed by Satan.

Jesus uses logic to refute their accusations. He says it is foolish to think that someone possessed by the prince of demons would go around casting demons out of other people. He uses three consecutive short parables to make His point (3:25–27). The first two are self-explanatory. The third one, however (3:27), can be confusing. The "strong man" is a reference to Satan, who possesses a number of people. The one capable of entering his house and carrying off his possessions is Jesus, who came to earth and began setting people free by exorcising demons. He would soon break the hold of sin and death for good with His sacrificial death.

Jesus' statement in verses 28–29 has been a source of discussion and debate for centuries. To begin with, we should not miss the emphatic opening that all the sins and blasphemies of people will be forgiven. Jesus' use of "Verily" (KJV) (or "Truly" [NASB, ESV, NRSV] or "I tell you the truth [NIV]") is a declaration that what follows is absolute truth. The term *blasphemy* refers to slandering another, in this case, being irreverent or defiant toward God. It is the notion of abusing the name of God by something one says or does. And what Jesus is stating so strongly is that such offenses will be forgiven.

It's the second part of His statement that creates the confusion, that whoever blasphemes against the Holy Spirit will never be forgiven (3:29). To understand this verse, we have to understand the context. Jesus has recently cast out a number of demons, using the miraculous power of God. But the scribes accuse Jesus of acting under the power of evil. Jesus explains that those who attribute the power of the Holy Spirit to Satan have no way of being forgiven. This sin is apparently quite rare because it requires being faced with the power of Jesus and then declaring it the work of the devil.

Demystifying Mark

Blasphemy was a serious sin, punishable by death in the Old Testament (Leviticus 24:10–16). The people took this matter so seriously that they would not speak the name of God at all. At the same time, it was rather easy for accusers to charge someone with blasphemy. It would be the official charge at Jesus' trial (Matthew 26:64–66) as well as the reason Stephen was stoned (Acts 6:11), even though in both these cases those accused were speaking only truth.

Verse 30 clarifies this a bit more. Mark tells us that Jesus' statement was made in response to the scribes saying that He had an evil spirit. Theirs was not a single act, but a habitual attitude that was influencing their actions. And it's noteworthy that the sin was committed by religious scholars and authorities, not laypersons.

📄 3:31–35

AN EXPANDED DEFINITION OF FAMILY

As Jesus faces skeptics and doubters both within and outside His family, we see quite a difference in scale. Jesus' family members thought He was crazy, yet they weren't as off-base as the scribes.

Still, when His family members show up asking to see Him, He doesn't give them priority. It seems they didn't want to go inside and get Him personally, so they sent someone with a message that they were waiting for Him outside. Jesus' response (3:33–35) shows a shift in thinking. Jesus is now speaking of God's family, not His own human family unit.

This passage surely encouraged Mark's Gentile readers, as it does modern Christians. It is difficult to think of a more meaningful symbol than inclusion in the family of God. Jesus came to bring salvation to the world, not just to a single family unit or ethnic subgroup. As a result, every new day brings additional growth to the family of God.

Take It Home

Jesus redefined family, expanding it to include everyone who responds to His message and does God's will. Mark's account suggests that being part of God's family may require adjusting or even severing relationships with one's earthly family. Have you found this to be true at all? And how do you feel about being in God's family? Do you feel more like a full-fledged child with all the rights and privileges, or more like a distant cousin or ugly stepchild? What could you do to feel more at home in God's family?

MARK 4:1–25

THE PARABLE OF THE SOWER

Setting Up the Section

To this point, Mark has been providing a narrative account of Jesus' public ministry. Here, however, he inserts a series of Jesus' parables, the first being the Parable of the Sower. Mark's point is to announce the gospel of Jesus Christ and to help explain why Jesus' message will receive mixed reviews.

📄 **4:1–9**

MASTER OF PARABLES

When we think of biblical parables, we tend to immediately think of Jesus. While parables can be found in the Old Testament and were used by other teachers, Jesus carefully employed this literary device. His parables weren't intended as entertainment; Jesus used them for a very specific reason, as Mark will explain.

The "lake" (NIV) where Jesus is teaching (4:1) is the Sea of Galilee. The miracle ministry of Jesus has become so popular that it has spawned a following of mass proportions. Because of the size of the crowd, Jesus teaches from a boat in the lake while the people stand ashore. But His teaching this day is about farming.

Jesus begins and ends the parable by telling His audience to listen thoughtfully (4:3, 9), indicating that the meaning of parables is not always self-evident. The Parable of the Sower is short, clear, and true to what is known about Palestinian agriculture. Unlike the modern method of planting, seeds were first sown and then plowed underground. The sower held a quantity of seed in an apron with one hand and used his other hand to broadcast it. Naturally, some seeds would fall on the hardened path through the field, some where the soil was too shallow, and some among thorns. (The stones and thistles that infest Palestinian fields to this day are legendary.)

Critical Observation

The one atypical element in the parable is the abundant harvest (4:8). Due to primitive agricultural techniques, an average harvest in ancient Palestine was probably no more than seven or eight times the amount of seed sown; a good harvest might yield ten times more. So the parable makes a significant point: To achieve so high a return, much of the seed needs to take root in good soil. Even as He was speaking this parable, Jesus' words were like the seed being scattered and taking root only in the hearts that were fertile soil—which turned out to be quite a small percentage in this case.

Even though most everyone can understand what Jesus is saying about farming, they can't comprehend what He really means by telling the parable.

WHY PARABLES?

Some may assume that Jesus used the simplicity of parables to clarify what He was saying, but that's not the case. After He tells the Parable of the Sower, His disciples immediately asked about its meaning. Before answering, Jesus tells them that the mystery of the kingdom of God will be revealed in the form of parables. The parables serve to reveal truth to those with spiritual insight, those who have been redeemed by placing their faith in Jesus. Indeed, many parables are set in the context of a confrontation between Jesus and the religious leaders of Israel. Jesus condemns the rebellious religious elite while initiating a new covenant with Israel, as promised in Jeremiah 31:31–34.

In addition to revealing truth to those capable of understanding, parables also *conceal* truth from the rebellious. Quoting Isaiah 6:9–10, Jesus reminds His listeners of a time when God, as a form of judgment, said He would not allow the people to hear the word of salvation. Their pride had drawn them away from Him, and He would allow them to experience the consequences. The same was true of those too arrogant or insensitive to comprehend God's truth contained in the parables. Martin Luther wrote that the use of Isaiah 6:9–10 by Jesus shows that "divine foreknowledge is referred to, that God conceals and reveals to whom He will and whom He had in mind from eternity" (*Complete Sermons of Martin Luther Vol. 1.2* [Grand Rapids: Baker Book House, 2000], p. 123).

Demystifying Mark

The parables are the means through which God provides two opposing works: revelation and concealment. In the revelation of the kingdom of God, His people are trained and instructed in the requirements of the kingdom. In the concealment of the kingdom, those who oppose God are prevented, as a form of punishment, from ever understanding the true nature and requirements of the kingdom. Unless one understands this dual purpose of the parables, there will be no proper interpretation, and therefore the clear and intended meaning of the parables will be lost.

THE REAL MEANING

Jesus' questions to His disciples are not meant to discourage them, but to force them to consider the real meaning of parables as well as the state of their hearts. If they don't provide "good soil" for the seed He is spreading, how can they ever understand what He is trying to teach?

Jesus' explanation of the parable provides surprising insight. The symbolism of the sower is not explained, but the context indicates he is Jesus. Seed is the Word of God. Soils are different kinds of hearers. Birds represent Satan. Thorns are the worries of life. No wonder Jesus tells everyone to pay close attention!

Jesus seems to say that there are those who can hear His message, respond for days, months, or even years, and still not have the gospel take root in their lives. But those who hear and respond will bear spiritual fruit, with varying yields.

APPLYING THE PARABLE

The Parable of the Sower sets the stage for the ministry of Jesus and the kingdom of God on earth. Jesus' follow-up statements make direct application of the parable to the lives of the disciples. It is very important to understand the application because it lays the groundwork for the work of the apostles and believers who would follow.

Jesus explains that He and His followers are providing light to the world (4:21), yet light serves little use if it is hidden. Their challenge would be to let the light of God shine brightly. As spiritual light is provided, the hidden mysteries of God would be revealed. Although Jesus is using parables to intentionally keep some of the mysteries of God hidden from those who resist His ministry, soon the truth will become clear and brought out into the open (4:22).

Jesus concludes with another warning to pay close attention to the Parable of the Sower, because the better His hearers understand the revelation of this mystery, the more opportunity they will have to proclaim it (4:24–25). As they respond to the teaching of Jesus, they will be given responsibility commiserate to their understanding. Verse 25 is frequently taken out of context and used to create unfounded financial formulas, but Jesus is speaking of comprehension and ministry. In what may be a veiled reference to Judas, Jesus concludes by warning that whoever does not understand these truths will lose his or her ministry.

Take It Home

The Parable of the Sower raises questions for every reader:

- Which of the soils best represents my responsiveness to the Word of God?
- Am I hard-hearted to the extent that it never sinks in to begin with?
- Was I eager to respond at one time, but now rootless and dry?
- Do I allow people and circumstances to capture all my attention, so that God's Word gets choked out?

MARK 4:26–34

MORE PARABLES ABOUT SEEDS

The Parable of the Growing Seed	4:26–29
The Parable of the Mustard Seed	4:30–34

Setting Up the Section

Mark follows Jesus' Parable of the Sower (4:1–25) with two more related parables about seeds. Both are short, yet each one provides a bit more information about the kingdom of God.

📄 4:26–29

THE PARABLE OF THE GROWING SEED

The Parable of the Growing Seed is the only parable unique to Mark's Gospel. Like the Parable of the Sower, it presents a comprehensive picture of the coming of God's kingdom: sowing, growing, and harvesting. The emphasis, however, is on the growing stage. The opening statement (4:26) could be literally interpreted "The kingdom of God is as follows: It is like. . . "

The initial phase of the growing seed occurs when the sower scatters seed on the ground. In phase two the sower is present, but not active. He has planted the seed and left it to germinate, sprout, and grow. Meanwhile, he goes about his other daily duties. The soil ("the ground") produces grain, which develops to maturity in successive stages in a way the sower cannot understand. The growth occurs without visible cause, without the help of human intervention. It is God who works in the life-bearing seed that, when planted in good soil, grows stage by stage and produces grain.

The sower's ultimate interest is in phase three, the harvesting of the seed. When the grain is ripe, the sower immediately puts the sickle to it.

The point of this parable is that as the disciples work to "scatter the seed" (NIV) of the gospel, the ultimate results are the work of God. The sowers are not in charge of the hearts of the people, nor can they change others. All they can do is scatter the seed and trust God for the outcome. Followers of Jesus must understand that they do not cause the harvest; but they must spread the seed.

📄 4:30–34

THE PARABLE OF THE MUSTARD SEED

Although an herb, the mustard plant begins as a tiny seed and can grow to heights of ten to twelve feet with a stalk three to four inches in diameter. It is clear that the mustard plant symbolizes the extreme contrast between the tiny beginning and ultimate result of the kingdom of God. Mark is writing his Gospel at a time near the beginning of the growth cycle when the kingdom might not have appeared very significant in contrast to other earthly kingdoms such as the Roman Empire. Yet this parable points to a much greater impact to come.

Critical Observation

The mustard seed was not literally the smallest seed in the world (though it may have been the smallest known in Palestine). However, it was used proverbially to indicate small size (much as we might refer to the head of a pin). Bible critics might point to Jesus' statement that the mustard seed is "the smallest of all seeds" (4:31 NLT) and declare that the Bible contains errors. But Jesus was merely using a popular idiom to better communicate with His listeners.

Some people misinterpret this parable, questioning whether the growth depicted is desirable and pointing out that birds are sometimes symbols of evil. They suggest that an abnormally large herb with its branches filled with birds represents an overgrown, apostate, institutional church.

Yet such an interpretation is completely at odds with the two previous parables and as a description of "the kingdom of God" (4:30). The reference to the birds merely implies that just as birds inhabit a large tree, so, too, will people take rest and comfort in the great work of God that had such a humble beginning.

Mark concludes this section by pointing out that he is only recording a few of the parables that Jesus told (4:33). And he makes it clear that even though the crowds might have been confused by some of the things Jesus was saying in His parables, He later explained everything to the disciples when they were alone.

Take It Home

Jesus compares the growth of the kingdom of God to a seed that is planted and then grows on its own. Nothing people do can hasten its growth. In light of this teaching, how do you feel about the emphasis many churches put on growth and the tendency to measure success with numbers? Do you think Jesus was downplaying evangelism? If not, how do you think evangelism fits into what He is saying?

MARK 4:35–5:20

JESUS' ACTIONS VERIFY HIS TEACHINGS

Even the Wind and Waves Obey Him!	4:35–41
Helping a Wild Man	5:1–20

Setting Up the Section

Mark follows three parables about the kingdom of God (the Sower, the Growing Seed, and the Mustard Seed) with accounts of four miracles of Jesus. The miracles are signs that the kingdom of God is near, revealing the power of Jesus as the Son of God. It would take a long time for people to truly understand, but from the beginning, Jesus' works vindicated His words.

4:35–41

EVEN THE WIND AND WAVES OBEY HIM!

Most of the recorded miracles of Jesus were healings and exorcisms. This miracle, however, is important because it establishes Jesus' authority over nature just as His healings show His power over humanity. Jesus is the Lord of nature as much as He is Lord of individuals.

Jesus had been teaching in a boat (4:1). When He finished, He and the disciples decided to cross the Sea of Galilee and leave the crowd behind.

Critical Observation

The Sea of Galilee was—and still is—infamous for sudden squalls. Surrounded by mountains at most points, the waters swirl violently when a strong wind bears down. A storm can swell up with little advance warning.

After a long day of ministry, Jesus is tired and fell asleep. He continues sleeping even as a furious squall arises, nearly swamping the boat. Jesus' sound sleep demonstrates two things: (1) His humanity, as He felt fatigue just as humans would; (2) a confidence in God that allowed Him to rest as those around Him were panicking.

Finally the disciples wake Him, filled with fear (4:38). Remember that the group included a number of veteran fishermen, so this must have been quite a severe storm. The disciples rebuke Jesus for not caring about them. Jesus responds by rebuking the storm. (He had used very similar words to cast out an evil spirit on a previous occasion [1:25].)

The disciples should have been catching on by this point that Jesus was doing things only God could do. God's power to calm a storm is mentioned specifically in Psalm 107:29–30, so Jesus rightly questions the disciples on their faith. Their "terrified" response (4:41 NIV) reveals that they acknowledged an experiential glimpse into the real nature of Jesus. Their fear stemmed from a sudden understanding that they had met divine power in this teacher. They knew Jesus was a great man with great power, yet they never imagined *this* kind of power could exist.

They were astounded, but their faith remained weak. Mark will show his readers that the mystery of who Jesus is will continue to be an issue up to His death, resurrection, and beyond. It would take the resurrection of Jesus and the indwelling of the Holy Spirit to get His followers to see Him clearly.

📖 5:1–20

HELPING A WILD MAN

After the brief but terrifying storm subsides, Jesus and the disciples continue sailing across the lake. No sooner do they get out of the boat than Jesus is encountered by a man with an evil spirit. Based on their locale, the possessed man is probably a Gentile.

Demystifying Mark

Ancient Greek manuscripts, translations, and quotations vary on the location of this passage. Most likely, Mark is referring to a known village on the eastern shore. The village has steep hills and cave-tombs about a mile to the south. But one thing is for sure: This event occurred in Gentile territory—the first of Mark's account set outside of Palestine.

The word translated "evil spirit" (5:2 NIV, NLT) literally means "unclean spirit" (KJV, NASB, NKJV, NRSV, ESV). The ancients believed that the caves where people were buried were dwelling places of demons. The description of the man (5:3–5) emphasizes the demonic destruction of his personality to the point of insanity and the ostracism and brutal treatment he had received from his townspeople.

The demon within the man recognizes Jesus (5:7) and is afraid. In contrast to the disciples' recent fear that was based on their ignorance, the demon's fear is a result of knowing with whom he is dealing.

The spirit gives his name as "Legion," which was a term used to describe a Roman force of 4,000 to 6,000 men. It is unclear whether the word in this sense refers to a proper name, an arrogant boast, or an attempt to avoid providing an actual name. The usual interpretation is that many demons actually possessed this man.

The demon(s) realize Jesus is in complete control of what is going to happen. Rather than being cast out of the area, they beg to move into a nearby herd of pigs. When Jesus grants them permission, the entire group of 2,000 pigs runs directly into the lake and drowns (5:13).

The man, now freed of his demonic tormentors, is most grateful. He begs to go with Jesus, an indication that he realizes Jesus is not only a miracle worker, but someone to be followed. Jesus denies his request but gives him a different mission—one that is assigned to every disciple (5:19).

The surrounding townspeople are not so happy, however. They have not only just lost a significant source of income, but they are afraid of Jesus. Because of their superstitions, they are terrified of anyone displaying so much power, so they beg Jesus to leave.

This account shows that, even as important as Jesus' miracles are in Mark's presentation of the ministry of Jesus, they do not always serve to prove who Jesus is or to compel faith. The primary response in this case was fear. Yet the wild man was widely known, and the personal testimony of his healing would have a dramatic effect in the area.

The Decapolis (5:20) was a loosely connected group of ten Gentile cities that had been set free from Jewish domination by the Roman general Pompey when he occupied Palestine in 63 BC. Mark probably saw the healed man as the first missionary to the Gentiles and a preview of the Gentile mission that flourished during the quarter century before the writing of his Gospel.

Take It Home

As Mark shows us, ignorance of who Jesus really is can create a response of fear. However, clear insight into who He is can as well. Which case do you think is true of more people you know today? Is the fear of God based on what they don't know about Him, or on what they do?

MARK 5:21–43

A PLANNED AND AN IMPROMPTU MIRACLE

Setting Up the Section

Mark has been presenting Jesus as the Son of God, and as such, the only way to salvation. He has just shown Jesus' power over nature (4:35–41) and over demons (5:1–20). He continues now by emphasizing Jesus' power over sickness and death.

Here is another example of Mark's sandwiching technique. In this case, he interposes the story of the woman with the bleeding disorder into the story of the healing of Jairus's daughter. Examples of Mark's sandwiching in the Gospel are 4:1–20; 5:21–43; 6:7–29; 11:12–25; 14:1–11; 14:53–72.

📖 5:21–24

A HELPLESS FATHER

Jesus and the apostles have come back across the Sea of Galilee (5:21) after His healing of the demon-possessed man in Gentile territory. He is quite possibly back in Capernaum, and certainly among another Jewish crowd that knows His reputation and is eager to be around Him.

One who came with a specific request is a synagogue ruler named Jairus, but his request is not for himself. He knew of Jesus' reputation for laying hands on people to heal them, and his twelve-year-old daughter (5:42) is near death.

A synagogue ruler was an important and highly respected person. In some cases, Jesus faced strong opposition from leaders of synagogues (Luke 13:14), but this man shows surprising faith. What set Jairus apart from other leaders, and from the scribes and Pharisees in general, is that he believed Jesus could, and would, heal someone he loved.

Jairus implores Jesus to come heal his daughter, and Jesus starts off with him. As usual, a large crowd presses in on Jesus as He walks.

📖 5:25–34

A DESPERATE WOMAN

One person in the crowd actually shouldn't be there: a woman with a twelve-year bleeding issue. Mark isn't specific as to her problem, but it was probably uterine bleeding, which would have made her ceremonially unclean. She would have been an outcast for twelve years, with people having no contact with her, and yet here she is among the crowd.

Her desperation is understandable. She had been to numerous doctors and had only gotten worse (5:26). She had in mind to quietly walk up to Jesus, touch His clothes, and be healed. And as soon as she touched Him, that's exactly what happened (5:28–29)! Keep in mind that Mark has just shown how Jesus' family rejected Him, His disciples did not fully understand who He was, and the Gentiles were afraid of Him. Yet this unidentified, unclean, and very sick woman trusts Him completely.

The miracle is extraordinary because it takes place without conscious effort on Jesus' part. As Jesus realizes that healing power has left His body, He asks who has touched Him (5:30). It must have seemed a crazy question to the disciples and most of the swarming crowd. Yet the woman knew what He meant and confesses, somewhat fearfully.

Jesus gently assures her. He offers her more than just physical healing. He gives her peace of mind and security that her faith was placed in the right person. She goes away healed, both physically and spiritually.

📄 5:35–43

HOPE IN THE FACE OF DEATH

Just as the woman is leaving with fresh joy and peace, some messengers from Jairus's house are arriving to let him know it is too late, that his daughter has died. They assume Jesus' time would be better spent elsewhere (5:35). Jesus hears, but ignores them. He tells Jairus to "just believe" (5:36 NIV).

Upon arrival at Jairus's house, Jesus' comment about the girl not being dead but asleep (5:39) is met with scoffing laughter by the mourners. So He takes only the girl's parents along with Peter, James, and John into the girl's room with Him. This inner circle of disciples is singled out on other significant occasions as well (9:2; 14:33; etc.).

Consider that Jesus could have made a public display of bringing the girl back to life, silencing and shaming His critics. But it is a private moment, an incredible miracle to be witnessed only by those with considerable faith. At Jesus' command, the dead girl immediately stands up and walks (5:42).

Critical Observation

It was not unusual to have professional mourners at funerals to provide profuse commotion and wailing (5:39), although in this instance there might not have been time to procure them. The Jewish *Mishna* (completed about AD 220), quotes Rabbi Judah as saying that for a burial, even the poorest in Israel should hire two or more flutes and one weeping woman. A ruler of the synagogue, of course, was not likely a poor man and could probably afford professional mourners.

Jesus instructs the parents to feed the girl and not to tell anyone what He has done (5:43). He wants no publicity. Yet this healing—the resurrection of the dead—represents a crescendo of Jesus' ministry. Mark emphatically makes his point that Jesus is the Son of God, proven by His power over nature, evil spirits, disease, and even death.

Take It Home

Both of these miracles require an undistracted faith. Is your faith distracted by love of this world or fear that God's plan is not the best plan for your life? What might you do to remove the distractions that hinder your faith?

- How strong would you say your own faith in Jesus is at this point in your life?
- On a scale of 1 (least) to 10 (most), how would you rate it?
- What might you do to increase your faith?

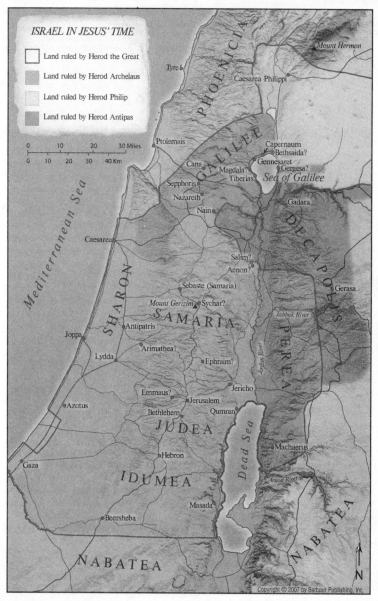

ISRAEL IN JESUS' TIME

Land ruled by Herod the Great

Land ruled by Herod Archelaus

Land ruled by Herod Philip

Land ruled by Herod Antipas

MARK 6:1–30

REJECTION INCREASES

Setting Up the Section

As more and more people who witnessed Jesus' ministry struggled with their faith, it was natural to expect a degree of rejection. We have seen that the Gentiles responded to Him in fear, the disciples are running hot and cold, and the Jews see Him as a miracle worker but are slow to respond in obedience and faith. This passage will provide some additional instances of rejection—a preview of what will become an increasing trend.

This section includes yet one more example of Mark's tendency to sandwich one story into another in order to make a point. In this case, both episodes—the news about John's death in the midst of the sending out of the disciples—demonstrate the role of a true disciple.

📖 6:1–6

REJECTION AT HOME

In bringing a fearful father's daughter back to life and healing a woman who had suffered for twelve years (5:21–43), Jesus witnesses two examples of great faith followed by gratitude for what He has done. He then goes home to Nazareth (6:1), where things change drastically.

Because He is a well-known speaker and healer, Jesus is invited to speak at His hometown synagogue. A large crowd is there. The people are amazed at His teaching (6:2), but not in a positive way. Instead, they question His credentials. They knew Him as well as anyone and were aware that He had never studied with a rabbi. They consider Him nothing more than an ordinary craftsman—no different than His brothers and sisters, and no better than anyone else in Nazareth.

This is Mark's last reference to Jesus' teaching in a synagogue. Jesus knew the people were offended, so He quotes a popular proverb (6:4). In spite of all the acclaim He is receiving throughout Israel, He is utterly rejected in His hometown. As a result of the lack of faith, He heals only a few people and then moves on (6:5–6). In fact, there is so little faith that Jesus is *amazed* (6:6). They don't merely doubt Him; they aggressively reject Him.

📖 6:6–13

THE APOSTLES ARE SENT OUT IN PAIRS

After such rejection in Nazareth, Jesus and the disciples start going from village to village. His emphasis during this time is on teaching. It is through His teaching that people hear the

Word of God, and through hearing the message of salvation that they can respond in faith (Romans 10:14–15).

At this time Jesus sends out the disciples to share the message He has been preaching. They travel in pairs, which was a common Jewish practice. Jesus gives them authority to speak for Him, and power over evil spirits.

Jesus' instructions (6:8–11) suggest the urgency of their mission and the necessity of trusting God for provisions. The bag they are prohibited from taking might refer to either a beggar's bag or a knapsack. The extra tunic probably is an outer garment often used as a blanket. This is a mission of faith in which the disciples will be dependent on God providing for them through the hospitality of their hosts.

The purpose of the injunction in verse 10 is to prevent the travelers from moving if they happen to find better accommodations in the same town. Yet they weren't expected to stay where they weren't welcome. In that case, the disciples were to move on.

Demystifying Mark

Jews returning to their homeland from other countries would remove the foreign dust from their shoes and clothing in order not to defile the land. Jesus adopted this symbolic action in the tradition of the ancient prophets to indicate first a warning and then judgment if rejection of the message and messengers persisted.

The six pairs of disciples go out with the same message of repentance (6:12) that had begun with John the Baptist (1:4) and Jesus (1:15). They heal the sick and drive out demons (6:13). Oil (usually olive oil) was often used medicinally, although here the anointing probably serves as a symbol of the presence, grace, and power of God.

📖 6:14–29

THE DEATH OF JOHN THE BAPTIST

When Herod hears of the power of Jesus and His followers, he grows worried that John the Baptist has risen from the dead, so Mark provides us with the account of John's death at this point. It's also an early warning that the preaching of the gospel can be so offensive to some that it would cause those who proclaimed the truth to lose their lives.

Critical Observation

The Herod of this account was Herod Antipas, the tetrarch of Galilee and Perea from 4 BC to AD 39 (Luke 3:1). He should be distinguished from Herod the Great, his father, who was the Roman client-king of all Palestine from 40 BC to 4 BC and from Herod Agrippa I, who was client-king from AD 41–44. Herod is called "king" (Mark 6:14), but the title is a token of respect. Technically, Herod was only the regional governor.

It seems that Herod has fallen in love with his sister-in-law, Herodias, and has divorced his wife and convinced Herodias to divorce her husband in order to get married. John the Baptist has criticized the marriage, and Herodias wants to have him killed. Herod believes John to be a righteous and holy man (6:20), but he has him arrested and imprisoned to keep him out of the public eye. But even in prison, Herod likes to listen to John preach.

However, Herodias sees an opportunity at Herod's birthday banquet. She has her daughter (named Salome, according to the historian Josephus) perform a dance for the assembled group of "leading men of Galilee" (6:21 NIV, NASB, ESV). We can speculate that the dance was seductive and the dinner guests inebriated. At any rate, Herod promises the young dancer anything. At her mother's urging, she asks for the head of John the Baptist on a platter (6:25). With all eyes on him, Herod has little choice but to comply, even though he is distressed. John's disciples come to claim his body and bury him.

📄 **6:30**

THE REPORT OF THE DISCIPLES

It's interesting that Mark inserts the story of John the Baptist between the sending out of the apostles and their report. No doubt they were encouraged and amazed to have experienced the power of Jesus in their individual ministries. But the death of John seems to foreshadow their report. Indeed, most of them would also eventually die martyrs' deaths.

Take It Home

Do you know anyone who has at some point attempted a purely faith-based ministry like the apostles did in this account? If so, what was the result? How do you think it would feel to go from town to town with no assets and no plans? What do you think Jesus was trying to teach His followers?

MARK 6:31–56

AN UNUSUAL STROLL AFTER AN UNUSUAL MEAL

The Miraculous Meal	6:31–44
The Miraculous Lake Crossing	6:45–56

Setting Up the Section

Mark has just reported on the death of John the Baptist and the sending out of the apostles. Now he returns to focus on Jesus. With two more amazing miracles, Jesus is still trying to teach His disciples who He really is, yet they are still slow to comprehend.

THE MIRACULOUS MEAL

After their return from ministering to the surrounding villages, the apostles are weary. They had hoped to retreat to a quiet place and rest (6:31), but the crowds won't allow it. Even when they leave on a boat, the people note the direction they are headed and run "from all the towns" (6:33 NIV, NASB, ESV) to get there ahead of them. But arriving to find large crowds doesn't upset Jesus. Instead, He sees their spiritual need, has compassion, and begins to teach them.

Demystifying Mark

"Sheep without a shepherd" (6:34 NIV) is an Old Testament image of Israel without spiritual leadership (Numbers 27:17; 1 Kings 22:17; Ezekiel 34:5). Jesus is pictured as the Good Shepherd who feeds the new Israel since its current spiritual leadership was not doing the job. Jesus understood the excitement of the people as they listened to the Word of God and saw His power applied to the sick and hurting among them.

The word translated "compassion" is used in the New Testament only by or about Jesus. It is an emotion that compels action, not merely a feeling of pity. Jesus saw not only physical need but also spiritual lostness. So first He feeds the crowds with His teaching and then addresses their physical hunger.

The disciples see a problem arising, and try to head it off (6:35–36). But rather than sending the people home, Jesus tells the apostles to feed them. Having just returned from their mission, they should have had a sense of what God was capable of doing. But rather than using faith, they figure out how much it would cost to feed everyone and determine it can't be done!

Jesus sends them to collect whatever food they can find, which turns out to be meager indeed (6:38). The loaves are smaller and flatter than modern bread. The fish are dried and salted. And the headcount is 5,000 men (plus women and children).

The "green grass" (6:39) suggests springtime in Palestine, which would have placed this event sometime around Passover. And the terminology befits a Passover meal, as it does the Lord's Supper: "taking," "gave thanks," "broke," "gave" (6:41 NIV). Jesus miraculously provides not only enough food to fill everyone but also enough to collect baskets of leftovers (6:42–43). Parallels to this event include Elisha's feeding of a hundred men with twenty barley loaves and some grain (2 Kings 4:42–44) and the miraculous feeding of the people of Israel with manna in the desert (Exodus 16; Numbers 11).

THE MIRACULOUS LAKE CROSSING

The disciples were tired before this event, so afterward they must have been exhausted. Jesus has them get in a boat and head toward Bethsaida. He was going to spend a little more time with the people and then have a private time of prayer. From His prayer spot on the mountainside, Jesus can probably see His followers struggling to row against the wind.

Critical Observation

Mark used Roman standards of timekeeping in this passage. The Jews divided a night into three watches, the Romans four. The first watch was 6:00 p.m. to 9:00 p.m., the second 9:00 p.m. until midnight, the third midnight until 3:00 a.m., and the fourth between 3:00 a.m. and 6:00 a.m.

In the wee hours of the morning, Jesus walks across the lake, catching up with the disciples. The Old Testament spoke of God walking on water (Job 9:8; 38:16), and Jesus is proving it true. It is debated what is meant by, "He was about to pass by them" (6:48 NIV). Some suggest it means He was going to outpace them so they would acknowledge His greatness. More likely, He simply wanted to pass in view of the disciples so they would see Him.

They certainly see Him, and they become terrified (6:49–50), thinking He must be a ghost. Mark makes a somewhat harsh notation that the apostles' hearts were hardened and that they didn't really understand the miracle that Jesus had just performed with the loaves and fish (6:52). So when Jesus identifies Himself with "It is I" (6:50), perhaps it is a reflection of God's identification of Himself to Moses as "I AM WHO I AM" (Exodus 3:14).

The notation that the disciples were "greatly amazed" (6:51 NKJV) makes the point that they should have learned by now that nothing was beyond the power of Jesus, because the power of Jesus was the power of God.

In contrast to the developing faith of the disciples is the response of the crowds when the boat lands (6:53–56). What is not stated, but implied, is that their reaction to Jesus is faith-inspired. The "fringe of his cloak" (6:56 NASB) was probably the tassel that pious Jews wore in accordance with Numbers 15:38–41 and Deuteronomy 22:12. And the word translated "cured" can also be interpreted as "saved," indicating that Mark saw in physical healing a sign of spiritual healing as well.

Take It Home

One might think that the apostles would have the best insight into the true character of Jesus and what He was capable of doing. Yet in spite of everything they had seen to this point—healings, exorcisms, the calming of a storm, feeding the 5,000, and even a resurrection from the dead—they were still disturbed and amazed to see Him walking on water. Why do you think this was true? And do you think the same thing happens today? In spite of their personal experience, do believers still tend to place limits on what they feel God can or will do?

MARK 7:1–23

CLARIFYING SOME TWISTED LAWS

Setting Up the Section

Mark has just described a phenomenal response to Jesus' healing ministry (6:54–56). The stir concerning Jesus has led to the hope—if not outright belief—that the Messiah had arrived. But the ruling religious authorities would never support anyone who did not believe exactly as they did. The things Jesus did were always within the law God had given Moses, yet they did not always conform to the numerous laws that had been tacked on over the centuries. Consequently, a perpetual state of conflict resulted.

📖 7:1–13

TO WASH OR NOT TO WASH

This time the Pharisees' complaint is that Jesus' followers eat meals before washing their hands. The issue is not one of hygiene but of ritual purity and is an excellent case in point to describe how oral law had become much more stringent than what Moses had recorded. In the Old Testament, priests had been instructed to wash prior to certain ceremonies (Exodus 30:17–21; 40:12). But by the first century, the scribes and Pharisees had started washing before every meal and apparently expected everyone else to do so as well. In addition, they call for the washing of "cups, pitchers, and kettles" (7:4 NIV, NLT). Mark provides a parenthetical explanation of their habits (7:3–4).

The "tradition of the elders" (7:3) is a reference to the oral, scribal interpretation of the written, Mosaic law. These laws were later collected and recorded in the Mishna (ca. AD 220). The "elders" were scribes, Pharisees, leaders of synagogues, and revered persons in general.

In response to the Pharisees' query, Jesus quotes Isaiah 29:13 (Mark 7:6–7) to clarify that external observance of religious ceremony is no substitute for inward piety. Their insistence on external righteousness is not in accordance with the scriptures, and they are missing the whole point. It is they who were unclean and not Jesus' disciples.

Critical Observation

Not every Old Testament passage quoted in the New Testament is word for word. That's because the New Testament writers used the Septuagint—a Greek translation of the Hebrew Bible.

But Jesus doesn't stop with the Isaiah passage. He labels His critics as hypocrites (7:6) and accuses them of substituting human tradition for God-given law (7:8). He also gives a specific example to show how ludicrous their traditions have become.

Demystifying Mark

"Corban" (7:11) is the English transliteration of the Greek transliteration of a Hebrew word meaning "a gift dedicated to God." The Hebrew word occurs about 80 times in Leviticus, Numbers, and Ezekiel. Corban was an offering that involved an irrevocable vow of dedication to God. As a result, the thing offered to God could not be used for any other purpose. However, there was no prescribed way the offering had to be used, so what was supposedly a sacred vow to God had actually become a loophole to impede observance of other clear laws of God.

It seems that it had become common practice to make an offering of one's financial wealth and devote it to God by invoking a vow (Corban). It sounds quite spiritual and selfless. But what such an action actually meant was that the person would retain his wealth throughout his life, and it would go to the temple/priests when he died. If his parents needed assistance in their old age, the person could refuse to provide funds because they were set aside for God. This twisted tradition was just a way to sidestep the clear command to honor one's mother and father.

Notice the progression Jesus describes: First the Pharisees have "let go" of God's law (7:8 NIV), then have become experts at "setting aside" the commands of God (7:9 NASB), and eventually "making void" the word of God (7:13 NRSV, ESV) with their improper traditions. Furthermore, the rigidity of the Corban vow was not an isolated instance of scribal manipulation of the law, but only one of many instances. The Pharisees used their traditions for their own profit and glory—not God's.

7:14–23

THE SOURCE OF "UNCLEANNESS"

At this point Jesus broadens His conversation from just the Pharisees to include the surrounding crowd. The scriptures dealing with "clean" and "unclean" foods (Leviticus 11; Deuteronomy 14:1–21) had been creating questions and confusion that would continue to be addressed by the early church for a number of years. But here Jesus makes it clear that food is not the real issue. Impurity, He says, is not the result of failing to follow a ritual, but rather is the condition of an unredeemed and unregenerate heart.

(Depending on the manuscript used for translation, some Bibles omit 7:16. This statement is not found in the earliest and best manuscripts.)

Jesus' disciples seek further clarification of what He is saying (7:17). Jesus thinks they should comprehend Him by now, yet explains that the real problem with uncleanness is not the result of eating an unclean animal or eating approved food with unwashed hands. Such food goes through the body without affecting the state of the heart. The "heart" in the Bible is a symbol of the rational, intellectual, decision-making element in human beings rather than the emotional, affectionate element.

Jesus goes on to explain that the source of uncleanness is already inside a person. He provides specific examples: evil thoughts, sexual immorality, theft, murder, adultery, greed, malice, deceit, lewdness, envy, slander, arrogance and folly (7:21–22). His point is that uncleanness is moral rather than ritual.

At this point in his Gospel (7:19), Mark inserts a parenthetical comment that Jesus' statements are a declaration that all foods are from then on considered "clean." After Jesus' resurrection, Peter will soon receive a confirmation of this new concept (Acts 10:9–23).

Take It Home

The religious segment of society had gotten off track in Jesus' time. By trying so hard to adhere to rules and laws, the religious had gone astray. Spiritual laws had been stretched so far that they became a burden for people. Legalism impeded the freedom God intended for His people—and perhaps it still does. Do you see similar problems in the church today? In your own life, do you find following God to be something of a burden, or is it a freeing experience?

MARK 7:24–37
OVERWHELMED WITH AMAZEMENT

Crumbs Are Enough   7:24–30
Deaf and Speechless No More   7:31–37

Setting Up the Section

After Jesus' debate with the religious leaders over the issue of "clean" versus "unclean," Mark follows with two accounts of miracles in Gentile territory. Jesus is teaching that purity has more to do with the condition of one's heart than the adherence to legal rules and ceremonies. This concept will become clearer as a ministry to the Gentiles is initiated.

📖 7:24–30

CRUMBS ARE ENOUGH

Tyre was a city on the Phoenician coast about thirty-five miles northwest of the Sea of Galilee. No explanation is provided for why Jesus goes there, other than perhaps to attempt to escape the crowds and be alone for a while. If that is His intent, it doesn't work (7:24).

A woman finds out Jesus is in the area and rushes to ask Him to heal her daughter who is possessed by an evil spirit. Prostration (7:25) was a sign of both grief and reverence. By falling at His feet, the woman is showing the utmost respect for Jesus.

This woman was from Syrian Phoenicia, not to be confused with Libyan or Carthagenian Phoenicia, which was located in North Africa. Phoenicia (modern Lebanon) was part of the Roman province of Syria. It was Gentile territory. That fact, coupled with the condition of her daughter, would indicate an emphatic state of ritual uncleanness. Still, the woman approaches Jesus with a request.

Critical Observation

Jews often used the word *dogs* to refer to Gentiles, and even though it seems out of character for Jesus to have done so, He almost certainly used it in this way (7:27). The harshness of the statement is softened somewhat by the use of the diminutive form that could indicate "puppies" or "house pets." In context, Jesus' comment was not an insult, but a comparative statement to say that the Jews, for a while, would take precedence over the Gentiles. Paul later echoed this same sentiment (Romans 1:16). And perhaps Jesus' apparent harshness in this case was to test the woman's faith.

When Jesus challenges her "right" to His attention, she responds with intelligence and determination. She does not deny the precedence of Israel, but also suggests that the Gentiles can be included as well. Even "dogs" get scraps under the dinner table, she says, indicating that Jesus' willingness to perform a miracle for her daughter will not in any way diminish the ministry He is doing among the Jews.

Although this account says nothing about the woman's faith, it is certainly implied in Jesus' statement. Jesus responds to her and grants her request. When she gets home, she finds her daughter well, with the demon gone (7:30).

📖 7:31–37

DEAF AND SPEECHLESS NO MORE

Mark describes Jesus as traveling from Tyre to Sidon and then to the Sea of Galilee and the region of the Decapolis (7:31). This would be like going from Chicago to Dallas via Minneapolis. We can speculate that since Jesus has been hoping to escape the crowds (7:24), He may have chosen a circuitous route. He is still beyond Israelite territory in the lands of the Gentiles.

A group brings a deaf and mute man to Jesus (7:32), but He takes the man aside, away from the crowd. Jesus is going to heal the man, but doesn't want the crowds to misinterpret the miracle. The miracle will be a sign authenticating Him as being the Messiah, not an indication that the earthly kingdom of God had arrived in its fullness where everyone could expect to walk around in perfect bodies.

Demystifying Mark

Ancient healing practices included touching a person, using saliva, uttering deep groans—all of which Jesus did in this account. However, this in no way suggests that Mark invented the details to conform to the usual practice. Because Jesus could not communicate with the man through ordinary methods (speech and hearing), it would be natural for Him to express His concern through touch.

Jesus first opens the man's ears. Mark provides us the interpretation of the Aramaic word *Ephphatha* (7:34). Only after his ears are "opened" is he able to speak. This miracle illustrates a running theme in Mark: Only those who have ears to hear can speak with faith.

After enabling the man to speak clearly, Jesus commanded him and his friends not to tell anyone (7:36). But who could blame this no-longer-mute man for telling others what had happened to him? The witnesses were "overwhelmed with amazement" (7:37 NIV), and the miracle could not be concealed. Mark quotes the people who said, "He has done everything well," (ESV) and "He even makes the deaf hear and the mute speak" (NIV, ESV). These are poetic references to the messianic age (based on Genesis 1:31 and Isaiah 35:5-6). Jesus' admonition to the people to keep quiet is another example of what some refer to as the Messianic Secret. Jesus did not want people talking about His miracles—He did not want His miracles to be seen as the central piece of His ministry. Jesus' miracles were only meant to confirm that He was who He said that He was. Until the cross, the miracles could not be placed within their proper context.

Take It Home

The response of the crowds to the miracles and ministry of Jesus was that they were overwhelmed with amazement (7:37). When is the last time you can remember having a similar response to a work of God in the world or in your life? What might you need to do to be more aware of God's work in life and in the world? Try keeping a record of prayer requests and answers to prayers for one year. How would that help you become more aware of God's work in the world?

MARK 8:1–26

REPEAT PERFORMANCES

Setting Up the Section

Mark 8 includes events similar to those he's already recorded. Mark wanted the reader to see and understand that Jesus was more than a good teacher and was indeed the Lord of the universe. As the disciples witnessed repetition of His miracles, this truth was being reinforced in their lives.

📖 8:1–13

ANOTHER FEEDING OF THE MASSES

Jesus and His disciples are still in the region of the Decapolis, a group of cities populated mainly by Gentiles. Crowd after crowd forms to see and hear Him. In this case, a group has been with Him for three days (8:2). Mark doesn't even mention whether Jesus is teaching or healing. Instead, he moves right to the compassion Jesus feels for the people, who are surely hungry after such a long time.

It is hard for those in the modern western world to perceive a time when food was not readily available, although the same conditions exist in many places outside the western world today. There was a very real danger of collapsing from hunger and exhaustion on the way home, and Jesus wasn't willing to send everyone away without a meal.

The disciples are woefully shortsighted. As soon as Jesus expresses the desire to feed the crowd, they immediately respond with the impossibility of finding enough bread "in this remote place" (8:4 NIV). Lest we forget, they had not so long ago witnessed Jesus feeding a larger crowd with less food (6:30–44). It seems that even though the disciples have witnessed a great number of Jesus' miracles, they are still perceiving them as one-time events rather than seeing Jesus as the divine Son of God.

Jesus instructs the people to sit down, and He gives thanks for the seven loaves and few small fish that are available (8:5–7). He is about to multiply the food, but He does so out of a thankful heart for the provision of His heavenly Father.

The word used to indicate a basket here (8:8) is not the same as the one used previously (6:43). This time the reference is to a large basket made of wicker or rope, used for carrying provisions. So the seven basketfuls of leftovers in this account may well have contained more than the twelve basketfuls in the previous miracle.

The exact location of Dalmanutha (8:10) is not known. A cave in the area called Talmanutha may indicate where Jesus goes with His disciples.

The "sign" the Pharisees request there (8:11) is not another healing, exorcism, or feeding. They want to see some kind of apocalyptic manifestation (the sun disappearing, angels appearing, or some similar sign) that will prove beyond all doubt that Jesus has God's approval. Jesus' response (8:12) is likely a sigh of anger because He knows they aren't sincere in their request—they only want to trip Him up and lessen His influence on the crowds. Jesus did not perform miracles to convince the hard-hearted; He used them to cure those in need and to show compassion on those hurt by sin.

Mark almost certainly sees an indication of Jesus' displeasure toward the Pharisees in His departure (8:13) and perhaps even a symbolic picture of the rejection of Judaism as the divinely approved religion.

📖 8:14–21

THE PROBLEM WITH YEAST

As Jesus and the disciples go back across the sea, He warns them to beware of the "yeast" (or "leaven") of the Pharisees and Herod (8:15). Most references to yeast or leaven in the New Testament almost always are symbolic references to evil. (Matthew 13:33 is one exception.) Just as a little yeast changes the complete nature of dough, so, too, a slight influence of pharisaical teachings could corrupt the truth of the gospel.

In spite of everything the disciples have seen Jesus do, they are coming dangerously close to unbelief. Even in response to Jesus' comment, they misunderstand and think He is speaking about their shortage of bread. The disciples no doubt are aware of the evil influence of Herod, but Jesus is saying the evil of the Pharisees is just as bad. He chides those closest to Him for still being hard-hearted and failing to see and hear all He has been doing.

Critical Observation

Some people speculate that Jesus may have only performed one great miracle of feeding the masses, which is reported more than once. But in His reasoning with the disciples (8:17–21), He speaks clearly of two separate events.

Jesus' references to eyes that fail to see and ears that fail to hear are reminiscent of Old Testament judgment passages such as Isaiah 6, Jeremiah 5:21, and Ezekiel 12:2. The disciples, like the people of ancient Israel, are failing to comprehend God's presence. In fact, at this point the unbelief of the disciples is bordering on that of Jesus' enemies!

📄 8:22–26

A MIRACLE IN STAGES

This is the one time when Jesus conducts a healing that requires additional attention. Because of where it is in the narrative, it can be considered an object lesson—a physical demonstration of the spiritual condition of Jesus' disciples.

Some people of Bethsaida ask Jesus to heal a blind man. Jesus applies saliva to the man's eyes, lays His hands on him, and asks what he saw (8:23). The man's vision has improved because he can see the shapes of people, but they look "like trees walking around" (8:24 NIV, NLT). Jesus again places His hands on the man, and this time the man can see clearly. Similarly, although the disciples' spiritual "vision" is not yet 20/20, they will eventually come to see clearly who Jesus was.

Take It Home

It's easy to be critical of the disciples who, even after seeing Jesus feed a crowd of at least 5,000 people, were helpless when He gave them the opportunity to feed a smaller crowd. Yet perhaps we do no better. Do you know anyone who has had an encounter with Jesus where they came face-to-face with His greatness, and then went on to live as if it were a one-time event? Or can you recall a recent, seemingly impossible event where you were quick to panic rather than call on the God for whom nothing is impossible?

MARK 8:27–9:1

THE BEGINNING OF THE END

Setting Up the Section

This section of Mark records a significant transition. To this point, Jesus' disciples have witnessed (and even initiated) a number of miracles. They have not only heard Jesus teach, but have also been privy to His interpretation of parables and other private instruction. Yet Jesus has repeatedly pointed out their inability to comprehend exactly who He was and what He was doing. They haven't acted in faith when given the opportunity. But here they begin to understand. As they do, Jesus reveals more of what they can expect ahead of them.

📄 8:27–30

THE GREAT CONFESSION

It was common practice in rabbinic circles for students to ask questions and have the teacher provide the answers. But Jesus would frequently pose a question, as in this case (8:27), and see what his students had to say. This was an essential question to help the disciples solidify who Jesus is, and this was one time when they come up with the correct answer.

Critical Observation

Caesarea Philippi (8:27) was a rebuilt, enlarged version of the ancient city of Paneas, the site of a grotto dedicated to the god Pan. When Herod the Great acquired the territory, he built a temple in Paneas and dedicated it to the emperor Augustus. His successor, Philip the tetrarch, renamed the city for Augustus (Caesar) and for himself. Another city named Caesarea was built on the Mediterranean Sea, but Caesarea Philippi was located in a beautiful setting at the foot of Mt. Hermon next to some gushing springs that were one of the sources of the Jordan River.

A number of popular opinions were being expressed about who Jesus was (8:28; 6:14–16), as had been the case with John the Baptist. While such beliefs expressed a degree of respect and acclaim for Jesus, they were still inadequate. So Jesus goes from the popular opinion to personal opinion by asking His disciples directly: "But what about you? . . .Who do you say I am?" (8:29 NIV).

The answer would reveal a lot in regard to the disciples' spiritual condition. It is not necessary to understand everything about what one believes. For example, a person can believe that a plane can fly and take a cross-country flight without fully understanding the mechanics involved. Similarly, someone can believe Jesus is the Messiah without comprehending all the "hows" involved.

Peter acts as the spokesman for the group, so his confession is as much theirs as it is his. And he affirms their belief that Jesus is "the Christ" (8:29). The term *Christ* has not been used in Mark since the opening verse, so it is especially noteworthy here. Peter's confession of Jesus as the Christ (or Messiah or Anointed One) went beyond that of popular opinion.

Yet we also discover that the disciples still have much to learn. They had a typical Jewish understanding of "the Christ" as a military conqueror who would free them from foreign domination (Acts 1:6). They aren't ready to spread the word about Jesus, so He warns them not to tell anyone (8:30).

SUFFERING AND DEATH

Up to this point Jesus had been revealing the Messiah's power and authority. Here, He begins to reveal His suffering role, clarifying for His followers what was involved in God's plan for the Messiah. It would involve not only suffering at the hands of others, but ultimately His death as well.

Demystifying Mark

We find three predictions of Jesus' death in the middle of Mark's Gospel: 8:31–32; 9:31; and 10:33–34. Clearly, Jesus foresaw His death and resurrection. It was planned, and no mistake or oversight. But because His role as Messiah/Christ was not what people had been expecting, they were slow to catch on to what He was teaching about having to suffer and die.

Jesus' teachings about His death are specific. He makes it clear that it is God's will, and that it will be at the hands of the Jewish leadership. The very nation that brought forth the Messiah will endorse His execution. Yet death will not be the end; "after three days" He will rise again (8:31).

But even after Peter's bold confession, he doesn't want to hear what Jesus is saying about suffering. He is envisioning a victory without suffering, and rebukes Jesus. But Jesus returns the rebuke. His comment to "Get thee behind me" (8:33 KJV) is commonly interpreted as a command for Peter to get out of sight and stop tempting Him. What Peter might plan was not what God had planned, as Jesus goes on to explain.

HUMILITY AND SACRIFICE

Not only will Jesus suffer, but so will His followers. To announce this new concept, Jesus calls the crowd to hear, along with His disciples.

To deny oneself (8:34) is not a call to asceticism, self-rejection, or self-hatred. Rather, it is to replace the desires of self with the will of God, to set aside all personal rights and live for the glory of God and the mission of extending His kingdom.

Denial of self might indeed involve taking up a cross, which would have had a much more severe implication in the first century. Many of Jesus' early followers literally died by crucifixion. Today the phrase is more symbolic, though it should never be cheapened by use in reference to minor irritations or common burdens.

Jesus challenges His listeners to think of long-term effects of their daily choices (8:34–37). Everyone either lives for self or lives for God. While living for self will have certain benefits, none come close to eternal life with a loving God.

Living for Jesus includes speaking up for Him, even when persecuted by a wicked and adulterous generation (8:38). But on the positive side, Jesus makes a promise to "some who are standing here" (9:1 NIV). What does Jesus mean that some will "not taste death before they see the kingdom of God come with power" (NIV)? The answer comes in the next section of Mark (9:2–13).

Take It Home

Peter's confession at Caesarea Philippi was a special moment in his relationship with Jesus (although a bit short-lived). Jesus' closest followers should have a different perspective on Him than the rest of the general population. If Jesus were to ask the same questions today, how would you respond? Who do people say He is? And how about you? Who do you say He is?

MARK 9:2–29

THE UNIQUENESS OF THE CHRIST

Jesus' Transfiguration	9:2–13
A Difficult Exorcism	9:14–29

Setting Up the Section

Context is always important in Mark's Gospel. In the previous passage Jesus has been quite frank about His impending death. Yet from the beginning of his writing, Mark's goal has been to show that Jesus is the Son of God, and death would not be the end. Ultimately, Jesus would be glorified, and we see a preview of that in this section.

9:2–13

JESUS' TRANSFIGURATION

The reference to six days (9:2) is significant. Jesus has revealed to His disciples that He will soon suffer and die, and He challenges the crowds to deny themselves, take up a cross, and follow Him. Yet He also promises that some of those present will not die before they witnessed "the kingdom of God come with power" (9:1 NIV, KJV).

Only six days later, three of those people—Peter, James, and John—are invited to climb a high mountain with Jesus. There He is "transfigured" in their presence. His clothes become supernaturally white, and Moses and Elijah appear and talk with Him.

Demystifying Mark

The "high mountain" referred to in verse 2 is traditionally thought to be Mt. Tabor in lower Galilee. Though only 1,929 feet above sea level, it is compared in the Old Testament to both Mt. Hermon (Psalm 89:12) and Mt. Carmel (Jeremiah 46:18). Mt. Tabor was beautiful, appealing, and convenient for pilgrims. Biblical references to a "high mountain" often indicate places of revelation, which was certainly true in this case.

Transfiguration refers to a radical change in form or appearance. In this account it was a physical change, as Jesus' appearance is temporarily transformed from that of a human being to a divine being in all His glory. In other places where the word is used, it refers to a dramatic moral transformation from sinner to saint (Romans 12:2; 2 Corinthians 3:18).

The Greek text implies that the garment of Jesus becomes "intensely white" (9:3 ESV). The brightness recalls the shekinah glory of God in the Old Testament—a glory beyond physical equal on earth.

Moses and Elijah (9:4) represent the law and the prophets. Jesus was the fulfillment of the ancient scriptures. Christianity would not be a new religion, nor a correction of Judaism. Rather, it is the fulfillment of what had been proclaimed through the Old Testament writings.

Peter isn't always presented well in this account, largely due to fear (9:6). First, on such a significant occasion, he addresses Jesus as "Rabbi," a less flattering title than Lord or Master. Then he asks to erect three "shelters" (9:5 NIV). What was likely intended as a tribute was actually something of a put-down because he was placing Jesus on the same level as Moses and Elijah—who were great men, to be sure, but only men. Peter wanted to capture and preserve the moment, but doing so would have short-circuited the cross. The transfiguration was just a *preview* of Jesus' glory. His true glory would come after, and as a result of, the completion of His mission by dying on the cross.

Critical Observation

The "shelters" Peter wanted to construct were probably similar to those used to commemorate the Feast of Tabernacles. During such times the Israelites would leave their homes to live in "booths" as a reminder of God's deliverance from Egypt (Leviticus 23:39–43; Hosea 12:9).

Even though Peter says and does the wrong thing in the presence of God's glory, we see the mercy of God in that there is no punishment or recrimination for his shortcoming. It *was* a lot to take in. Jesus is transfigured into a state of glory. A cloud envelops the group. A voice from the cloud declares that Jesus is the Son of God and instructs the disciples to listen to Him. No wonder Peter, James, and John are scared.

Then, abruptly, the event is over. The three disciples are alone again with Jesus. As they descend, Jesus is again discussing His death with them, instructing them not to tell anyone what they had just witnessed until He has risen from the dead (9:9). This is the last time Jesus will tell people not to relate what they had seen, and the only time He includes a time limit. But from this instance, we can infer that the reason He had prohibited people from talking (1:43–45; 7:36) was that the magnitude of His miracles could only be fully understood in the context of His death and resurrection. Still, the disciples have little idea what He means (9:10).

They are also confused about the prophecies that Elijah must come prior to the Messiah (9:11). They had just seen Elijah—was that what the prophecies meant? Or is all Jesus' talk of rising from the dead a reference to Elijah?

Jesus explains that Elijah had already come, meaning John the Baptist (Matthew 17:10–13). The prophesied suffering and death would be the burden of the Messiah, not Elijah.

A DIFFICULT EXORCISM

While the three disciples with Jesus are struggling to understand what He is trying to teach them, the nine they left behind are having troubles of their own. A man has brought his demon-possessed son for healing, and they are unable to cast out the spirit. A large crowd has gathered as the teachers of the law argue with the disciples.

The disciples had previously been able to exorcise demons (6:13), and apparently assumed they could do so whenever they wished. But in this case they lack faith. Spiritual power is not a resource that, once possessed, will always be available. It must be maintained and renewed.

Meanwhile, the young man with the spirit is in terrible shape (9:18, 20–22). As Jesus approaches, the evil spirit responds by throwing the youngster into a convulsion. The father feels helpless, and his faith is weak. But Jesus affirms that all things are possible to whomever believes. The father has wisely placed what faith he has in Jesus, so Jesus casts out the demon (9:25–26). The result is that the boy appears dead for a short time, until Jesus takes his hand and helps him up.

The disciples are frustrated and confused about not being able to cast out the demon on their own. While Jesus has spoken about faith on numerous occasions, here He adds the importance of prayer as well (9:29). The two go hand in hand. Prayer is the avenue to faith. The power the disciples lacked could come only from God, and therefore was available only through faith and prayer.

Take It Home

We can take comfort in seeing how long it took the disciples—those who spent the most time in direct contact with Jesus—to understand what He was trying to teach them. Similarly we can rest assured that God is patient and compassionate. We do not have to have everything figured out to be in a relationship with Jesus. What are some of the areas of spiritual life that you tend to struggle with? As you struggle, how strong is your faith? As you struggle, how distracted is your faith? Do you bolster your faith with prayer, scripture, Bible teaching, and Christian fellowship? How do those disciplines help create an undistracted faith?

MARK 9:30–50

GREATNESS: AN EXAMPLE AND SOME OBSTACLES

Setting Up the Section

At this point, Mark indicates that Jesus' public ministry in Galilee is over. This trip through Galilee will be the first leg of His journey to Jerusalem and the cross.

A MODEL OF GREATNESS

Jesus is again seeking privacy for Himself and His disciples, but this time it is not due to danger from Herod (6:14) or the teachers of the law (9:14). Rather, He wants to continue to instruct His disciples about His upcoming betrayal, death, and resurrection. The word *betrayed* (9:31) means "given over" or "handed over." The same word is used to refer to Judas' betrayal of Jesus as well as the fate of the Old Testament prophets, John the Baptist, and eventually Jesus' disciples. Some think the "handing over" in this case was God's delivering His Son over to sinful men to be a sacrifice for sins

Jesus' suffering and death would be the result of a friend's action. Yet Jesus was well aware of what was about to happen. His death was no mistake. It was part of the plan of God, the defining characteristic of His life. And His resurrection would prove that He is both the Son of God and the Messiah.

Mark again emphasizes the dullness of the disciples (9:32). By this time, they are even embarrassed to ask Jesus to explain what He means. Jesus knows their minds are on less noble things. When He asks what they are discussing, they won't respond. But Mark informs us that they are arguing about which of them is the greatest (9:34).

They have come to a house in Capernaum (possibly Peter's and Andrew's home previously mentioned in 1:29), so Jesus sits them down for a serious talk. Perhaps the disciples' debate on greatness was a result of three of them being chosen to accompany Jesus during His transfiguration (9:2–8). They believed Jesus was getting ready to establish an earthly kingdom (Acts 1:6) and were probably seeking key positions within that government. But Jesus quickly corrects their mistaken thinking. His use of a small child (9:36–37) is an object lesson to reinforce what He is saying. To welcome (9:37) such a person is a way of receiving both God and Jesus. Greatness in His kingdom consists not of position, but of ministry.

Critical Observation

In first-century society, the roles of both children and servants were considered lowly. Jesus elevated the role of the servant to the primary position in His kingdom. And He used a child as an example of someone whom His followers should care for, if indeed they cared for Him.

TEAMWORK OR COMPETITION?

The disciples were accustomed to thinking of spiritual leadership in terms of exclusivity. The scribes and Pharisees, for example, were exclusive groups. So when the disciples come upon someone else driving out evil spirits in the name of Jesus, they instruct him to stop. And they tell Jesus, thinking He would be pleased.

But Jesus makes it clear that anyone who does anything sincerely "in My name" is to be accepted as an ally. Jesus is beginning to promote a mind-set of acceptance rather than rejection.

Jesus' reference to "a cup of water" has come to be viewed as a symbolic act of hospitality. Yet in the semiarid climate of the Middle East, the act can just as rightly be interpreted literally. And Jesus quickly shifts the emphasis from the actions of one stranger to include "you" and "anyone" (9:41). While we have our own support groups, we should not be surprised to find people active for the kingdom of God whom we do not know. And perhaps we should be much slower to criticize than were Jesus' disciples.

📄 9:42–50

A STRONG WARNING AGAINST OFFENSES

"One of these little ones" may refer to the child Jesus is holding (9:36) or perhaps to new believers who are spiritually immature and weak. The word translated "millstone" (9:42) refers to a large stone that required a donkey to turn it (as opposed to a smaller stone that women sometimes used).

Jesus makes a subtle shift here, moving from actions that may cause someone else to sin to those that might allow oneself to sin. He uses hyperbole and metaphor (9:43–48) that should not be taken literally. Yet because of the emphasis He places on these instructions, neither should they be ignored. Followers of Jesus must not only watch over others; they must watch over themselves as well.

Believers should do away with harmful habits that endanger spiritual life as completely as a surgeon amputates a limb that endangers the rest of the body. Jesus speaks of hell as a very real place of very real torment, and something to be avoided at any cost.

Demystifying Mark

The word translated "hell" (9:43, 45, 47) is *gehenna*, a Greek transliteration of two Hebrew words meaning "valley of Hinnom." The site was a deep valley on the south and west side of Jerusalem. It had once been a place for child sacrifice to the god Molech, and certain Israelites seem to have adopted the practice during periods of spiritual decline (2 Kings 23:10; Jeremiah 7:31; 32:35). Later it became the garbage and sewage dump of Jerusalem and a symbol of the place of punishment because worms and fires were so closely associated with the location.

"Salted with fire" (9:49) is an unusual phrase, particularly in this context. Jesus has just mentioned *fire* in a sense of judgment and punishment (9:43, 48). Here, however, both fire and salt are symbols of refinement and purification. Jesus has been talking about His own suffering and death (9:31). Here He expands the possibility of persecution to everyone who follows Him.

In conclusion, Jesus teaches that the "salt" of the earth (believers) must not lose what makes it distinctive—its saltiness. The salt gathered from the Dead Sea contained so many impurities that much of it was essentially worthless for providing flavor or preserving foods. Pure salt, however, cannot lose its saltiness.

Jesus is saying that believers must strive to remain salty by welcoming all people, protecting the weak, acknowledging fellow believers, and watching out for their own souls. Much of this would occur·in the context of suffering, but truly "salty" believers would not lose their influence.

Take It Home

Jesus' teachings about greatness were not what His disciples were expecting to hear. Indeed, they still sound strange in modern culture. Can you think of any examples of someone attempting to be "first" by becoming the very "last," and a servant to all? And what do you think are the characteristics of a little child that Jesus wanted the surrounding group of adults to consider?

MARK 10:1–31

THE HEART OF THE MATTER

Setting Up the Section

Every story in Mark 10 deals with the heart of a person (or group) who comes into contact with Jesus. Some hearts are filled with arrogance and self-interest, while others contain childlike faith and eagerness to serve God and His kingdom. This passage (Mark 10:1–31) covers three stories; the following passage (10:32–52) will examine two more.

📖 10:1–12

DIVORCE: A TOUCHY SUBJECT

By this time, it seems that everywhere Jesus went He was the target of the Pharisees and other religious leaders. On this occasion, they "test" Him (10:2) on the topic of divorce. The matter is of extreme interest to the people in the crowd. Herod Antipas and his wife (Herodias) had both gotten divorced to marry each other. (John the Baptist had died for publicly pointing this out [6:17–29]). In addition, two prominent rabbis of the time expressed very different opinions. Therefore, much debate takes place to determine what constituted justifiable grounds for divorce, according to the scriptures.

Demystifying Mark

To better understand the test the Pharisees were giving Jesus, it helps to know that His peers would have been exposed to the teachings of Rabbi Hillel and Rabbi Shammai, two noted scholars born a generation or so before Christ. Both had great wisdom, though they disagreed on a great many topics. For example, after both rabbis had studied Deuteronomy 24:1, the conservative school of Shammai ruled that "something about her that he doesn't like" meant adultery. The liberal school of Hillel, however, claimed that a man could divorce his wife for *anything* that displeased him, even burning a meal. If Jesus had sided with either of these men's teachings on divorce, He might well have lost the following of all those who supported the other.

Jesus is in the territory of Herod, so perhaps His questioners hope to get Him to say something that will incur Herod's displeasure, as John the Baptist had done. But Jesus counters their question with one of His own (10:3), which sends them back to their scriptures. He then explains that Moses wasn't by any means promoting divorce, yet had allowed for it in extreme cases. It was God's intention for marriage to last a lifetime, yet He knew that people's "hearts were hard" (10:5 NIV) and had created a contingency plan.

The response of Jesus' critics is not noted. But Jesus goes into even greater detail when alone with His disciples. His comments (10:10–12) are quite contrary to the traditions of Judaism at that time. According to Jewish law, a wife could commit adultery by having relations with another man; a man (single or married) could commit adultery against another man by having relations with that man's wife. But a husband could not be charged with adultery against his own wife by being unfaithful to her. By insisting that a husband can commit adultery against his own wife, Jesus greatly elevates the status of wives and women in general.

Jesus' statement in 10:12 is found only in Mark. In ancient Jewish society, a wife did not have the right to divorce her husband. But in the first century, if a Jewish woman wanted a divorce, she could obtain one on the basis of Roman law even though her decision might cut her off from Jewish society.

We need to understand that the issue of divorce is complicated. Jesus was not saying all that could be said about divorce. He was speaking to people who would leave a spouse for no good reason and move from partner to partner. He condemned divorce as contrary to God's will and set forth the highest standards of marriage for His followers. But He did not address other potential reasons for divorce, such as spousal abuse and similar horrendous issues that have recently plagued society. We must be careful not to apply His teaching beyond its original context.

📖 **10:13–16**

LITTLE CHILDREN: A MODEL FOR US ALL

Jesus had recently used a little child as an example of a helpless, humble person who should be welcomed by His followers (9:35–37). But apparently His disciples had missed the point. In this case, people are bringing little children for Jesus to touch (bless), and the disciples are trying to discourage them. The disciples are probably trying to protect Jesus' time, assuming He is too busy or too important to be bothered by such trivial matters.

The Gospels contain only a few instances where Jesus expresses anger, but this is one of them. He grows "indignant" (10:14) with His disciples for their treatment of the small children. Anyone who comes to Jesus, regardless of age, should do so with the simple faith and trust of a child. He or she is not to be hindered, but encouraged and supported.

In ancient society, children were considered irrelevant, totally without social status. Here, the traits of children that Jesus is probably referring to are their lowliness and dependence on others. In essence, he is telling His disciples they must be humble and absolutely dependent on God to enter the kingdom. For us as well, these values help us find and enter the kingdom of God.

Note that God's kingdom is to be both received and entered (10:15). The blessings of the kingdom are to be received as a gift, yet we enter the kingdom through responsive faith. Jesus takes the children in His arms to visually demonstrate that the blessings of the kingdom are available to those who choose to come to Him (10:16). Through faith, all believers are accepted in the arms of Jesus and blessed by Him.

10:17–31

THE ONE WHO GOT AWAY

When Mark points out that Jesus is "on his way" (10:17 NIV), it is a reminder that Jesus is headed toward Jerusalem and the cross. On the way He encounters a man who asks what needs to be done to inherit eternal life. But the man's reference to Jesus as "Good Teacher" is what caught Jesus' attention.

In Jewish thought, God was preeminently "good"—so much so that it was unusual to apply the term to anyone else. So first, Jesus responds to the man with a query (10:18) that essentially asks, "Are you consciously calling me God, or was that just a mistake?"

Then Jesus continues with information from scripture that the man is already aware of. In fact, the man is convinced he has kept the laws perfectly since his childhood, which should certainly merit his entrance into God's kingdom.

He must have been sincere about his thinking, because Mark tells us that Jesus "looked at him and loved him" (10:21 NIV). Jesus goes on to explain how a true keeper of the law would behave (10:21)—with unbridled compassion for the needy. Jesus is expressing love and compassion for this man and asks him to do the same for others.

Jesus' command to "sell all you possess and give to the poor" (NASB) should not be applied literally to every professing Christian. It is used in this case to demonstrate that someone who obeyed the law to the point that this man *thought* he did would have such a heart of love for others that he would be ready to take the next step and give them all he had.

The man can't do as Jesus asks and "went away sad" (10:22 NIV). Even though Jesus promises him "treasure in heaven," he is unwilling to let go of what he already possessed. This is the only example in Mark of someone being called to discipleship, but refusing.

Critical Observation

The story of Jesus and the rich man must be understood in light of the Jewish attitude toward riches. The dominant Jewish view was that wealth was an indication of divine favor and a reward for righteousness. Although provision was made for the protection and assistance of the poor, rarely was poverty associated with piety. So the teaching of Jesus was revolutionary in its time, and remains scandalous even today.

After the man leaves, Jesus and His disciples discuss the difficulty of rich people entering God's kingdom (10:23). Jesus' comment about a camel going through the eye of a needle has prompted much discussion. The suggestion that He was referring to a small gate in the wall of Jerusalem called "The Eye of a Needle" has no supporting evidence, and first arose in the ninth century, long after the destruction of Jerusalem. But clearly, the contrast between the largest Palestinian animal and one of the smallest openings is meant to teach the impossibility of entering God's kingdom on our own merits.

This idea is confirmed in 10:26–27, which contain the key to understanding the entire passage. Salvation, eternal life, and entry into God's kingdom are impossible for any human being, but not for God.

After Peter takes a stab at saying the disciples had tried to do as Jesus said (10:28), Jesus turns from warning to promise. Jesus is not encouraging people to walk away from their families (10:29–30), but is telling His followers to keep their priorities straight. Following Jesus can be costly, because along with blessing comes persecution. Yet ultimately the eternal rewards will far outweigh any sacrifices made in order to obtain them.

Finally, Jesus doesn't intend for us to be preoccupied with rewards (10:31). As we learn to serve the people He places in our path, He will see to rewards beyond anything we can ask or imagine (Ephesians 3:20).

Take It Home

Wealth can be a temptation, a hindrance, and a diversion from ongoing spiritual maturity. It provides false security that makes radical trust in God difficult. Yet Jesus never condemned riches as evil in themselves. Have you experienced any personal tension between your assets and your spiritual growth? How do you maintain a balance you feel good about? Do you perceive a need to make any changes in your financial attitudes or practices in order to become a more dedicated follower of Christ?

MARK 10:32–52

LEARNING TO SEE STRAIGHT

Unclear Spiritual Vision	10:32–45
Unclear Physical Vision	10:46–52

Setting Up the Section

As he did in the previous section (10:1–31), Mark continues to provide his readers with stories that reveal what is in the hearts of those who surrounded Jesus. While Jesus appears to know what people want from Him, He still encourages them to verbalize their desires before He responds.

🖹 10:32–45

UNCLEAR SPIRITUAL VISION

Jesus and His disciples are "on their way up to Jerusalem" (10:32 NIV)—a literal statement in this case. The road from Jericho to Jerusalem climbs about 3,300 feet in a twenty-mile stretch. The phrase is also used as a common expression for going to the Holy City on a pilgrimage or for some other important purpose.

Demystifying Mark

Several times in Mark's Gospel, Jerusalem is used as a symbol of opposition to Jesus. See, for instance, 3:22 and 7:1. And in this account, Jesus is heading to Jerusalem to die.

Mark describes Jesus leading the way, resolutely pressing toward His goal, deliberately striding toward His death (10:32). Twice already Jesus had begun to instruct the disciples about His upcoming death (8:31–32; 9:30–32). This time, however, He provides many more details (10:33–34), including being handed over to the Gentiles and suffering a number of humiliating indignities.

Yet again, Jesus' disciples demonstrate complete incomprehension. No doubt Mark's readers/hearers had difficulty understanding the full significance of Jesus' death and resurrection, and they benefited by realizing that Jesus' original disciples had a similar difficulty.

The disciples are still anticipating an earthly reign, and they want positions of authority when the time comes. In Jewish thought, the right hand (10:37) of the king was the place of greatest prominence; his left hand was the second most coveted seat. But James and John are missing the point. Jesus doesn't rebuke them directly, but indicates they do not realize the implications of their request.

The "cup" that Jesus refers to (10:38) symbolizes the wrath of God. His use of "baptism" is not the sacrament we know, but a metaphor for being immersed in calamity. It is ironic that even though James and John don't know what they are asking, Jesus foretells their participation in His "cup" and "baptism" (10:39).

By aspiring to positions of greatness, the disciples are thinking like Gentile rulers (10:42). And as a result, dissention runs through their ranks (10:41). Jesus emphatically states that His disciples must be like servants—even slaves (10:44). And He is about to demonstrate just what He is teaching them.

Jesus' subsequent statement about His own purpose—to serve and give His life as a ransom—is often considered an appropriate theme verse for Mark's whole Gospel (10:45). Humankind was in bondage to sin and pride, but Jesus' sacrifice was the necessary ransom. This usage of the word *ransom* indicates the price paid to free a slave or someone in prison. Jesus not only demonstrated humility but also freed us, enabling us to see what true humility is and then strive to emulate it.

🔖 **10:46–52**

UNCLEAR PHYSICAL VISION

When Jesus and His disciples reach Jericho, they encounter a blind man name Bartimaeus among a large crowd (10:46). Bartimaeus addresses Jesus as "Son of David" (10:47–48). The crowd tries to shush the blind man, but he is determined to get Jesus' attention. Jesus finally calls him forward. Mark provides the interesting detail of the man casting off his cloak (possibly used as a pallet), showing that Bartimaeus was casting aside everything to stand before Jesus. He had real and passionate faith. And when Jesus asks what he wants, he is quick with his response (10:51).

Critical Observation

Just as the healing of the blind man at Bethsaida (8:22–26) introduces the second major division of Mark, so the healing of Bartimaeus concludes it. Both stories contain exact geographical references—something unusual in Mark. Bracketing this section of Mark as they do, these accounts tie together the work of Jesus in providing physical sight for the blind and spiritual insight to His disciples. Bartimaeus becomes a picture of what was happening to the apostles—they were beginning to understand who Jesus was and what He came to do.

Again Mark emphasizes the importance of faith (10:52). The man calls out to Jesus, and Jesus saves him. His eyes are opened. He is healed physically and saved spiritually. And he immediately begins to follow Jesus.

Take It Home

The story of Bartimaeus is the last healing miracle in the Gospel of Mark. It provides an example of someone who understood who Jesus was, responded immediately to His call despite discouragement from others, believed in Him, and followed Him as a disciple. And it remains as an example for others to follow. Suppose you were to encounter Jesus today and He asked, "What do you want Me to do for you?" What would you say? What is it that Bartimaeus saw in Jesus that excited his faith to call out to Jesus?

MARK 11:1–10

JESUS' FINAL TRIP TO JERUSALEM

Humble Service	11:1–6
Necessary Deliverance	11:7–10

Setting Up the Section

For a while now, Mark has emphasized that Jesus was deliberately moving toward Jerusalem, where He would suffer and die. In this section, He arrives on what will become the original Palm Sunday. The focus of Mark's Gospel is on the humility of Jesus during His entry into the city. In Jesus' humility, we begin to see the foundation for victory in our own Christian lives.

📖 11:1–6

HUMBLE SERVICE

Jesus is making His way to Jerusalem to prepare for the single most important moment in human history, the moment when He would take the place of sinful humankind and die. His entry into the city is of extreme importance because it sets the stage for how He is going to carry out the work He was called to do.

Jesus is fully in control of this moment. From His perspective, the event had been planned and prepared far before the foundations of the world. It had been prophesied more than 400 years previously by the prophet Zechariah (Zechariah 9:9). Jesus is not improvising as He goes along.

A common question is how Jesus knew about the colt, and why someone would just give it away when the disciples asked for it (11:2–3). Had Jesus made arrangements with the owner ahead of time, or was this some kind of divine miracle? There is no record of Jesus talking to the man beforehand. With the long anticipation of the moment, it is not too much to believe that God worked in the man's heart to let him know that his animal would be used to fulfill the Old Testament prophecy. Regardless, it is certain that Jesus is fulfilling the scriptures to the letter. So the disciples do as Jesus instructs and obtain the colt (11:4–6).

Critical Observation

The fact that the colt used by Jesus had never been used has symbolic overtones. In the Old Testament, whenever God designated an animal to be used for religious purposes, it was always without defect and never previously used for other purposes (Numbers 19:2; Deuteronomy 21:3). So the donkey's colt chosen by Jesus would be appropriate for His mission.

Jesus' choice of a donkey's colt is very important because it demonstrates an unusual level of humility. Those who rode donkeys were usually people of humble means. If a king rode a donkey into a city, it was to proclaim peace rather than to declare war. Therefore Jesus enters Jerusalem, making a statement of humility and peace. He is not coming to claim the military or political leadership of Israel.

Without such a display of humility by Jesus, we would never be able to understand the level of humility that God loves and expects from us. Jesus humbly served God so that we might receive the power to choose humility as well. If He had not humbly entered Jerusalem to willingly die on a cross, we would have been swallowed up in our own pride and left to our many selfish ambitions.

Although Jesus is exemplifying complete humility, He enters Jerusalem fully intending to look like the Messiah. Until this point, Jesus had been reluctant to tell the crowds following Him that He was the Messiah. Here, His bold approach to the city finally confirms their thoughts, but it also sets into motion His death. Jesus knows this dramatic entrance will trigger a response from the religious leaders.

📖 11:7–10

NECESSARY DELIVERANCE

The crowds recognize the significance of Jesus' entrance into Jerusalem and respond with signs of respect (11:8–10). The spreading of garments pays homage to royalty (2 Kings 9:13), as do the waving of branches (Psalm 118:27 NIV). The verbal shouts (11:9–10) are additional signs of honor. Although Jesus demonstrates complete humility in what He is doing, He is also fulfilling the mission He has come to do, and is glorifying God in the process. So God ensures that, at least for this short ride into Jerusalem, Jesus receive worship and honor.

The cries of the people are meaningful. *Hosanna* is Hebrew for "Save us, now." Originally a cry for help, it had become a shout of praise for deliverance. "Blessed is he who comes in the name of the Lord" was a cry that applied to every pilgrim who approached the temple, but no doubt Mark intends his readers to understand that the phrase has particular significance when applied to Jesus. And "Blessed is the coming kingdom of our father David" expresses the expectation that Jesus will not only deliver, but also bring the kingdom of God to earth.

Demystifying Mark

It is important to keep in mind that Jesus was entering Jerusalem just prior to the Passover celebration. As the Jewish people recalled and celebrated God's deliverance of Israel from Egypt, their hopes for the eventual deliverance from Rome naturally ran high. In fact, the Roman Empire maintained troops in Jerusalem during this time in case riot control became necessary.

Although the people are celebrating Jesus' appearance, most of them miss the significance of the deliverance He is bringing. They are looking for political deliverance, but Jesus is bringing spiritual deliverance, which is much more essential. He is the only One capable of removing the oppressive burden of sin under which humankind suffers and struggles. Yet when He doesn't do anything about the oppression of Rome, many of the same clueless people who were cheering Him on this Sunday are crying for His execution less than a week later.

Take It Home

In spite of all the excitement of the people, they would eventually reject Jesus because He did not meet their expectations. When you think of the Savior, what image comes to mind? Are you willing to respond to someone who sets you free from pride and the burden of sin, or are you holding out for someone who allows you to hold on to your pride and is still willing to make your life better? What preexisting ideas, thoughts, dreams, plans, or agendas in your life keep you from seeing Jesus as a humble servant who obeyed God in order to follow His example in a greater humility and obedience?

MARK 11:11–26

A NONPRODUCTIVE FIG TREE AND A DISRESPECTFUL TEMPLE

The Cursing of the Fig Tree, Part I	11:11–14
The Expulsion of Merchants from the Temple	11:15–19
The Cursing of the Fig Tree, Part 2	11:20–26

Setting Up the Section

Upon reaching Jerusalem, it doesn't take Jesus long to begin to address things that need attention and correction. The improprieties He witnesses in the temple cause His immediate response, and His cursing of a fig tree serves to symbolize the unfruitful spiritual state of the religious leaders of His day.

This section includes yet one more example of Mark's tendency to sandwich or bracket one story into another in order to make a point. In this case, He first tells of Jesus cursing the fig tree, then moves on to His experience in the temple. Then Mark again returns to Jesus at the fig tree, stacking the image of the fruitless fig tree against the image of the fruitless religion found in the temple.

🗎 11:11–14

THE CURSING OF THE FIG TREE, PART I

If Jesus and His disciples have walked the twenty-one miles from Jericho to Jerusalem—most of it uphill—it makes sense that it would be late by the time He arrives (11:11). It also explains why the crowd disperses and Jesus takes no public action. Still, note that He doesn't just enter the city that evening, but the temple as well. Then He and the disciples go on to Bethany (about two miles away), where they will stay during this final week of Jesus' life.

It's not surprising that Jesus is hungry. The first meal of the day wasn't eaten until mid-morning, and the prospect of figs is encouraging. Israel had been compared to a fig tree throughout the Old Testament (Jeremiah 29:17; Hosea 9:10, 16; Joel 1:6–7; Micah 7:1). So "not the season for figs" (11:13) is as much a reflection on the spiritual state of Israel as for the fruitless tree. Both the tree and the nation appear to be healthy and complete, but neither is in season or productive. Both create disappointment rather than satisfaction.

Jesus addresses the fig tree (11:14) within earshot of the disciples. This will be important the following day, as will be seen (11:20–26).

📄 11:15–19

THE EXPULSION OF MERCHANTS FROM THE TEMPLE

The event in this passage is frequently called "the cleansing of the temple." In this case, the temple or temple area refers to an outer court—the only place Gentiles are allowed to worship. Yet it is here where the moneychangers provide shekels required for the temple tax in exchange for Roman currency. Other sellers provide doves, the prescribed offering for the poor who cannot afford a larger animal to sacrifice.

Critical Observation

The Tyrian shekel was the closest equivalent for the annual temple tax payment required from all Jewish males. According to the Jewish *Mishna*, the tax was due two weeks before the Passover, so exchange tables were set up in the temple five days prior to the due date.

Jesus takes immediate action to rid the temple of the moneychangers and animals (11:15–16). As He drives them out, He quotes Isaiah 56:7 and Jeremiah 7:11 to remind everyone that God's house is intended to be a place of worship, not business. Mark is the only Gospel writer with the reference to all nations (11:17) in Jesus' quotation. Perhaps he had in mind Isaiah's prediction that the Gentiles would one day have a place among the people of God and in the temple of God (Isaiah 56:6–7).

While the pilgrims in Jerusalem would have benefited from the services of the moneychangers and animal sellers, the temple was not a proper location to conduct business. Even if the merchants weren't price gouging, they were "robbers" (11:17) in the sense that they were robbing the Gentiles of unhindered worship opportunities.

The responses to Jesus' actions are quite mixed. The crowds are amazed at His "teaching" (11:18), a word that probably indicates both His words and His symbolic act of expelling the merchants. In contrast, the chief priests and teachers of the law are afraid of Him, and begin to look for a way to kill Him.

Perhaps Jesus waits until evening to leave (11:19) for His safety, as the time for His crucifixion has not quite arrived.

📄 11:20–26

THE CURSING OF THE FIG TREE, PART 2

After witnessing the clearing of the temple, the disciples may have had second thoughts about the significance of Jesus' previous cursing of the fig tree. When He had said, "May no one ever eat fruit from you" (11:14), did His meaning extend beyond the single tree to include the nation of Israel? And if so, what did that mean to the apostles, who were from that nation?

When Peter sees that the tree has indeed withered by the following morning (11:20–21), he brings it to Jesus' attention. Jesus minimizes the alarm and fear the disciples may be feeling by focusing on the importance of faith. Despite the cursing of the fig tree (Israel), God was still accessible. The temple would no longer be the way to Him, however. Faith and prayer would be the way to God—an approach equally available to Jews and Gentiles.

Jesus' words (11:22–23) are sometimes taken out of context. They are not intended to apply to spectacular miracles, but as an encouragement in accomplishing the Christian mission. He is saying that if a person walks by faith, no difficulty can overwhelm him or her—not even a mountain-sized one.

Similarly, His statement on prayer (11:24) is not to be universalized and applied without exception. But neither is it to be limited to the original disciples and ignored as having no current practical value. Faith is an indispensable element in prayer. When faith is exercised, the pray-er can be confident of an answer.

In addition to faith, forgiveness is also an essential aspect of prayer (11:25). Believers must pray in a way that reflects the gospel they promote. A healthy relationship with God cannot be maintained apart from proper relationships with one's fellow human beings. Standing (11:25) was probably the most common posture for prayer at the time.

Verse 26 has been omitted from some Bibles. The sentence is found in a large number of medieval manuscripts, but not in the older and more reliable ones. It reads, "But if you do not forgive, neither will your Father in heaven forgive your trespasses" (NKJV).

It was most likely added under the influence of Matthew 6:15. But Jesus' point is not to be missed: Forgiveness is critical to every part of our relationship with God.

Take It Home

What are some of the obstacles in your life that get in the way of sharing the gospel with a family member or a friend? What encouragement comes from this text as you consider the hope of this passage? Who do you need to forgive so that you can carry on God's will in an undistracted manner?

MARK 11:27–17

CONTROVERSIES IN THE TEMPLE, PART I

Setting Up the Section

This section begins a series of seven conflicts between Jesus and the religious authorities. (Three will be examined in this segment; four in the next one.) These stories show how Jesus refutes the errors of the Jewish leaders and why they reject Him. The accounts were also helpful for first-century readers in seeing how Jesus faced opposition to His teachings, something the early church had to do as well.

📄 11:27–33

CONTROVERSY: JESUS' AUTHORITY

Upon Jesus' return to the temple, He is confronted by a delegation of chief priests, teachers of the law, and elders (11:27) from the Sanhedrin—the Jewish religious ruling body. They want to know by whose authority He had driven out the temple moneychangers and animal sellers.

Authority was a big issue, as Mark has regularly noted (1:22, 27; 2:10; 3:15; 6:7; etc.). The religious leaders feel Jesus had gone too far—they were supposed to be in charge of the temple. But Mark is seeking to demonstrate that Jesus is the Christ, the Son of God. As such, He possesses all authority.

Rather than defend His actions, Jesus answers their question with a question of His own (11:29-30), posed to show that their motives are not about seeking the truth as much as staying in power and maintaining popularity. He isn't attempting to evade their question, but rather to establish the source of His authority in the spiritual realm.

At issue is the authority of John the Baptist. The clear implication of Jesus' question is that John's ministry was divinely authorized. And if so, since John had endorsed the ministry of Jesus, then the religious leaders should recognize Jesus' authority. Of course, the religious authorities would never concede that John was a prophet from God. But John had been popular with the crowds, so the religious leaders don't dare voice their opinion. Their only option, in response to Jesus' question, is to say, "We do not know" (11:33).

In rejecting John, they have rejected God's truth. So Jesus refuses to respond to them. They already know the answer to their question of authority (11:28). But if they hadn't listened to John, neither will they listen to Jesus.

📄 12:1–12

CONTROVERSY: THE REJECTION OF ISRAEL

This parable of the wicked tenant farmers is very similar to a prophecy of Isaiah (Isaiah 5:1-7). In both cases, the vineyard clearly represents Israel, and the owner, God. In the Isaiah account, the problem was that the vineyard failed to produce the fruits of righteousness. In Jesus' variation, the problem is with the overseers (the religious authorities) who refuse to serve the owner due to their wickedness (greed, dishonesty, violence, and murder). The servants (12:2-5) are the prophets whom God had sent, yet who had been rejected, abused, and sometimes even killed. And the owner's beloved son is Jesus (1:11; 9:7).

Jesus is saying that the current tenants (the Jewish religious authorities) will lose their coveted position. God's vineyard will soon be the church, which He will use rather than the nation of Israel to advance His kingdom. Yet the church will include both Jewish and Gentile believers, grafted into the same olive tree (Romans 11:17–24).

Demystifying Mark

If no living person claimed ownership of a piece of land, its occupants could acquire it. By doing away with every representative of the owner, the tenants in the parable thought they could possess complete control over their land. To kill the owner's son was bad enough, but to leave a corpse unburied was the ultimate insult and showed complete contempt.

The "cornerstone" or "capstone" reference (12:10–11) is a quote from Psalm 118:22–23 used two other times in the New Testament (Acts 4:11; 1 Peter 2:7) in addition to the parallel Gospel accounts (Matthew 21:42; Luke 20:17). The Jews had understood the prophecy to refer to their nation, which was rejected by other nations but would be restored by the Lord. The early Christians, however, realized the rejected stone was a reference to Jesus (Ephesians 2:20).

The religious leaders who continue to oppose Jesus realize this parable is about them (12:12). If Jesus was right, it meant that God would soon reject them. But rather than change their opinion, they are all the more determined to have Jesus arrested. This is an irony in Mark's Gospel that while previous parables concealed the truth from the religious leaders, this one reveals it to them and so provokes Jesus' crucifixion.

📖 **12:13–17**

CONTROVERSY: THE PAYMENT OF TAXES

A short time later a group of Pharisees and Herodians (see "Critical Observation" for Mark 3:1–6) go to Jesus in an attempt to "catch Him in His words" (12:13 NIV, KJV, NKJV). Although what they say about Jesus (12:14) is true, Mark reveals their shady motives by showing that it is insincere flattery.

Jesus sees right through their hypocrisy and calls them on it. Ironically, Jesus doesn't have a coin, but His opponents do. The insertion of this fact might be another indication that they implicitly recognized the authority of the emperor, therefore exposing them as hypocrites.

Critical Observation

A poll tax was imposed on all residents of Judea, Idumea, and Samaria in AD 6. Although the tax was only one denarius a year—a day's wage for an agricultural laborer—it was a symbol of foreign domination. In addition, the tax had to be paid with a coin bearing both the image of the emperor (in this case, Tiberius) and an offensive inscription claiming a status of deity for the ruling emperor.

The Pharisees think they had Jesus in a no-win situation. If He advises them to pay the tax, He will surely lose much of His popularity with the people. If He advises against it, He will become a target of Rome. But Jesus ingeniously sidesteps their trap (12:15–17).

A coin minted by the emperor with his picture was considered his property even while in circulation. So Jesus says to give it to him, acknowledging that God's people have an obligation to the state. But a far greater obligation is to God. If coins bearing the image of an emperor ought to be returned to him, how much more should human beings bearing the image of God devote themselves to their Lord? Believers should present their lives to God as an act of worship (Romans 12:1).

Jesus teaches that obedience to a secular power does not necessarily conflict with one's obedience to God. Later New Testament writings would reaffirm this fact (Romans 13:1–7; 1 Timothy 2:1–3; Titus 3:1–2; 1 Peter 2:13–17).

People who hear Jesus are "amazed" at Him (12:17). But that doesn't stop His opponents from trying to trap Him. More controversies follow in the next section of Mark.

Take It Home

Not many people live under the rule of an emperor these days, but we can still encounter situations where faith and secular authority create conflict. Can you think of any such circumstances in your own experience? How do you handle situations where your faith and your other commitments seem to be at odds with one another?

MARK 12:18–44

CONTROVERSIES IN THE TEMPLE, PART II

Controversy: Marriage at the Resurrection	12:18–27
Controversy: The Greatest Commandment	12:28–34
Controversy: The Identity of David's Son	12:35–37
Controversy: The Scribes Contrasted with the Widow	12:38–44

Setting Up the Section

The conflict between Jesus and those hoping to destroy His credibility continues in this section of Mark. The previous section (11:27–12:17) contained three separate controversies. But in the four that follow, we find a few positive examples amid the attempts to discredit Jesus.

📄 12:18–27

CONTROVERSY: MARRIAGE AT THE RESURRECTION

The Sadducees (12:18) are mentioned only here in Mark's Gospel. Little is known about them, but they had some different viewpoints on certain matters of theology. One distinction was that they did not believe in the resurrection of the dead.

Demystifying Mark

The Sadducees seem to have emerged as an identifiable party during the second century BC. They were wealthy aristocrats who were politically liberal and theologically conservative. They were usually associated with the temple and the office of the high priest, although only one high priest was explicitly identified as a Sadducee. (Their name may have derived from Zadok, a high priest in David's time [2 Samuel 20:25].) None of their own literature has survived, so all references to them are in the writings of their adversaries, and therefore questionable. One thing for certain is that they rejected the oral tradition of the scribes and Pharisees, which created some interesting discussions and debates.

The preposterous supposition they have concocted (12:20–23) has probably been used many times in their debates with the Pharisees. It is based on a teaching found in Deuteronomy 25:5–10, intended to provide for any widow who had been left childless after her husband's death.

Jesus again uses a question (12:24) to reveal ignorance and take the discussion to a higher plane. He points out two errors of the Sadducees: (1) not knowing the content and/or proper interpretation of the scriptures; and (2) not having personally experienced the power of God in their lives. Therefore, they are missing the whole point of the argument.

Jesus teaches that resurrection life will be different from earthly life. "Like the angels" (12:25 NIV, NLT) may indicate either a sexless state or an emphasis on serving and worshiping God. Relationships in heaven will be of such a degree that they will satisfy better than the best relationships on earth. Sin, grief, and loss will be left behind as believers experience the surpassing joy of new and more powerful relationships.

And as far as the Sadducees' disbelief in resurrection, Jesus quotes from Exodus 3:6 (12:26). When God spoke in present tense of being the God of Abraham, Isaac, and Jacob, He indicated that those patriarchs were still alive—an implication of resurrection. And to make things perfectly clear, Jesus emphasizes that the Lord is not God of the dead, but of the living (12:27).

📄 12:28–34

CONTROVERSY: THE GREATEST COMMANDMENT

No sooner has Jesus answered the Sadducees than a scribe approaches with another question. But this time, the questioner seems to be more sincere. He wants Jesus' opinion on which He considers to be the greatest commandment, and quite a challenge it is. The scribes had gone through the law and identified 613 separate commandments: 365 prohibitions and 248 exhortations to obey. They also categorized them as "heavy" or "light" based on what they felt was more or less important.

Jesus quotes from Deuteronomy 6:4–5 (the first part of the Jewish *Shema*) and Leviticus 19:18. In doing so, He teaches that in loving God and one's neighbor, a person fulfills the entire law of God. Jesus brings together and virtually merges the commands to love God and to love fellow human beings.

Critical Observation

The Shema is the declaration of Deuteronomy 6:4–9. Its foundation is Deuteronomy 6:4 which declares that God is the one true God. The name *Shema* is derived from the first Hebrew word of the verse, "hear." This passage is recited three times a day as part of the religious Jew's spiritual practice. It is also part of the synagogue Sabbath service.

The response of the scribe (12:32-34) is found only in Mark. It is the only place in the Gospels where a scribe is described as being favorably disposed toward Jesus. But it's enough to demonstrate that not all scribes and Pharisees were unwilling to listen and respond to what Jesus had to say.

And it's noteworthy to notice exactly what they agree on: the elevation of an ethical quality over sacrificial worship. This scribe understands that Jesus is exactly right—love for God and for one's neighbor is more important "than all burnt offerings and sacrifices" (12:33).

By deeming the man "not far from the kingdom of God" (12:34), Jesus is encouraging him to go the rest of the way with wholehearted devotion. Whether he did so cannot be known.

📖 **12:35–37**

CONTROVERSY: THE IDENTITY OF DAVID'S SON

Jesus has proven Himself authoritative on taxes, resurrection, and the law, so at this point He raises a question of His own (12:35). Throughout the Old Testament, the prophets had written that the Messiah would be from the line of David, and "Son of David" would be a regular title in the New Testament. However, fathers in ancient Israelite society did not refer to their sons—much less their distant descendants—as "lords." So why did David refer to his future descendant as "Lord" (12:37)?

Critical Observation

When David wrote, "The LORD said to my Lord. . ." in Psalm 110:1, quoted by Jesus in Mark 12:36, two different words are used for "Lord." The first usage is a clear reference to God (Yahweh). The second word (*Adonai*) is sometimes used of God, but not always. So a paraphrase of the statement might be, "God said to my superior. . ."

Jesus is not denying that He is David's descendant or the Messiah. However, those terms were too limiting. Jesus is more than the "Son of David." He is also the "Son of Man"—the representative of all humanity who has to suffer before He is exalted at God's right hand (Daniel 7:13-14). Still more importantly, Jesus is the Son of God!

In a veiled way, Jesus is telling everyone that the Messiah is not to be a warrior-king like David. And yet He will be greater than David. To hear such deep thoughts explained brings "delight" to Jesus' listeners (12:37).

CONTROVERSY: THE SCRIBES CONTRASTED WITH THE WIDOW

Jesus refutes the showiness that has come to symbolize "proper" worship (12:38-39). The reference to long or flowing robes probably refers to the *tallith*, a shawl worn during formal prayers and ceremonies. Some scribes might have worn one to attract attention. "Greetings in the market places" (NASB) were expressions of deference to a religious authority. The "most important seats" (NIV) in the synagogue were on the bench facing the congregation or near the chest that contained the scrolls. At a banquet, the choicest seats were near the host.

But such religious gestures were hollow. The same people putting on such a pretense would "devour widows' houses" (12:40). Scribes were forbidden to receive payment for their teaching. However, some may have ingratiated themselves to widows in hopes of being willed their homes. Others might have found technicalities in the law, allowing them to lay claim to the houses of defenseless persons, or perhaps expected generous sums from widows after praying for them.

In contrast to this unscrupulous habit of taking from helpless people stands the example of the widow (12:41-44). The "treasury" (12:41) where this takes place appears to be in the court of women where thirteen trumpet-shaped receptacles were placed to collect both the temple tax and money given voluntarily for various purposes.

The amount of each of the widow's two coins (12:42) would have been 1/64 of a denarius— a denarius being equal to a day's wage. Jesus observes her selfless gift and points out that the amount of a gift is weighed by how much remains for one's personal use afterward. The widow's giving of everything she has to live on demonstrates her absolute trust in God—a far more significant gift than anyone else had given.

Take It Home

There were no shortage of controversies between Jesus and the established religious leaders of His day. What controversies are you aware of in the church today? Based on what He said to His critics, how do you think Jesus would respond to each issue that confronts the church today?

MARK 13:1–13

WATCH AND WAIT

Setting Up the Section

Mark 13 has been given a variety of names, including the eschatological discourse, the prophetic discourse, the Olivet discourse (since it was given on the Mount of Olives), and

the "Little Apocalypse." Jesus foretells God's judgment, a great cataclysm in the world, and Jesus' eventual return. This passage is the longer of two of Jesus' extended discourses found in Mark's Gospel (the other being 4:1–34). At this point in Mark's account, Jesus begins to reveal to the disciples some of the specifics of what will happen as the ministry of the church begins to unfold in the world.

📖 13:1–11

THE DESTRUCTION OF THE TEMPLE

The Olivet discourse is initiated by a random comment by one of the disciples about the temple (13:1). Jesus acknowledges the greatness of the buildings, but predicts a day when "not one stone here will be left upon another" (13:2). Naturally the disciples want more details (13:4), so Jesus sits them down on the Mount of Olives where they can look down on the temple and the city of Jerusalem. The Mount of Olives was also prominent in Old Testament prophecies about the return of the Lord (Zechariah 14:4).

Critical Observation

The "massive stones" of the temple (13:1 NIV) were indeed magnificent. According to the writings of Josephus, a first-century historian, some of the stones were thirty-seven feet long by eighteen feet deep by twelve feet high. The few stones that remain from portions of the southeast corner and the western wall are not quite that large, yet are still considerably larger than the stones used during the medieval rebuilding of the walls. In Jesus' day, before its destruction, the temple was truly a masterpiece of architecture.

Jesus gives His followers signs to look for, but not specifics. He *doesn't* say that the Jews will rebel against the Romans in AD 66 and that the Romans will obliterate the temple in AD 70 as a result. Yet the disciples realize that if the temple were to fall as Jesus said, it would surely be as a result of greater events that would throw the world they know into chaos. So Jesus lays out a number of events for them to watch for.

📖 13:5–13

SIGNS TO WATCH FOR

In Jesus' expansive answer to the disciples' questions (13:4) He identifies four signs that will indicate the coming destruction of Jerusalem and/or the end of the world.

(1) False Messiahs (13:5–6)

It's interesting to note that Jesus' first warning sign is deceit—many people will come, claiming to be the Christ, and will recruit a lot of followers. One of the ongoing challenges of living in a fallen world is discerning false teaching that appears to be true. At the heart of this false teaching will be people who claim to be (or to represent) the Messiah. So Jesus repeats the warning to "watch out," "beware," and "be on your guard" throughout the discourse

(13:5, 9, 23, 33, 37). Despite the horrendous physical calamities He is about to describe, the spiritual dangers are far greater.

(2) Wars (13:7–8)

The Roman Empire had risen to greatness through conquest, and would continue to do so. The reference in 13:7 is to the war soon to be fought between Israel and Rome. After the Jewish rebellion of AD 66 and fall of the temple in AD 70, Jewish opposition to Rome will be ultimately quashed at the fortress of Masada in 73 or 74. Although it will be hard for Jewish people to believe at the time, Jesus indicates that these events will *not* be a sign of the end of the world or of His return. Wars will continue and worse things will happen.

(3) Natural disasters (13:8)

Earthquakes and famines will be only the beginning of the problem. The reference to birth pains (or pangs) should have been familiar to any Jewish people with a knowledge of their scriptures. It was a common metaphor to symbolize anticipation of a significant event (Isaiah 13:8; 26:17–18; Jeremiah 4:31; 50:43; Hosea 13:13; Micah 4:9–10; etc.).

(4) Persecution (13:9, 11–13)

The followers of Jesus will be opposed and handed over to the courts where they will be sentenced to punishment or death. The gospel will be rejected as the religious establishment seeks to silence the message of Jesus.

None of these signs can silence the gospel (13:10). Even in the midst of horrendous times and catastrophic events, God's Word will continue to be preached and His kingdom will advance. Consequently, persecution won't be just one of the signs of the end of the world, but a way of life for believers. So Jesus includes some guidelines for handling persecution: Continue to testify for Him (13:9), depend on the Holy Spirit to know what to say (13:11), and stand firm to the end (13:13).

Demystifying Mark

Verse 11 is one of the few references to the Holy Spirit found in Mark's Gospel. It is not a prohibition against preparation, but against anxiety.

When Jesus tells His followers to endure "to the end" (13:13), He likely means the end of each individual's life rather than the end of the age or any other specific date. The promise of being saved is in a spiritual, not a physical, sense.

The readers of Mark's Gospel were facing the birth pangs of persecution. These words were no doubt of great comfort to them as they were assured that God would certainly reward those who are faithful to Him.

Take It Home

Mark's purpose in writing was to provide assurance about the true identity of Jesus and confidence about His eventual return. Yet his repeated warnings against being deceived were intended to dampen

CONTINUED

uncontrolled enthusiasm and speculation about the future. In the 2,000 years since Jesus died, many groups and individuals have been deceived and/or mistaken about the end times. When you think about such things, what is your response? (Some may want to hide, others want to talk about nothing else, etc.) What do you think Jesus' intent was in sharing so much general information with His followers, but not giving them (us) a detailed schedule of when everything would take place?

MARK 13:14–37

THE END OF THE AGE

Setting Up the Section

Whenever the return of Jesus is discussed, it's not unusual to find a number of different opinions. Mark reports what Jesus has to say, but it is interpreted in different ways by different people. This passage almost certainly refers to the coming siege of Jerusalem in AD 70. Even so, it's a debated passage that looks far ahead into our future.

🗎 13:14–23

TRUE SIGNS OF THE END OF THE AGE

"The abomination that causes desolation" (13:14 NIV) is a phrase found in Daniel's prophecies (Daniel 9:27; 11:31; 12:11). The word *abomination* indicates something repulsive to God and His people. *Desolation* suggests that as a result of its profanation, the true people of God abandon the temple. Daniel's prediction came true when Antiochus IV Epiphanes of Seleucid Syria erected a statue of Zeus Olympus in the Jerusalem temple in 167 BC.

Demystifying Mark

In addition to the "abomination that causes desolation" of Antiochus IV Epiphanes, later temple desecrations (prior to Jesus' statement in Mark) included one in 63 BC when the Roman general Pompey conquered Jerusalem and entered the Most Holy Place, and another when the governor, Pilate, introduced idolatrous standards into the city in about AD 26–27. Later ones would include the unsuccessful attempt by Caligula to erect his statue in the temple (AD 40) and the intrusion of the Zealots when they gained control of the temple during the Jewish rebellion in AD 66–70.

Jesus' use of the phrase most likely refers to the coming profanation of the temple by the Romans just prior to its destruction in AD 70. During this siege, Titus will enter the Most Holy Place and remove various items, taking them to Rome to adorn his victory procession. However, a second meaning can also be taken to refer to a future sacrilege by another profane and oppressive person, possibly the one of "lawlessness" Paul writes about in 2 Thessalonians 2:1–12.

The call to "let the reader understand" may be an insertion by Mark rather than part of the statement of Jesus, calling the reader to think about the significance of this statement in light of previous revelation in Daniel 9:23, 25. Some scholars think that Mark is pointing the original readers to events taking place at that time, and that the destruction of Jerusalem is imminent. This would date the Gospel to the late 60s of the first century.

The danger Jesus describes (13:14–16) is so great that there is no time for any delay. Palestinian houses had flat roofs for relaxation and cooling off during summer evenings, and were built with outside staircases. Jesus' warning is to flee without even going inside. Nor should field workers stop to retrieve their outer cloaks (removed while working). The time will be especially bad for "pregnant women and nursing mothers" (NIV) because of their weakened condition and inability to hurry. And winter will be an especially bad time because rivers will be high and hard to cross.

The "days of distress unequaled from the beginning, when God created the world, until now" (13:19 NIV) is another reference to Daniel (Daniel 12:1). This tribulation will be so severe that it could cause even the true children of God to despair (13:20), but God will not allow it to go that far.

One reason Jesus is being so frank with His disciples is that "false Christs and false prophets" will arise and deceive a lot of people. To prevent His followers from being misled, Jesus is carefully telling them "everything in advance" (13:23 NASB).

📖 13:24–27

THE RETURN OF THE SON OF MAN AND THE GATHERING OF HIS ELECT

Verse 24 signifies a contrast, showing that the return of the Son of Man (13:26) is a distinct event that follows the fall of Jerusalem and other sufferings of the present age, though no time frame is provided. The scene described in 13:24–25 is an allusion to Old Testament passages such as Isaiah 13:10; Ezekiel 32:7–8; and Joel 2:10, 31. Some people interpret these as literal events; others see them as symbolic. The point in either case is there will be a clear sign that precedes the return of Jesus Christ. God will make the event known.

The return itself will also be public (13:26). This presumably means that all persons—not just disciples—will observe Jesus' return. It is significant that the title "Son of Man" is used here. It means that the same One who humbly ministered on earth (10:45) and who suffered and died (8:31) will return with "great power and glory." Glory is an Old Testament characteristic of God, so Jesus' glorious return is further indication of His deity.

In Mark's account, Jesus says nothing about future judgment (either punishment or rewards), resurrection, or reigning. The emphasis is on the gathering of God's scattered "elect" (13:27)—those who are chosen and blessed. The word itself gives no indication of why this group is chosen, but the concept of gathering the scattered people of God runs throughout the Old Testament (Deuteronomy 30:3–4; Psalm 147:2; Isaiah 11:12; 43:6; Jeremiah 32:37; Ezekiel 11:17; 34:13; 36:24). The emphasis in Mark is that Jesus will regather His people from wherever they have been scattered. This will be comforting for Mark's readers who are about to be scattered due to mounting persecution.

13:28–37

CERTAIN AND UNCERTAIN TRUTHS ABOUT THE RETURN OF JESUS

Jesus concludes His Olivet discourse with a collection of sayings and parables that deal with the uncertainty of the end times and the need to be ready. The mini-parable in 13:28–29 compares the coming of the Son of Man with the approach of summer. Jesus uses a fig tree in His example because so many other trees in Palestine are evergreens. But the fig tree loses its leaves in winter, and the reappearance of leaves is a sign of summer. Similarly, the signs Jesus has been describing are certain to lead to His return.

Critical Observation

This is an important teaching: As the condition of the world goes from bad to worse, it is not a sign that Jesus is losing the spiritual battle, but that His victorious return and final judgment are only getting closer.

"This generation" (13:30) refers to the contemporaries of Jesus. Some of them—particularly some of His disciples—will not die until the events of 13:5–23 have taken place, including the destruction of the temple. To a limited extent, 13:30 is the answer to the question asked in 13:4.

Verse 32 affirms that no one except God knows the exact time of the coming of Christ. But by referring to the event as "that day," Mark taps into the richness of the Old Testament writings about the Day of the Lord—a day of judgment for both Israel and the surrounding nations (Amos 5:18–20; Zephaniah 1:7, 14–16). The day marks the end of the present evil age and the beginning of the coming age of righteousness.

Another mini-parable in 13:34 once more reminds Mark's readers to be watchful. People in his day didn't usually travel by night (13:35), but might do so if returning from a late banquet or from abroad. They were not to sit around doing nothing while waiting for something to happen. The proper way to be prepared was to go about one's assigned tasks (13:34). Ignorance of the date or laziness (13:36) was no excuse to be caught unprepared.

Finally, Jesus gives one concluding reminder to "Watch!" (13:37). And He makes it clear that He is not only talking to His disciples; the discourse is for all Christians of all times.

Take It Home

Jesus spent a lot of time trying to inform His followers about the end times. What is the variety of emotional responses to this teaching? Why are there a variety of responses? How have you responded to this teaching in the past? What is your response today? How is this teaching meant to encourage us?

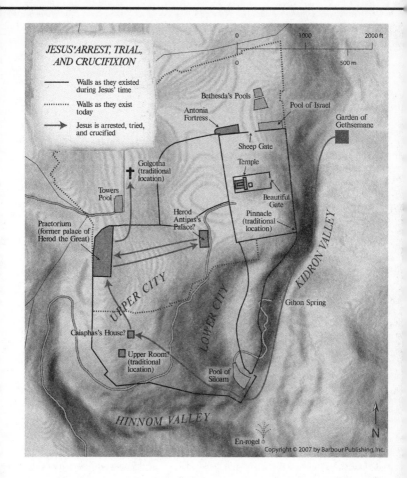

JESUS' ARREST, TRIAL,
AND CRUCIFIXION

——— Walls as they existed
during Jesus' time

·········· Walls as they exist
today

———▶ Jesus is arrested, tried,
and crucified

Bethesda's Pools

Pool of Israel

Antonia
Fortress

Garden of
Gethsemane

Sheep Gate

Golgotha
(traditional
location)

Temple

Towers
Pool

Beautiful
Gate

Herod
Antipas's
Palace?

Pinnacle
(traditional
location)

Praetorium
(former palace of
Herod the Great)

KIDRON VALLEY

UPPER CITY

LOWER CITY

Gihon Spring

Caiaphas's House?

Upper Room?
(traditional
location)

Pool of
Siloam

HINNOM VALLEY

En-rogel

N

Copyright © 2007 by Barbour Publishing, Inc.

MARK 14:1–26

A FINAL MEAL TOGETHER

Setting Up the Section

Two days before the annual celebration of Passover and the Feast of Unleavened Bread, the opponents of Jesus are still looking for an opportunity to arrest and kill Jesus—and finally come up with a workable plan. Yet others are beginning to recognize who He is, acknowledging Him in verbal and more emphatic ways.

📖 14:1–11

A REMARKABLE GIFT

During annual festivals, the population of Jerusalem swelled to three or four times normal. So even though a contingent of religious leaders is still looking for a way to put Jesus to death, it is afraid of a riot among the people.

Demystifying Mark

The Passover and the Feast of Unleavened Bread began on the same day, but the Feast of Unleavened Bread lasted seven days. It both celebrated the barley harvest and recalled the time when Israel ate unleavened bread during the exodus from Egypt. Passover commemorated the "passing over" of the angel of God who spared the firstborn sons in homes with blood on the door (Exodus 12:1–28). The Passover lamb could be killed only in the temple and eaten only within the city of Jerusalem. The emphasis on God's leading people from slavery to freedom, connected with the slaying of innocent lambs, made the timing and symbolism of Jesus' death highly significant.

Jesus is still popular, in large part due to His acceptance of people who were normally ignored or looked down on by other leaders. Here Mark shows that Jesus is at a party given by a man identified only as "Simon the leper" (14:3)—perhaps someone Jesus had healed.

While Jesus is reclining at the table (the traditional posture during more formal meals and dinner parties in that time and culture), a woman approaches Him. That is unusual in itself, because Jewish women didn't normally attend banquets for men except as servants. But in addition, she breaks a jar of very expensive nard (aromatic oil probably imported from India) and pours the entire contents on Jesus' head. Mark doesn't explain the woman's motives. (John indicates this woman is Jesus' friend, Mary [John 12:3]).

The woman's actions result in criticism from many of those present (14:4–5). But Jesus not only recognizes her motives, but also publicly defends her. It isn't that He doesn't share the others' concern for poor people, but the world would have only one Messiah and one death for their sins, so those facts were of greatest importance at this point. Only the woman had recognized the significance of the moment.

Verse 8 reveals Jesus' perception of the woman's actions, whether or not it had been her intent. And His prophecy in 14:9 was fulfilled as Mark recorded the event.

In stark contrast to the woman's devotion to Jesus, Mark inserts Judas's decision to betray Jesus at this point (14:10–11). Mark had only mentioned Judas once previously, and that was in a list of the disciples (3:19). Nothing is said of Judas's motive. Was he disappointed about Jesus' refusal to become a political Messiah? Was he attempting to force Jesus to take decisive action against His enemies? Had he been a spy all along? No one knows for sure. But Judas's cooperation sets in motion the plan of the religious leaders to have Jesus put to death.

📄 14:12–26

THE INSTITUTION OF THE LORD'S SUPPER

Three important aspects to this section support Mark's theme that Jesus is the Christ, the Son of God: (1) Jesus is the fulfillment of the Passover; (2) Jesus is not taken by surprise by His captors; and (3) Everything Jesus does is in accordance with the scriptures.

The unique manner in which a house was arranged for the Passover meal echoes the arrangements Jesus makes to secure the colt to ride into the city (14:13–16; 11:1–6). The "man carrying a jar of water" (14:13 NIV) should have stood out because women ordinarily transported water.

Large upper rooms (14:15) were rare in Palestinian homes, which usually consisted of from one to four rooms on a single level. A furnished room would have provided carpets, couches, and vessels.

Jesus has already made it clear that He will be betrayed and put to death. The observation that Jesus' betrayer is a close friend (14:17, 20) is intended to show the extent of Judas's crime. In ancient Semitic society, eating together was one of the most meaningful indications of friendship. Few actions were more despicable than betraying a friend at, or immediately after, a shared meal.

Critical Observation

The Passover meal was special. In addition to the main course of a specially sacrificed lamb, it began not with the traditional breaking of bread, but by dipping bread and bitter herbs into a bowl containing dried fruits, spices, and wine or vinegar. Wine was mandatory at Passover, but much more rare at other meals (at least among common folk). Passover was celebrated in the evening rather than late afternoon. Reclining while eating was more common at formal meals than ordinary ones. And a traditional dinner did not conclude with a hymn.

The very celebration of Passover is a reminder that death is necessary to provide salvation. Yet the one who betrays Jesus will face a horrible consequence. The word *woe* (14:21) carries with it intense condemnation. At the time, all the disciples are afraid Jesus might be talking about them (14:19).

At some point during this Passover, Jesus institutes a new meal for His followers (14:22–24). It begins with giving thanks, followed by the proclamation that the bread is Jesus' body and the cup (wine) His blood. Up until this point, Passover recalled the lamb that was slain to preserve life just prior to Israel's exodus from Egypt. In the future, however, the celebration would become a remembrance of the body of Jesus offered up as our substitute and His blood shed to provide the forgiveness for our sins. "Poured out" (14:24) indicates the shedding of blood would be violent.

This will be Jesus' last meal together with His disciples (14:25). The "hymn" (14:26) is probably Psalm 118. The Hallel, a Jewish prayer/recitation of Psalms 113–118, was used during Passover and other holidays.

Events will now unfold that bring about the death of Jesus. He has instituted a formal remembrance, but will continue to prepare those He loves for what is about to happen.

Take It Home

When this woman saw Jesus for who He was, she responded with a wholehearted act of worship. What did she see in Jesus that caused her to respond with such a sacrifice of worship? What do we learn about how a person views Jesus by his or her response of praise and worship? How would you evaluate your view of Jesus by your response to His person?

MARK 14:27–72

ARRESTED AND CHARGED

Setting Up the Section

After all the predictions and preparations by Jesus, the time has finally come for His arrest and trial. The whole process, including His death and resurrection, will only take a weekend. Yet the emotional toll of dread, denial, betrayal, physical abuse, and everything else will be horrendous.

📖 14:27–42

ABANDONED IN GETHSEMANE

At the Passover dinner Jesus had predicted His betrayal by "one of you" (14:18). On the way to the Mount of Olives He foretells that *all* His disciples will "fall away" (14:27). Yet Jesus is already looking beyond their failure to His reunion with them (14:8).

Peter makes a bold and arrogant claim (14:29), and Jesus just as boldly corrects him. This emphatic statement that Peter will deny Jesus not only once, but three times, is punctuated with Mark's final use of Jesus' phrase, "I tell you the truth" (14:30 NIV). It was certain to happen.

The vehemence of Peter's affirmation of loyalty (14:31) makes his failure all the greater. The fact that scripture portrays its main characters with such honest and unflattering examples is one indication of its trustworthiness. In addition, the Bible affirms that positive results can come from negative experiences, so the utter failure of Peter should encourage later followers of Jesus who fail in similar ways.

"Gethsemane" (14:32) is a transliteration of two Hebrew words meaning "oil press." It was probably an olive grove, and the exact location is unknown.

Another translation of 14:34 might be, "Horror and dismay came over Him." Jesus knows what it would mean to be forsaken by God, and He is seeking prayer support from His closest friends. The observation that Jesus "fell to the ground" (14:35 NIV) indicates a spirit of desperation.

In praying that "the hour might pass from Him" (14:35), Jesus is not regretting what He had come to earth to do. But in His humanity, He seeks another way to get the job done. When there is none, He leaves everything in His Father's hands: Yet "not what I will, but what You will" (14:36). Jesus' use of "Abba" in addressing God is unique in Judaism and shows His unique relationship to the Father.

The disciples, as usual, are lost as to what is really happening. When Jesus checks on them, they are sleeping off a good meal. The reason Peter (and all the others) will soon let Jesus down is that they are sleeping while Jesus is preparing His Spirit and His flesh to obey God. Even after Jesus specifically asks them to pray with Him, they fall asleep a second time. . .and a third (14:37–41).

By then, the hour has come—in a literal sense. The time is here for Jesus to be betrayed and put in the hands of sinful people.

📄 **14:43–65**

ARRESTED AND TRIED

Even as Jesus is waking Peter, James, and John for the third time, Judas appears with an armed crowd. Judas knows Jesus' specific plans and has arranged for Jesus' enemies to pick Him up when there won't be much of a crowd. Using a kiss as a sign—the way someone would greet a close friend—shows the ugliness of the betrayal (14:44–45).

We know from John's account of this story that the disciple with the sword (14:47) is Peter (John 18:10). He makes an initial futile effort to defend his Master, but he is a fisherman, not a soldier.

Jesus repairs the damage Peter has done to the servant's ear (Luke 22:51), and then addresses the crowd (14:48–49). His comments point out the wickedness and deception of His adversaries. It is safe to speculate that the guards and weapons were not present as protection against Jesus, but because the religious leaders feared His followers. Yet being so outnumbered, Jesus' disciples "all forsook him, and fled" (14:50 KJV).

Demystifying Mark

The unusual notation about the young man who ran away naked (14:51–52) has led to much speculation that he was John Mark, the author of the Gospel. The upper room where Jesus had celebrated Passover might have been owned by Mark's mother, and Mark could have followed the group after dinner. The word translated "naked" could mean completely naked, or wearing only a loincloth.

Peter has run away, yet he trails the crowd and follows Jesus all the way into the courtyard of the high priest. He can't witness the trial, but it isn't going very well from the perspective of the prosecutors.

They have made an arrest, but have no evidence to formally charge Jesus. The trial should have been public, but they are trying to get it done under the cover of night. Before imposing a death penalty, Jewish law required the agreement of two (if not three) witnesses, but no two people will agree (14:56). The religious leaders' scheme is backfiring, so Jesus has no need to speak. His silence during this period fulfills prophecies such as Psalm 38:13–14 and Isaiah 53:7.

Finally the high priest asks Jesus directly, Are you "the Son of the Blessed One?"(14:61). The question is phrased this way because the Jews did not like to speak the name of God, lest they accidentally profane it. But Jesus knows what he means, and gives a direct and detailed response (14:62) which references the Old Testament prophecies of Psalm 110:1 and Daniel 7:13–14. After so much secrecy about His identity to this point, His openness seems quite surprising. But He is leaving no doubt—neither for His accusers nor His followers. Not only is He the Messiah, but He is also going back to His Father and will return to earth one day in all His power.

That's all the high priest needs to hear. Tearing one's clothes (14:63) was usually a dramatic symbol of grief or alarm; in this case it was an official act expressing indignation. By claiming to sit at God's right hand, predicting a return from heaven, and using the divine name "I am," Jesus is clearly claiming to be God. He is accused of blasphemy and "condemned. . .as deserving death" (14:64).

Critical Observation

Under Roman rule, the Jewish leaders could sentence someone to death, but could not execute him. That was left to the Romans, which is why Jesus was sent on to Pilate after His trial before the Sanhedrin.

The irony in 14:65 becomes apparent in retrospect. The hostile crowd beats Jesus and challenges Him to "prophesy" because they think He can't. Yet their very actions are fulfilling His own previous prophecy (10:33–34) as well as Old Testament prophecies such as Isaiah 50:6; 53:3–5 and Micah 5:1.

📖 **14:66–72**

PETER'S THREE DENIALS

Meanwhile, Peter waits in the courtyard. He is trying to remain anonymous, but to his credit, he has at least tried to stay close to Jesus. A servant girl thinks she recognizes him as a member of Jesus' group, but Peter claims ignorance. Later she asks him again, this time including "those standing around" (14:69 NIV). Peter responds with a second denial. But by then he is attracting attention. A group (presumably including men) tries to get him to admit an association with Jesus. This time Peter begins "to call down curses on himself" (14:71 NIV), and he swears he doesn't know Jesus. As soon as the words leave his mouth, a rooster crows a second time and Peter recalls Jesus' prediction that he would deny Him three times (yet another of Jesus' prophecies coming true even as a hostile crowd is challenging Him to "prophesy").

In response, Peter "broke down and wept" (14:72). His great failure is recorded in all four Gospels. There is no attempted cover-up of the fact that the man who insightfully confessed Jesus' messiahship at Caesarea Philippi (8:29) later denies Him three times.

Take It Home

Peter thought that he could follow Jesus everywhere in the power of the flesh—he failed to understand that following Jesus must be done in the power and strength of the Spirit. In your life have you ever sought to follow and serve God in the power of the flesh? What was the outcome? Have you ever served God in a spirit of dependence upon the power and strength of God? What was that like? How do you depend upon the Spirit in your life—what does it look like?

MARK 15:1–20

JESUS' ROMAN TRIAL

The Trial Before Pilate   15:1–15
Jesus Before the Soldiers   15:16–20

Setting Up the Section

Jesus has just been arrested, tried, and sentenced to death. Judas has betrayed Him, Peter has already denied Him three times, and the rest of His friends have deserted Him. That was the treatment He received from His own people. Now He has the Romans to deal with.

📄 15:1–15

THE TRIAL BEFORE PILATE

Mark makes regular notations about the time in this passage. Chapter 15 is divided into four periods of three hours each: "very early in the morning" (15:1), "the third hour" (15:25), "the sixth hour. . .until the ninth hour" (15:33), and "evening" (15:42).

As soon as it is morning, the chief priests meet with the scribes, elders, and the entire council to present the conclusion of their findings—that Jesus had declared He was God and therefore should be handed over to the Roman government for execution.

The Roman ruler at this time is Pontius Pilate, the fifth Roman governor of Judea after the deposition of Archelaus in AD 6 (Matthew 2:22). Although the governors usually resided at Caesarea, they often came to Jerusalem at festival times in order to be at the site should disorder arise among the thousands who attended the fest.

Critical Observation

Pilate was governor from AD 26–36. Both Josephus and Philo described him as being cruel and without any sensitivity for Jewish religious beliefs or practices. (One of his atrocities is briefly mentioned in Luke 13:1.) By the time of Mark's writing, Pilate was so well known in Christian circles that he needed no detailed description.

Pilate's first question to Jesus (15:2) gets right to the heart of the charge. The phrase *king of the Jews* doesn't appear in Mark until this point, yet it is used six times in chapter 15. By doing so, Mark calls attention to the fact that Jesus died as the king of the Jews.

Jesus' affirmative response is quick and direct (15:2). Pilate wasn't too concerned if Jesus were only a religious leader. But if Jesus saw Himself as someone seeking to overthrow the Roman government, He would surely be executed.

Mark doesn't specify what other charges the Jewish leaders bring against Jesus (15:3). Whatever they are, Jesus again remains silent (15:4–5; 14:60–61). Pilate is amazed, probably because he has never seen anyone refuse to defend himself in such a situation.

The custom of releasing a prisoner (15:6) is probably unique to Pilate. No records exist to suggest this was an official Roman practice. Most likely, it was a ploy for popularity.

Mark records another irony with his account of Barabbas (15:7–11). After showing how the religious leaders have gone to such lengths to position Jesus as a threat to Rome, Pilate then places Him up against an already convicted insurrectionist. It seems that Pilate is attempting to see that Jesus is set free.

Pilate's attempt to release Jesus is probably based less on motives of humanity and justice than his contempt for the men who are railroading Jesus. It surely wasn't hard for a politically astute ruler to see that the Jewish leadership was envious of Jesus and that the entire procedure was a sham. Just as clear to see would have been Jesus' pure and moral character. Indeed, if Jesus really had been vehemently opposed to Roman rule, it is highly unlikely that the Jewish leaders would have turned Him in.

The crowd's defense of Barabbas (15:11) is influenced by the chief priests. Pilate has unconditional power of amnesty and can release both prisoners if he wishes. But Mark suggests that Pilate sees the potential for a riot and makes the politically correct decision.

As the momentum shifts and the people turn against Jesus, they begin to demand His crucifixion (15:13). Yet when Pilate presses the point and asks what crimes Jesus has committed, they have no answer (15:14). As a result, Jesus is falsely accused by the Jews and condemned by Pilate for the very offense for which Barabbas is guilty.

🔖 15:16–20

JESUS BEFORE THE SOLDIERS

The Praetorium (15:16) probably refers to whatever building(s) constituted the residence and office of the governor. The Praetorium was not always a fixed place, but was designated wherever a high Roman official conducted business—many times outdoors.

The "whole company of soldiers" (NIV) was a cohort—a Roman force of between 200 and

600 men. It was typical of Roman soldiers to humiliate as well as torture condemned prisoners. Purple cloth was very expensive, so the color purple (15:17) is associated with royalty. The "crown" of thorns is a mocking parody of the emperor's laurel wreath. The soldiers' shout, "Hail, king of the Jews," is an imitation of their salute, "Hail, Caesar the Emperor."

During all this time of mocking, Jesus is also being beaten and spat upon. All had been prophesied in the Old Testament: the mocking (Psalm 22:7; Isaiah 53:3), the beating (Isaiah 50:6; 53:4–5; Micah 5:1), and the spitting (Isaiah 50:6). Jesus had also foretold these very offenses (Mark 10:33–34).

Demystifying Mark

Flogging was a severe punishment in itself, yet was also used as a preliminary to crucifixion (perhaps to hasten death). Roman flogging must be distinguished from the "forty lashes less one" that were sometimes administered as a synagogue punishment. The Romans embedded bits of metal, bone, or glass in leather thongs, which shredded the flesh of victims until bones or entrails were exposed. Occasionally flogging was fatal.

The usual Roman procedure was to strip the convicted person and flog him along the way to the place of execution. But Jesus has already been flogged (15:15) and can bear no more. He will even need help along the way to carry His cross.

Take It Home

How do you feel when you read about the different groups that mistreated Jesus: the so-called religious leaders who twisted truth and incited crowds; the Roman soldiers who were so merciless; and even the disciples who betrayed, denied, and deserted Jesus? Lest we be too hard on them, we need to realize that what they did would be no different than what *anyone* would have done. It is Jesus' sacrifice on the cross that allows us to find salvation and treasure the love of God within us. Barabbas was a symbol for us all. Our ongoing response should be one of wonder and gratitude.

MARK 15:21–47
JESUS' CRUCIFIXION, DEATH, AND BURIAL

Jesus' Crucifixion	15:21–32
The Death of Jesus	15:33–41
Jesus' Burial	15:42–47

Setting Up the Section

The plot to have Jesus put to death is finally implemented. After a number of debates, disagreements, and outright conflicts with Jesus, the Jewish religious leaders finally get

what they want. Yet even in His death, there is additional evidence that Jesus is who He claimed to be—the Messiah and the Son of God.

▤ 15:21–32

JESUS' CRUCIFIXION

We know that Jesus started toward Golgotha bearing His own cross (John 19:17). But the fact that Simon is recruited to help Him carry it (Mark 15:21) indicates that Jesus must be very weak at this point. Some people speculate that Simon was a Gentile, but a colony of Jews had lived in Cyrene, North Africa, since the fourth century BC, so Simon could just as easily have been a Jewish pilgrim in Jerusalem for Passover. The passing reference to "Alexander and Rufus" indicates they were probably church members who would have been familiar to Mark's readers.

Golgotha (15:22) is a Greek form of the Aramaic word for "skull." None of the Gospel writers provide a location or description of the place. Both Jews and Romans customarily executed people in public places, but outside the city. It is possible that the name reflects a place of unnatural death.

Crucifixion (15:24) was one of the most horrifying forms of execution ever devised. After being stripped and flogged, the victim was lashed and/or nailed to a wooden pole. Death usually came slowly as a result of exposure and exhaustion. Inasmuch as no vital organ was damaged, it often took two or three days for the subject to die, although death could be hastened by breaking the legs, making breathing much more difficult. The usual practice was for the condemned person to carry the crossbar to the place of execution where he was affixed to it before being hoisted upon the vertical pole that was permanently fixed.

Demystifying Mark

Crucifixion seems to have been invented by the Persians, adapted by the Carthaginians, and then learned by the Romans. It was the ultimate punishment for slaves and provincials, but never used for Roman citizens. There were different kinds of crosses, including a single upright pole with two crossed poles in the shape of an X. But the most common seems to have been a vertical pole with a horizontal crossbar on or near the top to form a T shape.

The Babylonian Talmud records a tradition of the women of Jerusalem providing those condemned to die with a narcotic drink—possibly based on Proverbs 31:6–7. The "wine mixed with myrrh" offered to Jesus (15:23) may have had this purpose, but He refuses it. He faces death in complete control of His senses and willingly endures the pain. Jesus endures the fullness of suffering and death so human beings would never need to. Because He has faced the worst, He can see us through any future sufferings.

Roman custom allotted the clothing of the victim to the executioner (15:24). Clothing held much more value in ancient times than today. Casting lots for Jesus' clothing calls to mind Psalm 22:18.

The "third hour" (15:25) was 9:00 a.m. The written inscription (15:26) was usually a placard containing the condemned man's charges that he wore around his neck to the execution site, where it was then affixed to the cross. However, we learn from other Gospel accounts that Pilate himself was responsible for the sign designating Jesus as "king of the Jews." Again, what he surely meant as something to aggravate the Jewish religious leaders, unwittingly proclaimed the truth about Jesus.

The word translated "robbers" (15:27) probably means "insurrectionists" or "rebels." Perhaps these men were among the group Barabbas was involved with (15:7). The statement, "one on his right" and "one on his left" recalls the recent request of James and John (10:37) and provides insight into what it means to occupy "places of honor" in the kingdom of God.

Verse 28, not found in all Bible translations, was probably a study note (a reference to Isaiah 53:12) inadvertently added to the text by a copyist at a date after Mark's writing.

While on the cross, Jesus is mocked yet again (15:29–32; 14:65; 15:16–20). The repeated taunts for Jesus to save Himself reveal much ignorance. If Jesus had miraculously come done from the cross, He would not have saved Himself *or* others. Only by dying on the cross could He "give His life as a ransom for many" (10:45).

📖 15:33–41

THE DEATH OF JESUS

Mark records two apocalyptic signs that accompany the death of Jesus. The first is eerie darkness (15:33) for three hours (noon until 3:00 p.m.). Jesus' cry out to God (15:34) reveals His mental state. Even throughout His horrendous physical and emotional ordeal, He has been quiet. But here, while He bears the sins of the world, God cannot be with Him. Jesus has to experience the abandonment that sin creates in order for the wrath and justice of God to be fulfilled. His quotation of Psalm 22:1 expresses His feeling of aloneness. Not only have His friends all deserted Him while His enemies have tortured and crucified Him, but now even His heavenly Father is distant.

As Jesus hangs on the cross, many diverse attributes of God are displayed at once. His love and mercy for sinners is clearly evident, as is justice and wrath against sin, which His righteousness demands.

The observers' mistaken belief that Jesus is calling for Elijah (15:35–36) is understandable. The Jews believed not only that Elijah would return, but also that one of his tasks would be to help those in need. The offer of wine vinegar fulfilled Psalm 69:21.

Most people who were crucified grew gradually weaker over a long time and quietly expired. But Mark's account suggests that Jesus' death is sudden and violent, that He voluntarily and deliberately dies with the forceful shout of a victor (15:37).

The second of Mark's recorded apocalyptic signs occurs at the moment of Jesus' death. The tearing of the temple curtain (15:38) represents the climax of the replacement of the temple motif throughout Mark (11:12–25; 13:2; 14:58). The death of Jesus removes the barrier to the Most Holy Place, opening the door to God.

Jesus' death has an immediate effect on one of the people closest to Him—a Roman centurion. Although crowds have mocked and taunted Him while He is on the cross, the centurion sees the way Jesus dies and is convinced of His deity (15:39). The fact that a Gentile is the first to recognize that Jesus' status as Son of God is confirmed through His suffering is quite significant. In fact, it foreshadows the expansion of the gospel mission beyond the Jews into the Gentile nations.

Mark also introduces a group of female disciples, three who are named, who are observing Jesus' death "from a distance" (15:40). Members of their group will also be at His burial and later at the empty tomb. Although Jesus has been forsaken by His male disciples, these women display great strength and courage.

15:42–47

JESUS' BURIAL

The Romans did not always permit burial of executed criminals, often leaving the bodies on the cross to rot or be devoured by animals and birds. But the Jews believed a quick and decent burial of the dead—including enemies and criminals—was an act of piety.

"Preparation Day" (15:42) was the Friday prior to the Sabbath. Since sunset was the starting point, Jesus' body needed quick attention to prevent profaning the Sabbath and to comply with burial instructions in Deuteronomy 21:22–23.

It was unusual to release a body to someone not a relative. Yet Jesus' mother seems to have left the scene (John 19:26–27) and nothing is said of His other family members. None of the Twelve have the courage to ask for the body, but a high-ranking Jewish leader steps forward. Joseph of Arimathea is a secret disciple (John 19:38) who volunteers to see to Jesus' burial, at risk to his own reputation, if not his life.

Pilate's surprise that Jesus is already dead (15:44) is not unusual. But the fact that he releases the body of one charged with treason may further indicate that he recognizes Jesus' innocence.

Critical Observation

Burial in caves or in rock chambers of abandoned quarries was much more common among ancient Jews than burial in the ground. Such tombs were sealed with large rocks to keep out animals and grave robbers. But upscale tombs often had a disk-shaped rock similar to a millstone that rolled back and forth in a channel. The channel sloped toward the opening so that it was easy to seal the grave, but difficult to remove the stone and uncover it.

As Joseph wraps Jesus' body and places it in his own tomb (Matthew 27:60), he is seen by two of Jesus' previously mentioned female disciples (Mark 15:40, 47). They note the location of the tomb and plan to return to anoint Jesus' body, but their plans will be surprisingly changed.

Take It Home

During His crucifixion, the worst experience known to humans, Jesus refused substances that would have deadened the pain. Why do you think He did so? What hope do you gain from knowing that Jesus endured the full pain of the cross? What help does this give to us as we face the trials and suffering that come from following Jesus?

MARK 16:1–8

BETWEEN DEATH AND RESURRECTION

Setting Up the Section

We are accustomed to moving quickly from any consideration of Jesus' death to the joy and certainty of His resurrection. But for His first-century disciples, the emotions following the death of their leader are dark and severe indeed. It is these emotions that help to put the significance of His resurrection into a clearer perspective.

📖 16:1–3

WORRY

Due to the onset of the Sabbath, the women who have followed Jesus' ministry have not been able to attend to His body after His death as they wished. But they are already set to go at sunrise on Sunday morning. They are prepared to anoint His body with oils and spices that were probably bought immediately after sunset the previous night when stores opened briefly after the close of the Sabbath.

The devotion these ladies feel for Jesus is evident in their purchasing of the spices and even more so in their willingness to anoint a body already dead for a day and a half. Also evident is the fact that they are certainly not anticipating a resurrection. They are prepared to see Jesus dead, in the grave, and already beginning to decompose in the Middle East heat. Mark shows his readers that not even Jesus' closest friends and most loyal allies truly understand what He had come to do, even when the great miracle of God was taking place right before their eyes.

Critical Observation

The Jews did not embalm. The use of spices was not to prevent decomposition of the body, but to offset its stench. John's Gospel informs us that Joseph of Arimathea, accompanied by Nicodemus, had already wrapped Jesus' body in about 75 pounds of myrrh and aloes (John 19:38–40). The women didn't seem to know about this, even though they had noted the location of Joseph's tomb (Mark 15:47).

In addition, they are worried about how they might be able to remove the stone that covered the grave (16:3). Tombstones were large to prevent grave robbers from taking clothes and other memorabilia placed in the tomb with the dead. It wasn't unheard of for murderers to hide their victims in tombs. And in Jesus' case, as we learn from Matthew's Gospel, the tomb even had the seal of Rome and guards stationed outside to prevent anyone stealing the body and creating a story that Jesus had risen from the dead.

The male disciples are still in hiding, so the women are on their own. It is natural for them to worry, and they are expecting nothing supernatural. But soon their worry will turn to alarm.

16:4–6

ALARM

On arriving at the tomb, they discover they had worried for nothing. The stone is already rolled away—not to make their access easier, but to reveal that Jesus is no longer there. The young man wearing a white robe (16:5) is an angel who confirms that Jesus has indeed risen from the dead. This unexpected event fills them with alarm. They are not only startled, but afraid as well.

The angel tries to comfort them by assuring them they will see Jesus again and by giving them directions (16:7). The oldest and most reliable versions of Mark's Gospel do not include any post-resurrection accounts of Jesus, but Mark makes it very clear in this passage that Jesus has risen. His body has not been stolen or misplaced. He has been resurrected and is alive again.

Demystifying Mark

The angel's reference to "Jesus of Nazareth" (16:6) is an ongoing reminder that Jesus was a real person who can be traced to specific history and geography.

And as miraculous and hard-to-comprehend as this event was, it rings true largely because of the presence of the women. Since women in the first century weren't even allowed to testify in court, no one would have made up a story where the primary witnesses were all female. The truth of this account is unusually verifiable because the story is too countercultural to be concocted.

Still, the events of the early morning are a shock to the women. Their alarm quickly intensifies into fear.

16:7–8

FEAR

The angel has attempted to comfort the women, and his instructions to them are intended to comfort others (16:7). The news is almost too good to believe: They will see Jesus again, "just as He told you." And this message is to be delivered immediately to the disciples (because they had all fled in Gethsemane) and specifically to Peter (because he, in particular, had denied Jesus). The angel's message implies forgiveness and eventual restoration to fellowship with their Lord. Jesus had previously shared this very plan with them (14:27–28), and it was still intact.

This should have been terrific news, yet the women flee from the tomb just as the disciples had fled from Jesus' arrest. They run out "trembling and bewildered," and "said nothing to anyone, because they were afraid" (16:8 NIV). Other Gospel accounts report that the women also experienced great joy intermingled with their fear. Why did Mark record only the fear? Perhaps he wanted his readers to see the humanity of the women and to comprehend the reality of human interaction with Jesus.

In some manuscripts, this was how the Gospel of Mark originally ended. He concluded with this stark reminder that human faith may fail at times, and trust will waver. Even so, Jesus had not deserted those He loved, and was planning to reunite with them soon.

Take It Home

The women and the disciples did not fully understand the full extent of the cross and thus fear overcame their hearts. How does our lack of understanding the cross bring about fear in our own lives? In light of this text, what insight can we gain from 1 John 4:18? Can you think of an example from the book of Acts where the knowledge of the cross gave the first century believers courage?

MARK 16:9–20
AN ADDENDUM TO THE GOSPEL OF MARK?

Setting Up the Section

Most Bible scholars feel that the Gospel of Mark ended at 16:8 and that verses 9–20 were added considerably later to smooth out the abrupt ending. Although these closing verses are not considered to be part of the scriptures to the extent of the rest of Mark's Gospel, they are an honest attempt to complete the story of Jesus.

Because the other Gospels provide such full accounts of appearances of Jesus after His resurrection, it is curious and somewhat frustrating that Mark's writing stopped at 16:8. Perhaps he had written more, but his ending was lost. The scribes who added verses 9–20 pulled from other scriptures as well as historical witnesses to the post-resurrection lives of the apostles. Therefore, the events recorded here are true, but not a part of Mark's original record.

It seems that two attempts are made to complete Mark's work: one in verses 9–18, and a second in verses 19–20. These passages are largely comprised of details taken from the other Gospels or Acts, with a few additions from early church traditions.

Verses 9–11, seemingly taken from John's Gospel, explain how Mary Magdalene is the first to see the risen Christ. The two of them mentioned in verses 12–13 are a reference to the appearance of Jesus to the two disciples at Emmaus (Luke 24:13–32). And verse 14 has parallels in the other Gospels, though the exact occasion referenced here is not clear.

Even though these verses were most likely added to Mark's Gospel as a footnote, they are still in harmony with the rest of the book. Themes of believing and not believing permeate this section. Although the verses may not be from the pen of Mark, they are nevertheless consistent with his previous writing and with the rest of the Gospels.

The great commission of Matthew 28:18 is reflected in verses 15–16. Belief in Jesus leads to salvation; unbelief is itself a condemnation.

Most of the signs mentioned in verses 17–18 are found either in the Gospels or the book of

Acts. The exception is drinking poison without being harmed, which is mentioned in writings of the early church. Yet the writer does not suggest that these particular signs are provided all the time and for everyone. They were unique events used to authenticate the message of the apostles (Hebrews 2:1–4).

Critical Observation

Though God still performs miracles today, we must not assume that the signs recorded in Mark 16:17–18 still apply in every instance today. The text describes what occurred after the gospel was preached, and does not prescribe action for the church. In other words, a believer bitten by a poisonous snake is not assured continued health should he choose not to seek treatment. We should accept the miracles of God gratefully if and when they occur. But our minds should be set on God's kingdom, not merely on its signs.

The final two verses (19–20) may have been a second addition to Mark's writing. They describe a brief triumphal ascension of Jesus, the apostolic mission of evangelism, and the manner in which the preaching of God's word was vindicated by the results.

The section of Mark 16:9–20 is not part of scripture, so should not be used as a basis for establishing doctrine. However, we may accept these closing verses because they agree with scripture and are a valuable summary of the beliefs of the early church.

Take It Home

Suppose this section of Mark had not been added and you were left hanging with the women "trembling and bewildered" as they fled from Jesus' tomb. What would you have wanted to recall, either from previous portions of Mark or your knowledge of other portions of scripture, to bring closure to this Gospel?

CONTRIBUTING EDITORS

Dr. Ian Fair was a missionary in South Africa for 14 years, has preached for 39 years, taught Bible classes for 39 years, and has served as an elder and deacon. Recently retired from Abilene Christian University, Dr. Fair continues to teach as an adjunct professor.

Dr. Stephen Leston is pastor of Kishwaukee Bible Church in DeKalb, Illinois. He is passionate about training people for ministry and has served as a pastor at Grace Church of DuPage (Warrenville, Illinois) and Petersburg Bible Church (Petersburg, Alaska).

CONSULTING EDITOR

Dr. Mark Strauss is a professor at Bethel Seminary's San Diego Campus. He is the author of *Distorting Scripture? The Challenge of Bible Translation and Gender Accuracy; The Essential Bible Companion,* and *Four Portraits, One Jesus: An Introduction to Jesus and the Gospels.* He is presently revising the commentary on Mark's Gospel for *Expositor's Bible Commentary.*